# The Actors of Postnational Rule-Making

## Contemporary Challenges of European and International Law

Edited by
Elaine Fahey



Routledge
Taylor & Francis Group
LONDON AND NEW YORK

First published 2016
by Routledge

2 Park Square, Milton Park, Abingdon, Oxon OX14 4RN

711 Third Avenue, New York, NY 10017, USA

*Routledge is an imprint of the Taylor & Francis Group, an informa business*

First issued in paperback 2017



*Library of Congress Cataloging in Publication Data*
A catalog record for this book has been requested

ISBN: 978-1-138-85666-0 (hbk)
ISBN: 978-1-138-71723-7 (pbk)

Typeset in Garamond
by Florence Production Ltd, Stoodleigh, Devon, UK

# The Actors of Postnational Rule-Making

Despite its centrality to academic discussions of power and influence, there is little consensus in legal scholarship over what constitutes an actor in rule-making. This book explores the range of actors involved in rule-making within European Union law and public international law, and focuses especially on actors that are often overlooked by formative and doctrinal approaches.

Drawing together contributions from many scholars in various fields, the book examines such issues as the accommodation of new actors in the process of postnational rule-making, the visibility or covertness of actors within the process, and the role of social acceptance and legitimacy in postnational rule-making.

In its endeavour to render and examine the work and effect of actors often sidelined in the study of postnational rule-making, this book will be of great use and interest to students and scholars of EU law, international law and socio-legal studies.

**Elaine Fahey** is Senior Lecturer at City Law School, City University London.

# Contents

# Notes on contributors

**Sabino Cassese** is Judge of the Constitutional Court of Italy and Professor Emeritus at the Scuola Normale Superiore of Pisa.

**Anna-Luise Chané** is a Research Fellow and PhD candidate in Law at the Leuven Centre for Global Governance Studies/Institute for International Law, University of Leuven.

Dr **Richard Collins** is Lecturer in International Law, UCD Sutherland School of Law, University College Dublin.

Dr **Elaine Fahey** is Senior Lecturer at City Law School, City University London.

Dr **Davor Jančić** is Senior Researcher in EU law, TMC Asser Institute, The Hague, Faculty of Law, University of Amsterdam.

Dr **Emilia Korkea-aho** is a Postdoctoral researcher, University of Helsinki/ European University Institute, Florence.

**Jed Odermatt** is a PhD candidate in Law, Leuven Centre for Global Governance Studies/Institute for International Law, University of Leuven.

Prof. **Matthias Ruffert** (Dr.iur) is Professor for Public Law, European Law and Public International Law at Friedrich-Schiller-Universität Jena, and holder of a Jean Monnet Chair for European Integration.

Dr **Ruth Sefton-Green** is Maître de conférences of comparative private law, Ecole de droit de la Sorbonne, Université Paris 1 (Panthéon-Sorbonne).

Dr **Rene Urueña** is Associate Professor and Director of the Master's Program on International Law, Universidad de Los Andes (Colombia), LL.D (*eximia cum laude*) and LL.M (*laudatur*), University of Helsinki.

Prof. **Henri de Waele** is Professor of International and European Law, Radboud Universiteit Nijmegen and Guest Professor of European Institutional Law, University of Antwerp.

Prof. **Jan Wouters** is Jean Monnet Chair and Full Professor of International Law and International Organizations and Director, Leuven Centre for Global Governance Studies/Institute for International Law, KU Leuven.

Dr **Jens-Uwe Wunderlich** is Lecturer in International Relations, Aston University.

# Foreword

## The new rulers: the actors and processes of the global space

*Sabino Cassese*

The phenomena of Europeanisation and globalisation are calling new actors to the collective decision-making processes at the global level, and are shaping the procedures through which they act in new ways.

Consider the following comments on globalisation by a German philosopher, by a Dutch-Argentine sociologist and by a Swiss-German political scientist, respectively:

> By 'globalization' is meant 'the cumulative processes of a worldwide expansion of trade and production, commodity and financial markets, fashions, the media and computer programs, news and communications networks, transportation systems and flows of migration, the risks generated by large-scale technology, environmental damage and epidemics, as well as organized crime and terrorism'.[1]

> A good part of globalization consists of an enormous variety of microprocesses that begin to denationalize what had been constructed as national.[2]

> [. . .] I suggest that we think of statehood as a product which is produced by the state in association with other actors [. . .].[3]

1 J. Habermas, *The Divided West*, Cambridge, Ciaran Cronin, 2006, p. 175.

2 S. Sassen, *Territory, Authority, Rights: From Medieval to Global Assemblages*, Princeton University Press, 2006, p. 1.

3 C. Zürcher, 'When Governance meets troubled States', in M. Beisheim-G. F. Schuppert (hrsg.), *Staatszerfall und Governance*, Baden-Baden, Nomos, 2007, p. 11. Zürcher continues by saying: 'It is sufficient to think of who provides security in Afghanistan or Tajikistan, domestic authority in Kosovo or Bosnia, or public services in Mozambique or Burundi. There are also international institutions and organizations in place to assume these functions – think of the UN transitional administration, the international forces in Afghanistan, or of the World Bank's suggestion to set up so called ISAs (Independent Service Authorities) in low income countries under stress (LICUS).'

These processes (denationalisation, communitarisation, Europeanisation and globalisation) bring new agents to the fore within the political arena, and require new procedures.

In studying these new realities, the first step must be to map the area, because, alongside States and international governmental organisations, there is a multitude of new actors, some of which do not have legal personality, such as epistemic communities; bodies that were once active only within States are now also active beyond their own territories. This book illustrates an initial sample of such highly diverse actors, together with their spheres of influence – regional authorities, the Presidency of the Council of the European Union, the European Union, EU lobbyists, the Inter-Parliamentary Union, academia. Preference is given to the European space, but some examples originate from other areas.

The second step is to enquire upon the nature of these new actors. The State is losing its central role, but through its fragmentation, it can ensure that its voice is heard in a different manner. For example, central banks are members of the Basel Committee, a global standard-setter. Global regulatory regimes include networks of national regulators, private regulators such as ICANN, and hybrid bodies such as the International Organization for Standardization (ISO). Behind the scenes, there are further actors, e.g. lobbyists, or the European Union when it acts in the United Nations arena.

The third step in studying this new geopolitical space requires an examination of the relations established by the new actors. While vertical interactions predominate in the State – due to the hierarchy of authorities – in this new space, horizontal relations prevail, as in the case of the EU and ASEAN. Horizontal links are functional to coordination or to other purposes, such as the export of one's own model.

The final problem concerns processes. It cannot be thought that new agents do not find new ways to interact and reach decisions together. In this respect, good examples are the EU's 'trilogue', contractual legislation, and the so-called 'postnational rule-making'. Just as the actors are not formalised, so too are the processes not formalised. 'Un-officiality' is the rule. Processes are complex and informal, and are based on bargaining and negotiation, as in the case of rule-making in the EU.

This book could not possibly cover this entire field, but provides a good set of examples as a starting point for research on the new rulers. Indeed, it is already possible to derive common patterns from the contributions collected herein, and attempt some generalisations.

The first conclusion that can be drawn is that the arrangement is fluid. As indicated in this book, the entire world of actors within this new space is in constant movement; suffice it to consider the EU, which was established by the treaties to be an 'ever closer Union'.

The second conclusion is that there is no eclipse of the State, but rather a restructuring of the State, which sheds the old paradigm of 'the State as a unit', but gains new roles as a disaggregated body.

The third conclusion is that it is a mistake to approach this area with the 'multi-level' paradigm. International and regional organisations, States and non-State actors are mutually interconnected within global governance structures, and follow the logic of collective action.[4]

> Global regulation typically does not operate on two distinct, vertically separated levels, international and domestic. Rather, it functions through a web of interactions and influences, horizontal, vertical, and diagonal, among a diverse multiplicity of different regimes and actors [. . .].[5]

The fourth conclusion is that we need also a new lexicon for these new realities. Because there is no unitary legal order beyond the State – except for a few general principles – it is better to speak of the global 'space' and of global 'regulatory regimes'. Because there are many, diverse and non-uniform actors, it is necessary to resort to the word 'constellation'. The subjects that are active in this space have different features, are not subjected to one national rule, and operate in various legal dimensions; therefore, it is necessary to use a neutral terminology when referring to them (hence the word 'actor'). In any case, these points are made very well in the Introduction, to which readers seeking a more in-depth discussion are referred.

4 P.G. Cerny, 'Globalization and the Changing Logic of Collective Action', in *International Organization*, 1995, vol. 49, n. 4, Autumn, p. 595.

5 R. Stewart, 'The Global Regulatory Challenge to U.S. Administrative Law', in *New York University Journal of International Law and Politics*, 2006, vol. 37, p. 703.

# Introduction

## Framing the actors of postnational rule-making

*Elaine Fahey*

This publication has its origins in a workshop held in Amsterdam in 2014 organised by the 'Architecture of Postnational Rule-Making' research project at the University of Amsterdam, devoted to dissecting new means and forms of actors engaging in rule-making beyond the Nation State. While there may be vast legal literature devoted to dissecting functional actors, courts and forms of private actors and legislative or executive power, legal scholarship rarely hones in on the precise idea of an actor in rule-making. Arguably, this publication takes an even narrower cut of the theme and selects predominantly – but not exclusively – two subject areas as its focus, which are European Union (EU) law and public international law (PIL) as manifestations of postnational rule-making. EU and PIL arguably constitute the leading contemporary sources of study for postnational rule-making, and for this reason are worthy subjects. However, this is not to suggest that it is the only or optimum take on postnational rule-making. Part of the difficulty targeted by this publication is that irrespective of the subject area, many of the most significant actors engaging in rule-making in contemporary times are not technically 'actors' in strict legal terms.

The publication thus focuses upon certain 'blind spots' in our understanding of actors in rule-making, that impact upon and even shape our analysis of conduct and the reasons for their status quo as blind spots. In order to further narrow the terms of the contribution, its focus is in large measure upon the analysis of practices of rule-making, specific behaviour and action taking place in what might be termed 'in the shadows' of other institutional components. Postnational rule-making is a term that may capture a vast range of rule-making beyond the Nation State. It may capture EU and public international law in their entirety. As living sciences, such subjects appear often highly flexible and innovative. And while postnational rule-making poses challenges for understanding the place of the Nation State, it also affords a useful *tabula rasa*. The *tabula rasa* of postnational rule-making must be approached by the user with caution. In this regard, part of the challenge of postnational rule-making may be empirical as much as metaphysical, i.e. as to what it is and what it could and should be are equally challenging.

# 1 On 'postnational' rule-making

## *1.1 An overview*

A 'constellation' is the infamous and commonly used construct of 'postnational' rule-making, embracing all transnational law and theory. It is often used to depict in all-embracing terms its components, by way of a term that specifically captures its spatial and theoretical complexity.[1] The lexicon of the 'spatial' is not unique to the transnational.[2] The appeal of spatial metaphors explains from assertions of its usefulness as to its methodological components.[3] Yet for all of its spatial associations, such a constellation encompasses a conglomeration of institutions, transnational and supranational organisations, private economic power, and, of course, the Nation State.[4] The vastness of the number of actors within this context may readily cause us to lose sharp focus. Moreover, the 'direction' of one's focus upon actors may be methodologically dominant.[5] For example, private economic power has tended to form the subject and object of much contemporary analysis, but in a 'unidirectional' fashion.[6] And newer actors and configurations of actors may attract more attention, than existing institutional entities or international organisations.

What this publication focuses upon is how the postnational 'constellation' comprises many active and 'living' institutional components. Institutional and specific forms of international law have traditionally been enacted so as to provide information for political actors in decision-making processes, to provide certainty for the global legal order, and to constrain, develop and evolve global politics. The goals of such changes have been shown to be easily overtaken over time, by time itself, power, politics and many other internal and external criteria. The postnational constellation inherently comprises active and living entities acting beyond the control of political processes or organised institutional design. There is an organic quality to it that is both challenging but also explanatory thereof. As a landscape, it operates within an uneasy actor-causative dynamic: it has resulted in the need for, or more so

1 P. Zumbansen, 'Transnational Law, Evolving' (2011) *Osgoode CLPE Research Paper No. 27/2011* accessed <http://papers.ssrn.com/sol3/papers.cfm?abstract_id=1975403>.

2 'Public administration' is similarly a space of proliferating actors, a proliferation that comes in waves of developments at national and international level – see D. Curtin, *Executive Power of the European Union: Law, Practices and the Living Constitution* (Oxford: OUP, 2009).

3 Zumbansen (n 1), see D. Chalmers, 'Post-Nationalism and the Quest for Constitutional Substitutes' (2000) 27 *Journal of Law and Society* 178.

4 A. Fischer-Lescano and G. Teubner, 'Regime-Collisions: The Vain Search for Legal Unity in the Fragmentation of Global Law' (2004) 25(4) *Michigan Journal of International Law* 999–1046.

5 K. Abbott and D. Snidal, 'International Regulation without International Government: Improving International Organization Performance Through Orchestration' (2010) 5 *The Review of International Organizations* 315–344.

6 Ibid.

the significance of, *more* actors in the rule-making space.[7] Least of all, it has not particularised our focus upon its components.

### *1.2 On postnational rule-making and its lexicon*

Terms such as 'postnational constitutionalism' or 'postnational democracy' have been deployed to depict 'the state of the State' as much as the *decline* of the boundaries of societal orthodoxy.[8] Yet there is no accepted normative idea of postnational 'law'. At its height, the deployment of the term postnational in legal scholarship has been critiqued as being both 'EU-centric' and 'Court-centric'. It has been dismissed as lacking relevance to any legal order or field outside of the context of the EU, constructed largely through judicialised understandings of conduct that may not be readily transposed elsewhere. Fundamentally, the postnational is perceived not to have a broad reach, precisely because, as has been wryly remarked, 'we have yet to arrive at a post-national world'.[9] Nonetheless, its context and lexicon indicates that the performance of constitutionalism and politics is no longer configured around or constructed *within* the territorial strictures of the Nation State. It signifies the importance of the proliferation of new forms of law and politics, interactions between legal orders and political disordering.[10] The study of the 'postnational' is arguably less a study of single or specific actors, instruments or policies, and instead is probably more accurately a broader methodology to study shifts in actors, norms and processes.[11]

Whatever about its overarching 'lexicon',[12] postnational rule-making as a process is more intrusive than ever, taking place under public scrutiny, around

7 B. Kohler-Koch and C. Quittkat, *De-Mystification of Participatory Democracy: EU-Governance and Civil Society* (Oxford: OUP, 2013).

8 K. Ladeur, 'The Theory of Autopoiesis as an Approach to a Better Understanding of Postmodern Law – From the Hierarchy of Norms to the Heterarchy of Changing Patterns of Legal Inter-relationships' (1999) *Law No. 99/3, EUI Working Papers* European University Institute, Law Department; E. Eriksen, C. Joerges and F. Rödl (eds), *Law, Democracy and Solidarity in a Post-national Union: the unsettled political order of Europe – Routledge Studies on Democratising Europe* (Oxford: Routledge, 2008); E. Eriksen, C. Joerges and F. Rödl (eds), 'Law and Democracy in the Post-National Union' (2006) *Arena/European University Institute Arena Report 1/2006*; N. Walker, 'Postnational Constitutionalism and Postnational Public Law: A Tale of Two Neologisms' (2012) 3 *Transnational Legal Theory* 61–86.

9 G. Shaffer, 'A Transnational Take on Krisch's Pluralist Structure of Postnational Law' (2012) 23 *European Journal of International Law* 565–582, 582; N. Krisch, *Beyond Constitutionalism: The Pluralist Structure of Postnational Law* (Oxford: OUP, 2011).

10 See Chalmers (n 3).

11 R. Urueña, *No Citizens Here: Global Subjects and Participation in International Law* (The Hague: Martinus Nijhoff Publishers, 2012).

12 'The vocabulary of a person, language, or branch of knowledge' accessed <http://www.oxforddictionaries.com/definition/english/lexicon>

or alongside the increasing openness of a digitally connected global society.[13] It is a change that is said to reflect the shifting empirical landscape of the exercise of authority beyond the Nation State.[14] The actors of this context may be said to have become more easily visible and more responsive to this scrutiny in recent times, in the era of transparency and public protests for accountability.[15] This leads to a consideration of the empirics of actors engaging in rule-making beyond the Nation State, as to, *inter alia*, what we measure and how we understand such measurement.

### *1.3 The empirics of what we speak about beyond the Nation State*

From an empirical perspective, our understanding of the 'postnational' or its constellation remains limited, variable and even haphazard. Despite the evolved state of transnational law as an established subject,[16] with its own communities, literature, esoteric publications across subject fields, there are comparatively few 'agreed' data sets, databases or agreed empirical sources used by lawyers as to the basis of our understanding of the operation of the subject.[17] The rising incidence of the delegation by Member States of authority to international organisations, the rising number of international organisations, the exponential rise of transnational non-governmental organisations (NGOs) and the increase of majority-voting in international organisations provide important empirical examples.[18] The number of transnational entities exercising political influence has increased considerably, from international courts and tribunals to rating agencies, accounting standards and education

13 See, for example, M. Zürn, 'The Politicization of World Politics and its Effects: Eight Propositions' (2014) 6(1) *European Political Science Review* 47–71.

14 Ibid.

15 See, for example, the evolution of the EU-US Transatlantic Trade and Investment Partnership (TTIP) negotiations and the place of transparency therein or the evolution of ICANN rule-making and its gradual openness for and to the world.

16 Which arguably has a much broader reach than postnational rule-making, but may be considered synonymous to a large degree.

17 See B. Koremenos, 'The Continent of International Law' (2012) *Journal of Conflict Resolution* 1–29.

18 See Zürn (n 13). See also M. Herdegen, *Principles of International Economic Law* (Oxford: OUP, 2014) at p. 29, where he notes how according to the Union of International Associations in 1909, the number of IGOS amounted to 37, while in 1999 this number had increased to over 3,637. See <www.uia.org/statistics/organiszations/ytb299/php>. See *Yearbook of International Organizations* (The Hague, Brill), listing 1,200 new organizations annually. It registers 64,000 transnational civil society organisations generally. The number of intergovernmental organisations listed in the *Yearbook of International Organizations* for 2013–2014 is 7,710, a dramatic rise from the 123 recorded in 1951 (Leiden, Brill: 2013); see the 'Continent of international law' project accessed <http://www.isr.umich.edu/cps/coil/>; the Authority of International Institutions, Transaccess accessed <http://www.statsvet.su.se/english/research/research-projects/transaccess>; PICT-PICT Project on international courts and tribunals accessed <www.pict.picti.org>; M. Zürn (n 13), L. Hooghe and G. Marks, 'Delegation and Pooling in International Organizations' (forthcoming) in *Review of International Organizations*.

setting bodies.[19] Allied to this is the so-called development of 'juristocracy', meaning the proliferation and the empowerment of international courts. Similarly, reflections on the authority of transnational and international bodies and their rising and measurable influence also proliferates.[20] The prominence of international bodies and courts within these disparate but unifying developments is apparent.[21] This has perhaps incited many to reflect on new metrics of global governance emerging, for example, indicators from technologies,[22] while older metrics ('hard' numbers) become part of a historical-sounding account of 'proliferation'.[23] One may pose the question as to whether sufficient empirical or conceptual clarity may be brought to bear upon 'the whole' and the sum of the parts together as one enterprise in the current status quo. This constitutes the context for the current contribution.

An empirical account of the circles of influence surrounding such rule-making practices: i.e. those such as private associations, private economic power, lobbyists and experts including academics, who initiate, bolster, support or sustain rule-making, arguably remains on the margins of our knowledge. It may also differ substantially between legal orders and legal cultures. The 'superstructure' of postnational rule-making may cause us concern because sometimes its components may seem more significant than the 'sum of its parts'. For instance, its actors comprise powerful and independent judiciaries, new manifestations of 'executive' actors after the State or transnational parliamentarianism. They may all be broadly understood as entities engaged in autonomous rule-making, to whatever degree.[24]

19 See Zürn (n 13).

20 R. Hirschl, 'Juristocracy vs. Theocracy: Constitutional Courts and the Containment of Sacred Law' (2009) 1(2) *Middle East Law and Governance* 129–165; R. Mackenzie, C. Romano, P. Sands, and Y. Shany, *The Manual on International Courts and Tribunals* (Oxford: OUP, 2010); see Yuval Shany, *Assessing the Effectiveness of International Courts* (Oxford: OUP, 2014); B. Kingsbury and C. Romano (eds), 'Symposium on Proliferation of International Tribunals: Piecing Together the Puzzle' (1999) 31(4) *NYU Journal of International Law and Politics*. K. Alter, *The New Terrain of International Law: Courts, Politics, Rights* (Princeton, NJ: Princeton University Press, 2014). M. Kanetake and A. Nollkaemper (eds), *The Rule of Law at the National and International Levels: Contestations and Deference* (Oxford: Hart Publishing, forthcoming).

21 See Alter (n 20).

22 See K. E. Davis, Benedict Kingsbury, Sally Engle Merry IILJ Working Paper 2010/2 Rev (Revised August 2011) Global Administrative Law Series Indicators as a Technology of Global Governance.

23 B. Kingsbury and C. Romano (n 20).

24 I.e. see R. D. Kelemen, 'Eurolegalism and Democracy' (2012) 50(1) *Journal of Common Market Studies* 55–71 and R. D. Kelemen, *Eurolegalism: The Transformation of Law & Regulation in the European Union* (Cambridge, MA: Harvard University Press, 2012) (on transnational courts and European courts in particular); D. Curtin, *Executive Power of the European Union: Law, Practices and the Living Constitution* (Oxford: OUP, 2009) (on the executive in the EU); see Walker (n 8) on transnational parliaments. See D. Jančić, 'The European Parliament and EU-US relations: revamping institutional cooperation?' in E. Fahey and D. Curtin (eds), *A Transatlantic Community of Law Legal Perspectives on the Relationship between the EU and US Legal Orders* (Cambridge: CUP, 2014).

Such institutional components of organisations exercising public authority after the State, constitute the institutionalised phenomena of this landscape.[25] These institutional components of organisations, not limited to the judiciary, may manage to engage in rule-making practices through exhibiting *inter alia* influence, independence, autonomy, contestation and an 'active' development of their functions and roles. So what could be an optimal means or method to capture them, collectively? Nevertheless, current descriptors (and metrics) of the 'postnational' may not give us adequate analytical tools to measure the intrusiveness of contemporary rule-making nor its actors. This provides more forceful reasons to sharpen our analytical and normative focus as to *actors*.

## 2 Actors in EU and international law: between formalism and flexibility

### *2.1 Overview*

The idea of '*actors*' is critical to the theorisation of power, autonomy, influence and even legitimacy in rule-making beyond the Nation State. However, there is no consensus in scholarship on what it means to be an actor, despite its centrality to discussions on rule-making, power and influence, across disciplines, not least in legal scholarship.[26] An actor engaging in rule-making is understood in this account as those who adopt acts, practices and/or standards in the exercise of legal authority. These challenges are felt acutely in rule-making beyond the Nation State, where the actors may either be fledging or evolving and where the rule-making practices may vary substantially from conventional practices. To view an institution as an actor in their own right is a technically rather inaccurate one from a legal perspective.[27] This is because legal doctrine employs formal and arguably limiting criteria to assess 'actor qualities', e.g. legal personality, legal authority to act and institutional autonomy. These criteria are heavily rooted in the *Trias Politica*.[28]

25 A. Bogdandy *et al.*, 'General Principles of International Public Authority: Sketching a Research Field' (2008) 9 *German Law Journal* 1909–1938, accessed <http://www.germanlawjournal.com/index.php?pageID=11&artID=1048>.

26 C. Hill, 'The Capability-Expectations Gap, or Conceptualizing Europe's International Role' (1993) 31(3) *Journal of Common Market Studies* 305–328; J. Jupille and J. Caporaso, 'States, Agency and Rules: the European Union in Global Environmental Politics' (1998) in C. Rhodes (ed.), *The European Union in the World Community* (Boulder, CO: Lynne Rienner, 1998, pp. 213–229); M. Barnett and M. Finnemore, *Rules for the World: International Organizations in Global Politics* (Ithaca, NY: Cornell University Press, 2004).

27 While it is difficult to find clear statements to this effect, it is perhaps a self-evident proposition within scholarship.

28 M. Cremona, 'The European Union as a Global Actor: Roles, Models and Identity' (2004) 41 *Common Market Law Review* 553–573; D. Sarooshi, *International Organizations and Their Exercise of Sovereign Powers* (Oxford: OUP, 2005); R. Collins and N. White (eds), *International Organizations and the Idea of Autonomy: Institutional Independence in the International Legal Order* (New York: Routledge, 2011).

The problem they pose is a circular one because such formalism may pose endless limitations. For example, one may consider in this light the challenges faced by those seeking to conceptualise actors in international law as 'participants' or those arguing for a departure from an understanding of international legal personality limited to State actors.[29] Or to similar effect, one might consider in public international law the complexity of the formulation of an 'international foreign fighter' in the UN Security Council Resolution or in EU law, the evolution of the European External Action Service (EEAS) as a 'legal actor'.[30] By contrast, other disciplines may appear often significantly less burdened by formalism. For example, emerging theories of international politics readily embraced the new phenomenon of secretariats of international organisations.[31] These practices cause us some difficulty in that they appear to open up a greater distance between law and other disciplines as to the lexicon of actors.

To put the issue differently, one may ask how malleable should legal principles be for each new actor as part of a system and/or organisation? For example, the autonomous 'arrangements' in multilateral environmental agreements averted to above have been accorded their own lexicon and are now the working language of international environmental law.[32] This in turn raises the question as to appropriate flexibility and pragmatism of legal theory as to actors. It has been argued that to construe public international law in overly simplified terms of 'subjects' and 'objects' would subject it to a form of intellectual prison.[33] Instead, many call for more elaborate conceptual tools

29 R. Higgins, *Problems and Process: International Law and How We Use It* (Oxford: OUP, 1994); C. Walter, 'Subjects of International Law' (2007) in R. Wolfrum *et al.* (eds), *The Max Planck Encyclopedia of Public International Law* (Oxford: OUP, 2012) vol. 9, pp. 634ff; A. Bianchi, *Non-State Actors and International Law* (London: Ashgate Publishing 2009); S. Woolcock, 'State and Non-State Actors' in S. Woolcock and N. Bayne (eds), *The New Economic Diplomacy* (London: Ashgate Publishing, 2nd edn, 2007); R. Hofmann, *Non-State Actors as New Subjects of International Law – from the Traditional State Order towards the Law of Global Community* (Berlin: Duncker & Humblot, 2000).

30 UN Security Council Resolution 2178 on foreign terrorist fighters S/RES/2187 (2014) (24 September 2014); see also <http://www.ejiltalk.org/security-council-resolution-2178-2014-the-foreign-terrorist-fighter-as-an-international-legal-person-part-i/>; <http://www.ejiltalk.org/un-security-council-adopts-resolution-2178-on-foreign-terrorist-fighters/>; M. Gatti, 'Diplomats at the Bar: the European External Action Service before the EU Courts' (2014) 39(5) *European Law Review* 664.

31 M. Barnett and M. Finnemore, 'The Politics, Power, and Pathologies of International Organizations' (1999) 53 *International Organizations* 699–732.

32 E.g. involving a conference or meeting of parties with decision making powers, a secretariat and specialist subsidiary bodies; see R. Churchill and G. Ulfstein, 'Autonomous Institutional Arrangements in Multilateral Environmental Agreements: A Little-Noticed Phenomenon in International Law' (2000) 94(4) *American Journal of International Law* 623–659; F. Biermann and B. Siebenhüner (eds), *Managers of Global Change: The Influence of International Environmental Bureaucracies* (Cambridge, MA: MIT Press, 2009).

33 See Higgins, (n 29).

to systematise the lexicon of non-State actors and their role played in contemporary international law.[34] Yet whether the solution lies in relativising the subjects or subjectivising the actors remains for some time open to doubt.[35]

One issue might be that legal scholarship lacks catch-all categories for actors, unlike, for example, in political economy. In political economy, 'actors' comprise State actors, international organisations, club forums, e.g. G7, 8 and 20, market actors, non-governmental organisations and, significantly, the catch-all category of 'everyday actors'.[36] As a science, it is a curious one because these categorisations are dependent upon which of them receives the most attention. Instead, we might argue that legal scholarship is much more matter of fact. International law traditionally recognises only a small number of entities capable of possessing international rights or duties and of bringing international claims because its primary subjects have always been States. Other traditional subjects of international law are insurgents or *sui generis* entities, e.g. the Holy See, the International Committee of the Red Cross. International organisations with international legal personality have followed thereafter, more prominently the UN and the number of international organisations has risen substantially over time – from the IMF, the Word Bank Group, and the WTO.

The problem lies in that international rules are shaped increasingly by actors *beyond* the traditional subjects of international law, e.g. international non-governmental organisations, transnational corporations, inter-agency cooperation. Private economic actors and companies have been strengthened by the rise of international investment protections. 'Actors' as a domain of study in legal scholarship tend to be depicted in esoteric subjects that have distinctive interactions between markets, private and public actors. For example, international economic law carves up actors to comprise States, State enterprises, International organisations, non-institutionalised forums of cooperation, international inter-agency cooperation, non-governmental organisations and private corporations and standard-setters for transnational cooperation.[37] Nevertheless, such analyses remain rooted in the 'subject' paradigm of public international law. This has an awkward relationship with 'standard-setting' and bottom-up practices or conduct that generates rule-making beyond these categories. No matter how vast the categorisation of actors appears, it arguably has a static quality to it.

34 S. Woolcock, 'State and Non-State Actors' in S. Woolcock and N. Bayne (eds), *The New Economic Diplomacy* (London: Ashgate Publishing, 2nd edn, 2007); R. Hofmann and N. Geissler (eds), *Non-State Actors as New Subjects of International Law – from the Traditional State Order towards the law of Global Community* (Berlin: Duncker & Humblot, 1999); see Bianchi (n 29).

35 See Bianchi (n 29).

36 E.g. A. Broome, *Issues and Actors in the Global Political Economy* (London: Palgrave Macmillan, 2014), Part I and Ch. 9. See the diagrammatic structure on p. 12.

37 M. Herdegen, *Principles of International Economic Law* (Oxford: OUP, 2014), Chapter 3.

The proliferation or 'pluralisation' of actors are also key concerns of contemporary EU law. Yet there is no agreed definition of an actor under EU law.[38] Instead, a sharp distinction is drawn there between the masters of the treaties and those amenable to judicial review or those with legal personality.[39] This concern is usually framed around the control of discretion or legality control of the powers of burgeoning agencies vis-à-vis the Commission, the Member States and national authorities. As a result of these developments, a permissive approach to the rule-making of the proliferating agencies has been recently adopted by the Court of Justice, where it has laid emphasis upon the importance of highly structured functionality rather than controls per se, even where extensive institutional design has been built up upon thin legal authority. [40] As will be discussed next, the grant of legal personality under EU law has been predominantly accorded to entities such as agencies in a wholly pragmatic rather than conceptual basis.[41] Similarly, the burgeoning use of the term 'non-State' actors as a term of art to comprise almost any entity *inter alia* contesting legitimacy, authority or accountability in public international law has followed a similarly pragmatic rather than conceptual path.[42] Flexibility and pragmatism are dominant and enduring themes in both subjects but do not necessarily provide analytical frameworks of any sophistication.[43] Instead they may be said to demonstrate the somewhat crudely factual understanding of actors in contemporary legal scholarship. However, such a conclusion would appear unduly harsh or quick to judge

38 See M. Ruffert, 'Personality Under EU Law: A Conceptual Answer Towards the Pluralisation of the EU *European Law Journal*' (2014) 20(3) *European Law Journal* 346–367; M. Ruffert and C. Walter (eds), *Institutionalised International Law* (Oxford: Hart Publishing, 2015).

39 See Ruffert, ibid. IV, (D).

40 E.g. Case C-270/12 *UK v. European Parliament and Council* (Judgment of the Grand Chamber of 22 January 2014), on the basis of Article 114 Treaty of the Functioning of the European Union

41 It arguably also reflects the under-developed conceptualisation of institutional balance in contemporary EU law: J. Jacqué, 'The principle of institutional balance' (2004) 41(2) *Common Market Law Review* 383–391; J. Monar, 'The Rejection of the EU-US SWIFT Interim Agreement by the European Parliament: A Historic Vote and Its Implications' (2010) 15(2) *European Foreign Affairs Review* 143–151; P. Craig 'Institutions, Power and Institutional Balance' in P. Craig and G. Búrca (eds), *The Evolution of EU Law* (Oxford: OUP, 2011) pp. 41–84; R. Dehousse, 'Misfits: EU Law and the Transformation of European Governance' in C. Joerges and R. Dehousse, *Good Governance in Europe's Integrated Market* (Oxford: OUP, 2002); B. Smulders and K. Eisele, 'Reflections on the Institutional Balance, the Community Method and the Interplay between Jurisdictions after Lisbon' (2012) College of Europe, European Legal Studies, 04 Research Papers in Law accessed <http://aei.pitt.edu/39285/1/researchpaper_4_2012_smulderseisele_final.pdf>; G. Conway, 'Recovering a Separation of Powers in the European Union' (2011) 17 *European Law Journal* 304–322; J. Ziller, 'Separation of Powers in the European Union's Intertwined System of Government – A Treaty Based Analysis for the Use of Political Scientists and Constitutional Lawyers' (2008) 73 *Il Politico* 133–179.

42 See above, n 34.

43 The rise of pragmatism is further evident in recent debates on the possible decline of formal treaties as a mechanism for cooperation in international law.

and reflects little upon the question of methodology. This would seem to lead to the question of the method to identify actors in EU and international law.

## *2.2 Functional and technical identification of actors in EU and international law*

The criteria for identifying actors in EU and public international law are dominated by legal personality. Methodologically, it plays a highly relativist function. Legal personality is a quality granted by certain legal norms and is exclusively recognised in the light of a respective norm. As a result, legal personality is frequently 'sidelined' as a highly technical, doctrinal or functional issue. Personality in the EU legal order often appears to be granted less on a conceptually reflected basis and rather for pragmatic reasons, thereby enabling entities to perform legal activities.[44] Thus, it is a 'doers' vision of functionality, rather than a 'thinkers' one. For example, while all 35 regulatory agencies of the EU have legal personality and independence,[45] many non-independent executive agencies established to perform programmes on behalf of the European Commission also have legal personality.[46] Some agencies have explicit clauses granting powers of legal supervision to the Commission, others not, but such distinctions are not necessarily perceived to have any significance.

And if personality is 'granted' by public international law, this signifies recognition of an entity in the international sphere and direct submission of the entity under the principles and rules of public international law.[47] Public

44 Ruffert, (n 38) pp. 350; M. Cremona, 'The European Union as an International Actor: The Issues of Flexibility and Linkage' (1998) 3(1) *European Foreign Affairs Review* 67–94; R. Leal-Arcas, 'EU Legal Personality in Foreign Policy?' (2006) 24(2) *Boston University International Law Journal* 165–212; R. Wessell, 'Revising the international legal status of the EU' (2000) 5(4) *European Foreign Affairs Review* 507–537; P. Caldwell, *EU External Relations Law and Policy in the Post Lisbon era* (The Hague: T.M.C. Asser Press, 2012). Cf. The conference on 'The Category of the Person in EU Law' EUI/ University Paris 1 in 2014, focusing upon the protection of the person as the chief asset and interest of EU law, reflecting its shift from agency to identity, as well as the prominence of justice.

45 Ruffert n 38, pp. 349; E. Chiti, 'An Important Part of the EU's Institutional Machinery: Features, Problems and Perspectives of European Agencies' (2009) 46 *Common Market Law Review* 1395–1442; S. Griller and A. Orator, 'Everything Under Control? The "Way Forward" for European Agencies in the Footsteps of the Meroni Doctrine' (2010) 35 *European Law Review* 3–35; M. Busuioc, *European Agencies: Law and Practices of Accountability* (Oxford: OUP, 2013).

46 Article 4(2) Council Regulation (EC) No. 58/2003 of 19 December 2002 laying down the statute for executive agencies to be entrusted with certain tasks in the management of Community programmes.

47 J. Nijman, 'The Concept of International Legal Personality – An Inquiry into the History and Theory of International Law' (The Hague: T.M.C. Asser Press, 2004); D. Akande, 'International Organizations' in M. Evans (ed.), *International Law* (Oxford: OUP, 3rd edn, 2010); J. Klabbers, 'Presumptive Personality: the European Union in International Law', in M. Koskenniemi (eds), *International Law Aspects of the European Union* (The Hague: Nijhoff, 1998) at 231; C. Brölmann, *The Institutional Veil in Public International Law* (Oxford: Hart Publishing, 2007); G. Weissberg,

international law differentiates sharply between entities vested with personality and institutions acting on behalf of these entities. For example, the United Nations bear personality while the Security Council and General Assembly do not. Yet while the international legal capacity of the IMF is not disputed, there is dispute concerning the form of agreements that it enters with Member States.[48] And although there may be a 'notion' of personality under public international law or national private law, there is no concept of a legal person under EU law.[49] More practically, the EU does not become legally subdivided by institutions such as the European Central Bank or European Investment Bank and instead they gain such powers as functional or practical means to allow them to become active in the international field, indicating the dominance of pragmatism. The redundancy of legal personality as a functional tool might be emphasised by contemporary EU law. Many new actors created in recent times are not technical actors, e.g. the European External Action Service (EEAS), the European Cybercrime Centre (EC3) or the European Public Prosecutors Office (EPPO).[50] Instead, they are carved up in other ways, for example, in the case of the EC3 as 'desks' of other institutions, i.e. of the evolving entity, Europol. As practice demonstrates, this does not preclude their autonomous development as actors who litigate or can be subject to judicial review. Arguably, such developments serve to underscore the unhelpful limits of doctrinalism and legal formalism, lacking realism about autonomy and institutional behaviour.

*The International Legal Personality of the United Nations* (Columbia, NY: Columbia University, 1959); C. Jenks, 'The Legal Personality of International Organisations' (1945) 22 *British Yearbook of International Law* 267, at 270; M. Rama-Montaldo, 'International Legal Personality and Implied Powers of International Organizations' (1970) 44 *British Yearbook of International Law* 111–155; A. Reinisch, 'Securing the Accountability of International Organizations' (2001) 7(2) *Global Governance* 131–149; I. Seidl-Hohenveldern, 'The Legal Personality of International and Supranational Organisations' (1965) 21 *Rev Egyptienne Droit Int* 35–72; F. Seyersted, 'International Personality of Intergovernmental Organizations: Do Their Capacities Really Depend on Their Constitutions' (1964) 4 *Indian Journal of International Law* 1–74; J. D'Aspremont, 'Abuse of the Legal Personality of International Organizations and the Responsibility of Member States' (2007) 4 *International Organizations Law Review* 91–119; H. Aufricht, 'Personality in International Law' (1943) 37 *American Political Science Review* 217–243; D. Bethlehem, 'The End of Geography: The Changing Nature of International System and the Challenge to International Law' (2014) 25(1) *European Journal of International Law* 9–24; J. Klabbers, 'The concept of legal personality' (2005) *Ius Gentium, Journal of the University of Baltimore* 35–66; M. Sellers, 'Legal Personality: International Legal Personality' (2005) 11 *Ius Gentium, Journal of the University of Baltimore* 67–78.

48 E. Denters, *Law and policy of IMF Conditionality* (The Hague: Kluwer Law International, 1996), at 306; N. Wahi, 'Human Rights Accountability of the IMF and the World Bank: A Critique of Existing Mechanisms and Articulation of a Theory of Horizontal Accountability' (2005–2006) 12 *U. C. Davis J. Int'l L. & Pol'y* at 344; J. Jackson, T. Cottier, J. Jackson and R. Lastra (eds), *International Law in Financial Regulation and Monetary Affairs* (Oxford: OUP, 2012).

49 Ruffert (n 38).

50 See Proposal for a Council Regulation on the Establishment of the European Public Prosecutor's Office COM/2013/0534 final <https://www.europol.europa.eu/ec3>. See n 30.

### *2.3 The 'whole' and the sum of the parts: speaking about institutional components of international organisations as actors in rule-making*

One means to look beyond legal and doctrinal formalism might be to gauge how we have evolved our understanding of the measurement of entities *qua* institutions. In this respect, pragmatism remains a challenge to the measurement of institutions, as much as the malleability of language. For example, consider those who have argued that each piece of international law should be studied as an institution itself, such that the set of institutions comprises a 'continent'.[51] International and EU law have proven themselves both to be flexible and pragmatic projects and yet risk much analytical clarity through the dominance of this pragmatism.[52] We may observe how legal theory specifically adopts a highly *internal* analytical perspective that renders its evolution more challenging. So this raises the question as to the usefulness and workability of *external* perspectives.

Formalist understandings of those who are '*actors*' engaged in rule-making are unable to capture much about EU lawmaking with many new manifestations of 'executive' actors after the State, powerful and independent judicial components or the rise of transnational parliamentarianism, broadly understood as actors engaged in rule-making after the State. To be sure, some may act with considerably more institutional, social or political legitimacy than others. We may say that formalist criteria and theorisations operate to exclude the acts or practices of institutional entities or components that are part of international organisations who exercise public authority beyond the State, who are not regarded as unitary actors or equivalent to the organisation itself. Yet how do they in reality interact with private associations, unions or certain experts? What is their zone of influence? How do we assess the autonomy of these component parts?

The rise of transnational parliamentarianism – such as in the Transatlantic Legislatures Dialogues (TLD),[53] the Association of Southeast Asian Nations (ASEAN) or the Arctic Council assemblies – through embryonically formalised contacts and then rule-making initiatives, may indicate 'living' practices of actorness. Similarly, 'agencification' in regional, national and international legal orders – empowering many independent actors and according them legal personality with increasingly less checks – might lead us to draw similar deductions. Yet are they appropriately excluded from actorness as a result? Lexicon has provided with relative flexibility and creativity, which notably has not availed of actorness in its evolution. For instance, new entities labelled as 'quasi-autonomous' actors under EU law have generated a new lexicon of

51 See Koremenos, (n 17).
52 See Bianchi, (n 29).
53 See Jančić, (n 24).

accountability in EU law and governance.[54] It suggests a flexibility through law that is absent in actorness theorisations.

Courts are largely omitted from theorisations of actorness, even courts that are globally and/or empirically acknowledged to be powerful, independent bodies engaging in rule-making practices, directly or indirectly.[55] It raises the question as to when do courts act as actors in transnational rule-making, formally and informally and/or directly and indirectly inside and outside the courtroom? How are practices of judicial institutions changing? Are courts overlooked as actors outside their courtrooms, for example, their formal interventions in legislative processes? How does (such) actorness impact upon adjudication of such rules, as regards accountability? Do such questions detract from the usefulness of actorness or simply indicate its 'distance' from legal theory?

One such means to look beyond challenges posed by formalism is to consider understandings of actors and structural power, which is considered here next.

## 3 Looking through and beyond law in the conceptualisation of actors in rule-making

In non-legal scholarship on the study regions and organisations, the phenomena of '*actorness*' embraces less readily evolving organisations or their institutional components, even when they obtain legal personality or legal authority to act, e.g. the EU or ASEAN.[56] The criteria remain much disputed and in flux but paradoxically retain much significance across subject fields.[57] The conceptualisation of actorness capacity provides that four distinct dimensions be studied: authority, autonomy, external recognition and internal cohesiveness.[58] Yet the perspective of the 'poser' of the question is significant, if we may term it this way. Is actorness *actively* ever sought-after by either fledging or components of international organisations? Or both? Do events in the Crimea indicate to us that the external perspective, i.e. of recognition, remains the most dominant component for lawyers? Adopting a more *internal*

54 See the account of M. Bovens, 'Analysing and Assessing Accountability: A Conceptual Framework' (2007) 13(4) *European Law Journal* 447–468.

55 See in particular the work of Kelemen, (n 24); Alter, (n 19).

56 M. Cremona, 'The European Union as a Global Actor: Roles, Models and Identity' (2004) 41 *Common Market Law Review* 553–573; U. Wunderlich, 'The EU an Actor Sui Generis? A Comparison of EU and ASEAN Actorness' (2012) 50(4) *Journal of Common Market Studies* 653–669; T. Forsberg, 'Normative Power Europe, Once Again: A Conceptual Analysis of an Ideal Type' (2011) 49(6) *Journal of Common Market Studies* 1183–1204.

57 E. Conceicao-Heldt and S. Meunier (eds), 'Speaking with a Single Voice: Internal Cohesiveness and External Cohesiveness of the EU in World Politics' (2014) 21(7) *Journal of European Public Policy* 961–979.

58 See J. Jupille and Caporaso, (n 26).

perspective, however, we may observe that practices as to actorness could have a dramatic impact upon an international organisation vis-à-vis its constituent institutional components. But would this be a more 'valid' analytical frame?

The criteria of 'actorness' in non-legal scholarship often include *inter alia* the *de facto* or *de jure* recognition of its actions, the legal authority to act, its institutional autonomy or distinctiveness and the cohesion between its constituent parts in the formulation of policy.[59] Each of the criteria has a distinctive and formal legal component: for example, external recognition, *de facto* and *de jure*, external delegation of competences, institutional independence and competence-derived cohesion. If legal scholarship is largely 'fixated' upon formalist criteria of legal personality or legal authority to act, we might usefully consider whether non-legal scholarship may also be said to reify such criteria. There are descriptive and normative components to actorness that may appear to sit together uneasily from a legal perspective. For example, do the criteria logically and analytically flow from one another? Who is to judge the criteria? Which of them is most legally, socially or politically authoritative? It raises many other challenging questions for legal scholarship: for example, how do actorness practices impact upon rule-making itself? How has or should legal scholarship responded to the evolution of actorness? And how does and should the attribution of legal personality of an organisation strengthen its actorness vis-à-vis its institutions and other components? It also raises the issue as to whether there a distinction between *de facto* and *de jure* actorness? If so, is it pragmatic or valid? How do the actors advance the components of actorness through law? And how flexible is actorness? How does and should actorness influence theorisations of legitimacy and accountability?

The conventional conceptualisation of the actorness qualities of international organisations only embrace formal international organisations, and less so fledgling or new supranational organisations or their institutional components, however powerful. As a result, the conventional criteria for actorness are innately challenged by transnational rule-making practices. For example, evolving international organisations such as ASEAN or the EU bedevil characterisation in non-legal scholarship, even after the recent acquisition of legal personality by the latter and the adoption of settled practices of representation in the former.[60] It also poses the question perhaps as to whether a lack of general agreement on the actorness of an organisation may be said to be 'exploited' by the organisation itself or its components. In this regard, one could take as an example the EU's far-reaching efforts to legislate in

59 C. Bretherton and J. Vogler (eds), 'The European Union as a Sustainable Development Actor: the Case of External Fisheries Policy' (2008) 30(3) *Journal of European Integration* 401–417; C. Gebhard, 'Coherence' (2011) in C. Hill and M. Smith (eds), *International Relations and the European Union* (Oxford: OUP, 2nd edn, 2011), pp. 101–127.

60 U. Wunderlich, 'The EU an Actor Sui Generis? A Comparison of EU and ASEAN Actorness' (2012) 50(4) *Journal of Common Market Studies* 653–669.

environmental matters, with implications outside of its territory.[61] Or similarly, one could consider the increasingly 'tense' construction of territory in EU regulation of financial services.[62] Understandably, then, there is a movement to reconsider why 'actorness' *must* evolve. And such a movement takes as its starting point frequently the exceptionalism of the EU as a case study as a means to reconsider the content of actorness, one which legal scholarship may derive much benefit from engaging with.[63] However, one risks easily an 'EU-centric' theorisation.

Moreover, 'formal' actorness criteria are particularly 'after the fact' and do not necessarily explain how actorness emerges nor how it interacts with other institutions presently or in the future – or even generates other actorness fact matrixes.[64] In this regard, actorness has a very formalistic and descriptive character that can appear rigid and unhelpful. The enhanced international actorness of an actor such as the EU may enable it to act as a central player in the creation of new international bodies, e.g. the International Criminal Court. Such 'subsequently enacted' entities may, as this example might demonstrate, engender much critique as to legitimacy in the form of social acceptance as much as authority. Yet does actorness offer any real window of insight as to such developments? Or into the specific legitimacy (and also authority) questions that these developments provoke?

Actorness may not yet provide a suitably reliable framework for legal scholarship, but it is argued to offer an important example of disciplinary reflection as to the contours of rule-making. This publication seeks to look more broadly at conceptualisations of actors and rule-making, even beyond the subject areas of EU and public international law, particularly leading case studies of transnational law or of international relations, so as to identify common themes and possible alternative means to reflect upon the conceptualisation of actors beyond flexibility and pragmatism. Part of the challenge of evaluating how we understand actors in rule-making is the nature of the action itself, i.e. *how* it occurs matters. The next section thus considers the relevance of behavioural and sociological understandings of postnational rule-making in the subjects of EU and public international law.

61 The EU Emissions Trading System (EU ETS), accessed <http://ec.europa.eu/clima/policies/ets/index_en.htm>; D. Ellerman and B. Buchner, 'The European Union Emissions Trading Scheme: Origins, Allocation, and Early Results' (2007) 1(1) *Review of Environmental Economics and Policy* 66–87.

62 E.g. J. Scott, 'Extraterritoriality and Territorial Extension in EU Law' (2014) 62(1) *American Journal of Comparative Law* 87–126.

63 K. Čmakalová and J. Rolenc, 'The Dimensions of EU's Actorness: Internal Legitimacy' in Petr Kratochvíl, *The EU as a Political Actor – The Analysis of Four Dimensions of the EU's Actorness* (Berlin: Nomos, 2013), pp. 47–58.

64 M. Groenleer and L. Van Schaik, 'United We Stand? The European Union's International Actorness in the Cases of the International Criminal Court and the Kyoto Protocol' (2007) 45(5) *Journal of Common Market Studies* 969–998.

## 4 The behavioural dimension of postnational rule-making

### *4.1 Zooming in upon acting in the shadows*

Institutional components of organisations may manage to engage in rule-making practices through *inter alia* influence, independence, autonomy, contestation and an active development of their functions and roles. However, the nature of such rule-making may be said to occur 'in the shadow' of other institutions or bodies within organisations, who are formal actors, eluding thus a more doctrinal debate. It remains 'in the shadow' insofar as it may occur as part of a larger organisation or structure where it may have many informal influences, lack formal power structures, may operate with a grey-zone of autonomy or independence or may even be subject to multiple influences beyond other institutions.[65] For example, much emphasis in EU rule-making has been placed on regulating *ex ante* participation of stakeholders without formally regulation of lobbyists – and thereby makes distinct choices concerning the penumbra of 'legality'. The temporal choices exercises in our study of zones of rule-making can swiftly exclude the 'shadows'. The lexicon of 'foreground' and 'background' actors has been central to mapping the theorisation of the EU's composite executive, as much as 'high level' and 'low level' functionality thereof.[66] In this regard, spatial zones of rule-making can be shrouded in their own malleable lexicon – but paradoxically, also elucidated, often sharply, in this manner.

There are notably very few 'dedicated' or 'actual' inter-institutional bodies in the EU, save, for example, European Personnel Selection Office (EPSO) or the Publications Office. Such entities range in task from the technical to the functional to the wholly administrative. The evolution of inter-institutional agreements in EU law are considered as a 'constitutionalisation' process by lawyers and political scientists alike.[67] They are even theorised as action from 'below', whereby the institutions themselves have been empowered and autonomously steered the evolution of practice.[68] Current debates concern their actual opacity or transparency, given their tendency to evolve into hard law. Yet why should institutional action from 'within' an organisation be considered as being 'from below'? What does it indicate about our understanding of zones of action between legal orders?

65 See Biermann and Siebenhüner, (n 32); Chalmers, (n 3); Lescano and Teubner, (n 4); D. Curtin and I. Dekker 'The European Union from Maastricht to Lisbon: Institutional and Legal Unity Out of the Shadows' in P. Craig and G. Búrca (eds), *The Evolution of EU Law* (Oxford: OUP, 2nd edn, 2011), pp. 155–186.

66 Curtin and Dekker, (n 65); Curtin, (n 2).

67 See Curtin, (n 2); A. Heritier and D. Kerwer *et al.* (eds), *Differential Europe: The European Union Impact on National Policymaking* (Lanham, MD: Rowman & Littlefield, 2001). See their place in the political guidelines of the Juncker Commission, accessed <http://ec.europa.eu/priorities/docs/pg_en.pdf>.

68 E.g., B. Driessen, *Interinstitutional Conventions in EU Law* (London: Cameron May, 2007).

This raises the question as to the appropriate normative frame through which to understand EU action.

### *4.2 The centrality of social legitimacy for postnational rule-making*

In sociological terms, legitimacy may be an objective fact but it is socially constructed.[69] Legitimacy in this context means social credibility and acceptance. Of course, legitimacy may be pragmatic or normatively or cognitively based.[70] It is not necessarily a study of legal formalism or legal validity, a study which some suggest could be even irrelevant or unproductive. Legitimacy can differ across time and space and between actors, systems and contexts, and is characterised by malleability but also much semantic ambiguity. The concept of legitimacy has been argued to have been long neglected in public international law until more recently.[71] The three 'dominant' theoretical categorisations or taxonomies of legitimacy, of legal, moral and social legitimacy are not always regarded as self-contained.[72] There remain important distinctions to be drawn between normative and sociological legitimacy, between normative and empirical legitimacy, between de jure and de facto legitimacy and between moral and descriptive legitimacy, and perhaps also formal legitimacy.[73] Functional categorisations are argued to have driven the significance of mixed approaches. Legitimacy may change but may also be resilient. Legitimacy communications can 'forgive' individual transgressions.[74] In scholarship, there is a particular tendency to focus upon normative or cognitive bases of legitimacy rather than on whether it is regarded as legitimate.[75] And while the questions are analytically distinct, each may have a normative or cognitive basis, e.g. legitimacy that is so deeply

69 W. Scott, *Institutions and Organizations – Ideas, Interests and Identities* (London: Sage, 2001).

70 See Thomas on the usefulness of distinguishing between the concept of legitimacy and legitimation, citing A. Appelbaum, 'Legitimacy in a Bastard Kingdom' (2004) John F Kennedy School of Government Centre for Public Leadership Working Paper, Spring 2004, pp. 74–94, accessed <http://dspace.mit.edu/handles/1721.1/55927>; J. Weiler, 'Europe in Crisis – On "Political Messianism", "Legitimacy" and the "Rule of Law" (2012) *Singapore Journal of Legal Studies* 248–269.

71 Cf. Thomas, 'The Uses and Abuses of Legitimacy in International Law' (2014) 34(4) *Oxford Journal of Legal Studies* 729–758, to the effect that it is easier to make things legal than to make them legitimate.

72 Ibid., 744; see T. Franck, *The Power of Legitimacy Among Nations* (Oxford: OUP, 1990).

73 C. Thornhill and S. Ashenden (eds), *Legality and Legitimacy: Normative and Sociological Approaches* (Berlin: Nomos, 2010); A. Buchanan and R. Keohane (eds), *The Legitimacy of Global Governance Institutions* in Rudiger R. Wolfrum and V. Roben (eds), *Legitimacy in International Law* (Berlin: Springer, 2008); F. Scharpf, *Reflections on Multilevel Legitimacy* (2003) Max Planck Institute for the Study of Societies Working Paper 07/03 pp. 10–16.

74 J. Gibson and G. Caldeira, 'The Legitimacy of the Court of Justice in the European Union: Models of Institutional Support' (1995) 89(2) *The American Political Science Review* 356–376.

75 J. Black, 'Constructing and Contesting Legitimacy and Accountability in Polycentric Regulatory Regimes' (2008) 2 *Regulation and Governance* 137–164.

rooted as to be beyond question.[76] Social legitimacy is defined as its projection on to an action, rule, actor or system by an actor's belief that the action, rule, actor or system is morally or legally legitimate. It is argued that unlike legal or moral legitimacy, social legitimacy does not make a normative commitment to any relationship of power, it drops any sense of an objective ought. On the basis that social legitimacy is an empty concept without an account of the moral or legal framework to which the 'believer subscribes', social legitimacy is an empirical concept, but one that is concerned specifically with what forms of power people believe morally or legally justified.[77] Weberian legitimacy has historically been strongly tied to the analysis of legal structures.[78]

We may easily overlook the social dimensions and significance of '*acting in the shadows*' for rule-making and our understanding of who are actors engaging in rule-making. It is argued here thus that an analysis of actors in postnational rule-making benefits most obviously – and even realistically – from a *social* understanding of legitimacy. To open up the 'black box' of the shadows to daylight enables us to address further questions such as the acceptance of the practices of postnational rule-making, i.e. the social legitimacy thereof.[79] Given the dominance pragmatism as an explanation of the evolution of the EU and international legal orders, acceptance appears as a reasonable tool to measure contemporary practices. The social legitimacy of actors in rule-making may have a differing resonance in alternate areas of law such that it becomes even more challenging to transpose this to the transnational context. Take, for example, the greater social 'acceptance' and understanding of the work of lobbyists in rule-making in the US rather than in the EU.[80] However,

76 For example, challenging the validity of legislation that is in force for some time and around which considerable enforcement regimes are built: data retention.

77 See supra, Thomas (n 71), 741.

78 M. Weber and E. Fischoff (tr.), *Economy and Society: An outline of Interpretive Sociology* in G. Roth and C. Wittich (eds) (Berkeley, CA: University of California Press, 1978), p. 215.

79 E. Cohn and S. White (eds), *Legal Socialization: A Study of Norms and Rules* (United States: Springer-Verlag, 1990); E. Cohn *et al.*, 'An Integrated Model of Legal and Moral Reasoning and Rule-Violating Behaviour: The Role of Legal Attitudes' (2010) 34(4) *Law and Human Behaviour* 295–309.

80 M. Cowles, 'The Transatlantic Business Dialogue and Domestic Business-Government Relations' in M. Cowles, J. Caparaso and T. Risse (eds), *Transforming Europe: Europeanization and Domestic Change* (Ithaca, NY: Cornell University Press, 2001) pp. 159–179; J. Thurber, P. Griffin and M. Egan, 'Conference on Lobbying, Ethics Reform in US and EU' American University, 17 March 2014, accessed <http://www.american.edu/spa/news/lobbying-conference-2014.cfm>. Contrast the scrutiny on all actors involved in the Transatlantic Trade and Investment Partnership (TTIP) negotiations, which currently includes videoing all stakeholders meetings, registering participation, tweeting all details of meetings and negotiations, and feeding the public and civil society regularly with copious amounts of information; accessed <http://ec.europa.eu/trade/policy/in-focus/ttip/>. The substantive and procedural 'acceptance' of this transparency on either side of the Atlantic seems highly divergent; see A. Bunea, 'Issues, Preferences and Ties: Determinants of Interest Groups' Preference Attainment in the EU Environmental Policy' (2013) 20(4) *Journal of European Public Policy* 552–570.

theorisations unduly reliant upon sociological and/or behavioural analysis risks over-expanding the malleability of vocabulary at the expense of analytical sharpness. It is all too easy to become emasculated in the malleability of words in the depiction of behaviour. What this publication makes a case for is the relevance of social legitimacy for our understanding of actors in rule-making from the perspective of EU and public international law. The publication also draws attention and focus to new sources and autonomous actors engaging in rule-making, falling outside standard definitions thereof. Many chapters of this publication focus upon new actors and practices of behaviour arising.

This ties in with a movement in scholarship to reconstruct methodology and take into account the multi-disciplinarity of postnational rule-making, its highly diverse range of actors, instruments and processes.[81] It advocates approaches that accommodate *inter alia* the plurality of sources of EU law and which explicitly enunciate its method. There is a significant demand for attention to new methodologies in the direction of EU law, so as to move beyond doctrinal outcomes and understandings. The methodological focus required to pinpoint the actions of a new or underexplored actors, e.g. the academy, or the less than regulated (lobbyists) simply mapping a new phenomenon, e.g. transnational parliaments, is thus done here through the use of inductive accounts.

Accordingly, this publication seeks to focus upon many of the individual components of institutional organisations, as well as other actors within rule-making structures that may be readily overlooked by formalism and doctrinalism, such as lobbyists and academia. The publication aims to capture new practices and themes and reflects upon the tensions that they pose for old 'lenses' by drawing together scholars, senior and junior, of EU law, public international law, international relations, the doctrinal and non-conventional studies, those focused upon Asia and South America as much as the EU.

## 5 Overview of the thematic sections and individual chapters

By way of a background and then overview to the contributions to the publication, readers might find it useful to know that contributors to Section I, 'Framing actors in postnational rule-making: between doctrine and lexicon', were asked to reflect upon the following general themes or questions insofar

81 R. van Gestel and H-W. Micklitz, 'Why Methods Matter in European Legal Scholarship' (2014) 20(3) *European Law Journal* 292–316, at 313–316 ('An Agenda for a European Debate'); see Vauchez (n 1); T. Hervey, R. Cryer, B. Sokhi-Bulley and A. Bohm, *Research Methodologies in EU and International Law* (Oxford: Hart Publishing, 2011); R. van Gestel, H-W. Micklitz and M-P. Maduro, 'Methodology in the New Legal World', *European University Institute Law Working Paper* 2012/13; U. Neergaard, R. Nielsen and L. Roseberry (eds), *European Legal Method* (Copenhagen: DJOF Publishing, 2013); see 'The New History of EU law' project, of Copenhagen University, accessed <http://europeanlaw.saxo.ku.dk/>.

as this proved relevant and/or possible for them individually. These included the following issues:

- How limiting is doctrine or lexicon? Does it accommodate change and flexibility?
- How easily are new actors accommodated within postnational rule-making?
- How do you understand the postnational? Does it accommodate your subject or appear procedural? Limiting?
- Do you find 'lexicon' useful as a term of art?
- How do questions of legitimacy, e.g. social legitimacy and social acceptance, impact upon how you formulate doctrine and lexicon here?

Next, contributors to Section II, 'New institutional components and systems: establishing autonomy in postnational rule-making', were asked to reflect upon the following themes or questions:

- How is autonomy established or practised by new institutional components? How does this autonomy relate to rule-making? Formally, informally, etc.?
- Is it a zero-sum game/a loss and gain for other institutional components? How easily does a new institution(al component) become part of a system?
- Is postnational rule-making a help or a hindrance to reflect upon new institutions and institutional components? Is it embracing of the *sui generis*?
- How do you understand '*sui generis*' within such rule-making?
- How do you understand rule-making in this context?
- To what extent does a new institution or component seek to operate, function or act in the shadows? How evident is such behaviour? Is it covert? Does it raise legitimacy questions? Does it raise legitimacy questions more from an internal than an external perspective?

Contributors to Section III, 'Interactions between actors in postnational rule-making: framing practices "in the shadows" and beyond', were asked to consider the following themes or questions:

- What are practices 'in the shadows' of rule-making? What makes them 'shadowy'? Does your case study fall short of this? What could make the practices shadowy? Is there illegitimacy, malaise or malpractice arising from non-regulation? Or is it social acceptance? By whom? Does postnational rule-making incorporate 'shadows' or such zones of activity outside of our regular lexicon?
- What is a site of rule-making? How relevant is social acceptance?
- Are there legitimacy questions raised by the formulation of the practices?
- Is social acceptance useful to reflect upon?

- What makes certain actors interact in rule-making practices?
- Is postnational rule-making helpful to frame these practices? Does it embrace them?
- Are 'new actors' the chief source of concern in your case study?
- Is your case study a new method of interaction more than 'new actors'? How do you understand rule-making?

The fruits of the labours of the contributors are to be found in their individual contributions. Nonetheless, their contributions are summarised here briefly next.

In Section I, 'Framing actors in postnational rule-making: between doctrine and lexicon', Collins identifies the tension of the postnational with formalism in his paper 'International law: mapping the terrain of institutional "lawmaking": form and function in international law'. He argues that maintaining a limited, formal doctrinal perspective on subjects and sources is not to suggest the immutability or centrality of the State, but instead reflects the best approximation of a systemic construction of legality in a plural international community. He argues that this is not to suggest a fetishism of form over function, but rather an interrelation and tension between form and function in structuring an understand of the actors of postnational rule-making.

Ruffert, in his piece 'European Union law: the many faces of rule-making in the EU', demonstrates that there is a plurality, even a plethora, of rule-making actors, most of which are active in the executive but not the legislative field and tend to work in an informal way within their network. He demonstrates that when rule-making is governed by the European Council, these supranational institutions remain in the shadows.

Beyond the subjects of European and international law, Wunderlich reflects on what it means to be an actor in international scholarship and considers the concept of actorness and regional actorness using the case studies of EU and ASEAN actorness in a chapter entitled 'International relations and global governance: actors in global governance institutions: ASEAN and the EU'. Is ASEAN really emerging as an international actor in its own right or is it mimicking EU actorness by creating a hollow mirror image of the EU? He argues that it is often difficult to discern a common rationale underlying various EU interregional contacts. EU interregionalism displays a bewildering variety of institutional models defying any simple categorisation. It remains difficult to evaluate regional actorness because it is influenced by the EU model. Similarly, focusing upon institutional criteria ignores other aspects. He cautions against exchanging one 'black box' for another.

In Section II, 'New institutional components and systems: establishing autonomy in postnational rule-making', Jančić maps both theoretically and practically the phenomenon of transnational parliaments beyond the Nation State in 'Transnational and global perspectives: transnational parliamentarism and global governance: the new practice of democracy'. He reflects upon the challenges they pose for rule-making beyond the Nation State given that they are mostly score lowly in terms of influence, legitimacy, accountability and effectiveness. He outlines in detail categorisations of international parliamentary organs (IPOs). Despite their empirical surge, legal and political science approaches to the democratisation of global governance pay no more than marginal attention to the transnational parliamentary revolution. He argues that the externalisation of rule-making beyond the State brings sociological, non-constitutional functions of parliaments to the fore.

De Waele charts the rise of the most stark but arguably complex actor of the EU's executive, that is the European Council, to a formal institution of the EU in his chapter, 'European Union law: the practices of the "new" European Council'. He argues that the European Council is increasingly sidestepped under the pretext of the Union method, placing further strains on the institution's actorness. Rather, it might be assumed too quickly that the new European Council possess a genuine actorness.

Urueña focuses upon the dynamics of interaction in postnational rule-making. He argues that actors are part of a wider landscape that defines their actorness and are expressions of a changing global regulatory space in his chapter, 'Interaction as a site of postnational rule-making: a case study of the Inter-American system of human rights'. He selects the specific dynamics of interaction in a case study of Latin America, as to the Inter-American Court of Human Rights and domestic constitutional courts in the region. Using the regulatory space as a site of lawmaking, he argues that it allows us to better appreciate the complex dynamics of postnational rule-making. He argues that actors enter a populated regulatory space where they adapt to the other actors of that space as a subtle process of adaptation. Focusing upon events of conflict alone tells us little about the workings of postnational rule-making. His focus is a critical one upon the dominance of constitutionalism in the inter-American mindset and its conception of time and space, and even international norms. Instead, the global regulatory space is useful to conceptualise change and temporariness in international law differently. The interaction approach is premised upon actors interacting in an unknown number of interactions.

In Section III, 'Interactions between actors in postnational rule-making: framing practices "in the shadows" and beyond', Wouters, Odermatt and Chané outline how the EU struggles to become a more effective global actor in their contribution, 'The European Union: a shadowy global actor? The UN system as an example'. They depict how the EU can be viewed as a shadowy global actor both in light of its limited role and position and through the indirect influences that it exercises in internal law and policymaking. It examines the case study of the EU within the UN system and its relationship to the targets within the Barroso-Ashton Strategy. It considers specific developments as to the Food and Agriculture Organization, the International Atomic Energy Agency, and the UN Educational, Scientific and Cultural Organisation as a variety of agencies where the EU has varying statuses.

In her contribution entitled 'European private law: lawmakers in the shadows: legal academics in the construction of European private law', Sefton-Green provides a vivid account of the input of academia into rule-making and the place of expertise in the construction of European private law, with multiple actors. She maps the variety of roles that European academics play in the prior stages of EU legislation. She argues that the official and shadow actors may have political agendas that blow the winds in opposite and converging directions, each with a degree of power to influence each other in various ways.

Korkeo-aha considers the place of lobbyists in EU rule-making and their complexity as regards their socialisation, their legitimacy and their transparency practices in 'European Union law: lobbyists: rule-makers in the shadow'. She argues that lobbyists have become actors of rule-making by positioning themselves as either experts or stakeholders. She argues that the analytical challenge is our perception of lobbyists in these new roles and their acceptance as actors and draws upon Max Weber in offering a typology of a lobbyist, whereby the most pressing legitimacy concerns are raised by the practices of the expert lobbyist.

I am very grateful to Raluca Sterian and Justin Wong for their research assistance and to the editorial team at Routledge also for their support and assistance.

Dr Elaine Fahey
London, 30 January 2015

Section I

# Framing actors in postnational rule-making

## Between doctrine and lexicon

# 1 Mapping the terrain of institutional 'lawmaking'

## Form and function in international law

*Richard Collins*[1]

It has been common in recent years to contrast modern and classical international lawmaking, depicting the former as dynamic and heterogeneous, and the latter as State-centric and 'doctrinal'. This doctrinal image is characterised as State-centric both in terms of the actors involved in rule-making processes and the nature of the rules themselves. In short, an actor's ability to make law is limited by their international legal personality, while the rules that result have legal 'pedigree' only if traceable to one or more of the formal sources of international law. Accordingly, doctrinal understandings are often depicted negatively as cementing the hegemony of the State as (almost) the sole international lawmaker. For instance, in considering the extent to which individuals can be said to be international actors, Robert McCorquodale (quoting Alexander Orakhelashvili) decries this State-centric understanding of 'actorness' in international law:

> One of the essential aspects of an international legal person is 'the capacity to participate in international law-making and to enforce rules of international law' . . . From the classical definition of the sources of international law found in Article 38 of the Statute of the ICJ, where State practice and State treaty-making are pre-eminent, to the laws on territory and jurisdiction being about State boundaries, it is the State that appears to decide exclusively on the creation, development and enforcement of international law.[2]

However, the argument that I wish to defend in this paper is that these kinds of characterisation of doctrinal approaches not only fail to grasp the

1 The chapter was originally presented as a paper at the workshop: 'The Actors of Postnational Rulemaking', University of Amsterdam, 6 June 2014. Thanks to the participants there for their useful feedback and suggestions, and in particular to the editor, Elaine Fahey, not only for comments and suggestions, but also for her support (and patience) during the writing process.

2 Robert McCorquodale, 'The Individual and the International Legal System' in Malcolm Evans (ed.), *International Law* (4th edn, OUP 2010) 280, at 294–95.

openness of international law to other actors as participants in international lawmaking processes, but also miss what is important about doctrine in the context of international law.

Accordingly, the central question posed in this paper is how international law *should* accommodate the increasingly complex array of actors involved in normative standard setting (rule-making) within the international legal system, including how it absorbs or understands the nature of those rules themselves. In particular, I want to consider to what extent one can retain a formalist (doctrinal) understanding of the subjects and sources of international law yet at the same time account for the array of actors involved in postnational rule-making. I will argue that any attempt to absorb within international law the range of actors and forms of normativity that exist as a result of the increasing 'institutionalisation' that has occurred throughout the twentieth and twenty-first centuries creates a significant tension between legal form and function, particularly with regard to the roles that many of these regimes and institutions have come to fulfil within the international system. Nevertheless, I will argue that this tension between form and function is an important part of securing some measure of legal accountability in a decentralised legal order such as international law.

## 1 Subjects doctrine and the 'dead end' of international legal personality

It is perhaps trite to say that the main or most prominent subjects of international law – its actors – are States. For a long period of time, of course, there were doubts about the formal legal recognition of legal subjects other than States, though the steady 'institutionalisation' of international law from the late nineteenth century onwards brought this restrictive approach increasingly into question. With the creation of the Public International Unions, river commissions and other technical organisations of the late-nineteenth century, followed by the creation of the League of Nations and International Labour Organization in the wake of the First World War, attention turned to the question of how to make sense of this novel new actor on the international scene. A number of international lawyers began to pose questions about the extent to which these institutions possessed a will of their own such that they could be described as subjects in their own right, and how thereafter they should be absorbed within, and how they perhaps also altered, the inter-State structure of international law.[3] Initially, much of this

3 See e.g. Andrea Rapisardi-Mirabelli, 'Théorie Générale des Unions Internationales' (1925-II) 7 *Recueil des Cours* 345–391, who developed the idea of 'community will' propounded, in different ways, in the works of Triepel and Anzilotti: see Heinrich Triepel, *Droit International et Droit Interne*, Paris: A. Pedone, 1920, pp. 27–61; Dinisio Anzilotti, *Corso di Diritto Internazionale*, 4th edn., Padua: CEDAM, 1955, pp. 82–85; and see discussion in Richard Collins, 'Non-State Actors in International Institutional Law: Non-State, Inter-State or Supra-state? The peculiar identity

discussion saw these institutions as 'contractual' vehicles through which States, still the primary actors of the international system, were able to enhance their participation in international law,[4] at best giving the system a more administrative and communitarian flavour.[5] It was not until the interwar years that international lawyers began to take seriously the idea that the new institutions might themselves be discrete and separate international actors in their own right. In any event, to the extent that certain, particularly continental-European, scholars were enthusiastic adherents to a theory of the separate legal personality of intergovernmental institutions, this was still largely seen in derivative terms as a product of inter-State agreement, rather than being an objective characteristic determined by international law and opposable also to non-members or other institutions.[6]

It was not until the emergence of the United Nations (UN) and the acknowledgement of its international legal personality by the International Court of Justice (ICJ) in its 1949 *Reparations* Advisory Opinion that doubts were laid to rest about the possibility of actors other than States being recognised formally as subjects of international law.[7] The importance of this case should not be understated. As Bederman notes, with its recognition that actors other than States could possess international legal personality (and thus subjectivity in a formal sense),[8] the ICJ ultimately put an end to much of the interwar uncertainty and, therefore, 'signalled the final days of the "law of nations" and ushered in the era of "international law"'.[9] However, by so doing, the case also perpetuates some of the ambiguities and uncertainties that helped shape the prewar discussion of how to come to terms with these new actors. As Bederman equally recognises, the reasoning of the Court seemed to recognise that organisations such as the UN exist both as over-arching 'communities', through which States participate in the broader international legal system as a whole, and as independent legal persons coexisting on an equal plane to those same states.[10] Accordingly, the 'actorness' of the institution exists both as a formal quality and as a derivative expression

of the Intergovernmental Organization' in Jean d'Aspremont (ed.), *Participants in the International Legal System* (Routledge 2011) 311, at 313–14.

4 Catherine Brölmann, *The Institutional Veil in Public International Law* (Hart 2007), 42–43.

5 See e.g. discussion of Rapisardi-Mirabelli (n 3), 359–366; discussed further in Brölmann, ibid., 55–56.

6 Brölmann, ibid., 56–58.

7 Reparation for Injuries Suffered in the Service of the United Nations, Advisory Opinion, ICJ Reports (1949) 174.

8 The two are often used synonymously; see Roland Portmann, *International Legal Personality* (CUP 2010) 1. It is at least defensible that 'subjecthood' differs from personality as a more general descriptor for those actors which are recognised by international law, even if lacking the kinds of competencies which legal personality is said to bring.

9 David Bederman, 'The Souls of International Organizations: Legal Personality and the Lighthouse at Cape Spartel' (1996) 36 *Virginia Journal of International Law* 275, at 279.

10 Bederman, ibid., 371–375.

of the combined will of the Member States. The internal institutional dynamics of the organisation and its external competencies and capacities are interminably intertwined.

In many ways, therefore, the case introduced as many uncertainties as it did clarity in the recognition of the subjectivity of actors other than States. The Court's reasoning constantly oscillates between deriving personality from the nature of the institution brought into existence, in which case it stresses the *sui generis* characteristics of the UN in particular, and placing emphasis on the intent of the founding States in bestowing certain kinds of competencies on the UN.[11] As Klabbers recognises, the case really highlights the circularity of the issue of non-State actors as subjects of international law, as their international legal personality seems to be evidenced by the exercise of competencies and powers that, in turn, require for their existence the possession of such personality.[12] To the extent that questions of personality have been raised with regard to actors other than States or intergovernmental institutions, such questions seem capable of being answered only once such actors have already had certain capacities and competencies bestowed upon them. The problem here is that not only is legal personality not automatic on meeting certain criteria, but it is fundamentally limited, derived from prior-agreement, and in that sense seems to reconfirm the primacy of the state once more. Accordingly, it is difficult to say more on the potential legal personality of other actors in the international legal system – e.g. individuals, NGOs, indigenous peoples, etc. – other than that 'it depends';[13] that is, it depends upon the particular circumstances of each candidate entity, as well as the surrounding political context. For instance, individuals enjoy subjectivity in international human rights law or international criminal law to the extent

11 The court seems to move from the internal legal order to the UN's objective personality in international law solely on the basis of the particular tasks that the UN attempts to fulfil:

'In the opinion of the Court, the Organization *was intended to exercise and enjoy*, and is in fact exercising and enjoying, functions and rights *which can only be explained* on the basis of the possession of a large measure of international personality and the capacity to operate upon an international plane. It is at present *the supreme type of international organization*, and it could not carry out the intentions of its founders if it was devoid of international personality. It must be acknowledged that *its members by entrusting certain functions to it*, with the attendant duties and responsibilities, *have clothed it with the competence* required to enable those functions to be effectively discharged.' (179, emphasis added)

This stress on the 'supreme' nature of the UN and the particular competencies with which it has been equipped is borne out by the Court's conclusion, some pages later (at 185), which claims that:

'. . . fifty States, representing the vast majority of the members of the international community, had the power, in conformity with international law, to bring into being an entity possessing objective international personality, and not merely personality recognized by them alone, together with capacity to bring international claims.'

12 See *inter alia* Jan Klabbers, 'The Concept of Legal Personality' (2005) 11 *Ius Gentium* 35, at 49.

13 See Math Noortmann, 'Presentation' in J. d'Aspremont (ed.), (n. 3), xxxviii.

that this subjectivity is bestowed by the prior existing treaty regimes that are, at their source and inception at least, still governed by States.[14] Such an approach follows the 'functional' nature of legal personality in international law that was clearly recognised in *Reparations*.[15] As the ICJ itself concluded, '[t]he subjects of law in any legal system are not necessarily identical in their nature or in the extent of their rights, *and their nature depends upon the needs of the community*.'[16]

Acknowledging this limitation means not only is it impossible to say anything meaningful and general about the formal legal status of actors other than States (and the intergovernmental institutions of which they form a central part), but it is also difficult to determine any definitive competencies or capacities that an actor enjoys as a result of personality. More particularly, very little can be said to follow in terms of any particular actor's ability to make law (or rules) in either a formal or informal sense. Beyond States, of course, international organisations that possess legal personality have the ability to enter into treaties and in that sense make law that is binding upon them (and their members),[17] but that is very different from being an independent lawmaker with the ability to bind a given community in a general sense. Furthermore, an institution's capacity to 'make law' in this way is fundamentally limited by its function and purpose, dependent upon the recognition of either express or implied powers, i.e. those accepted in practice by the institution's membership (again, usually just States).[18] In this sense, Portmann is surely correct in his assessment that personality means very little in terms of specific competencies or capacities in the international legal system, and instead implies no more and no less than an entity being able to invoke, and have invoked against them, responsibility for any international legal obligations which they have assumed.[19]

Nevertheless, indirectly at least, the recognition of the distinct legal personality of international institutions as a product of their growing autonomy and influence is important in another, discrete sense, particularly in terms of how this autonomy changes the regulatory landscape of international law. The ambiguities in the *Reparations* opinion – oscillating between an image of institutions as separate legal actors and as vehicles for Member States – suggests that the lawmaking process, whether State-driven or not, has the capacity to be fundamentally influenced by a range of actors operating

14 For a general overview of this development, as well as the recognition of individual legal personality through international criminal law and human rights law, see Chapters 6 and 7, respectively, of Portmann (n 8) at 80–172.

15 *Reparation* opinion (n 7), as noted in Bederman (n 9) at 279.

16 *Reparation* opinion (n 7) 178 [emphasis added].

17 See e.g. Vienna Convention on the Law of Treaties between States and International Organizations or between International Organizations (1986), as discussed in Brölmann (n 4) 125–40 & *passim*.

18 On which, see the excellent study by Viljam Engström, *Constructing the Powers of International Institutions* (Martinus Nijhoff 2012).

19 Portmann (n 8) 3.

'in the shadows of the State'. The creation of new regimes and regulatory contexts through inter-State agreement also often opens up new spaces for the participation of a range of non-State actors beyond the institution itself, many of which allow input into formal lawmaking and more informal rule-making processes. In particular, organisational *fora*, assembles of States-parties and other institutional organs are deemed to play an increasingly important role in the processes of international lawmaking and application,[20] not only in the way that organs such as the UN General Assembly (UNGA) aid in the formation of rules of customary international law, but also with UN-sponsored conferences adding to the centralisation of multilateral treaty-making processes,[21] or 'democratising' these processes by engaging non-State actors, particularly NGOs.[22]

I will consider this more in the next two sections, first by considering how non-State actors contribute to international law's formal sources and, second, by turning to consider how the normative influence of such actors has grown to such an extent to challenge international law's formal sources as having a monopoly in terms of lawmaking at the global level.

## 2 Sources doctrine and the limitations of the lawmaking processes

Recognising that institutionalisation has over the years had a significant impact on the functional means of lawmaking within international law also seemingly calls into question the centrality of the State (and in particular the role of State consent), within sources doctrine as traditionally understood. As noted in the introduction, it has been a common criticism in recent years that sources doctrine is overly State-centric in terms of the relevant participants in international lawmaking processes. For instance, Alan Boyle and Christine Chinkin begin their chapter on 'participants in international lawmaking' with the following statement:

> The traditional statement of the sources of international law, the Statute of the International Court of Justice (ICJ), Article 38(1) assumes states to be the primary actors in international law-making and gives no indication of the ways in which non-state entities impact upon this function.[23]

20 See, perhaps most famously, Rosalyn Higgins, *The Development of International Law through the Political Organs of the United Nations* (OUP 1963); see also, more recently, Jose E. Alvarez, *International Organizations as Law-makers* (OUP 2006) 259–60; Jonathan Charney, 'Universal International Law' (1993) 87 *American Journal of International Law* 529, at 543–50; and Nigel D. White, 'Separate but Connected: Inter-Governmental Organizations and International Law' (2008) 5 *International Organizations Law Review* 175, at 181–87.

21 Brölmann (n 4) 101–12.

22 Steve Charnovitz, 'Nongovernmental Organizations and International Law' (2006) 100 *American Journal of International Law* 348, particularly at 359–63.

23 Alan Boyle and Christine Chinkin, *The Making of International Law* (OUP 2007) 41.

However, this accusation levelled at sources doctrine arguably misconstrues the function of sources as a means of general law ascertainment (an ontological enquiry), which has little to do with describing the processes of norm-formation (an epistemological enquiry). In particular, nothing in Article 38(1) assumes States to be the primary actors involved in the *processes* of international lawmaking, as this provision does not provide anything like a full account of those processes, nor does it purport to limit what may be *legally or normatively relevant* 'rules' within the international legal domain overall. It provides only a list of sources that can be applied by the ICJ in the context of the jurisdiction it enjoys vis-à-vis contentious disputes (between States!) and the giving of advisory opinions.[24] Of course, Article 38(1) has come to represent more than just a statement of a jurisdictional limitation *ratione materiae* being widely accepted as a statement of the formal sources of international law per se (a kind of proto-Rule of Recognition, in a Hartian sense).[25] However, while in this sense the doctrine of sources seeks to delimit the relevant from the irrelevant, and thus prioritises the juridical opinion and practices of States as key to the identification of the law, it does not seek to describe nor indeed limit the participation of other actors in the formation of the rules themselves. Accordingly, Samantha Besson is correct when noting that sources 'refer to' the processes by which international law is made, but as she also points out, it is necessary to distinguish the material from the formal lawmaking process – the material relating to all the factors relevant to the formation of a given law (e.g. a rule of custom); the formal relating to *the identification of validity*, that is, the truth conditions for an international legal norm's binding force.

It is tempting to conflate the two ideas, but one would discover little about the processes of, for example, treaty-making or custom formation from formal sources, *precisely because formal sources do not provide a description of those processes*.[26] Accordingly, the provision makes no explicit reference to non-State entities' involvement in international lawmaking because their involvement is not, in the main, seen as relevant to the *claimed* existence of any given norm. Of course,

24 Article 38(1) includes as the sources to be applied by the Court are limited to 'international conventions . . . establishing rules expressly recognized by the contesting states; . . . international custom, as evidence of a general practice accepted as law; . . . the general principles of law recognized by civilized nations; [and . . .] judicial decisions and the teachings of the most highly qualified publicists . . . as subsidiary means for the determination of rules of law'.

25 See e.g. Oscar Schachter, 'The Nature and Process of Legal Development in International Society' in Ronald St J. MacDonald and Douglas M. Johnston (eds), *The Structure and Process of International Law: Essays in Legal Philosophy, Doctrine, and Theory* (Martinus Nijhoff 1983) 745, at 762; Samantha Besson, 'Theorizing the Sources of International Law' in Samantha Besson and John Tasioulas (eds), *The Philosophy of International Law* (OUP 2010) 163–85; Thomas Skouteris, *The Notion of Progress in International Law Discourse* (TMC Asser Press 2010) 134.

26 As d'Aspremont notes, the role of sources doctrine is to provide content-independent criteria for the validity of international legal rules. See e.g. Jean d'Aspremont, *Formalism and the Sources of International Law: A Theory of the Ascertainment of Legal Rules* (OUP 2011).

Article 38 does refer to the role of scholars and international courts as material processes for the identification of international norms – and thus recognises the importance of these actors to rule identification – but both scholars and courts act as a *material source* for evidencing the prior existence of laws which are still deemed valid according to formal source criteria (e.g. ratification of treaties by states and/or international organisations, State *opinio juris* and practice as a means for the identification of customary law, or general principles of law evidenced by widespread acceptance within national legal traditions). In that sense, sources doctrine is State-centric, but I would suggest that this State-centrism is an important legitimacy condition for sources to act as a means for formal law-ascertainment (such conditions are not immutable, but nonetheless recognise the difficulties in otherwise determining legitimate authority in the processes of law-ascertainment within a decentralised legal system).[27]

Accepting this distinction, therefore, the criticism of State-centricity, even if not entirely missing the mark, certainly oversimplifies in what it purports to describe. For instance, even if a steady institutionalisation has undoubtedly intensified their involvement, there has long been recorded significant input from non-State actors in international lawmaking processes, particularly in the formation of key regimes and institutions of international law since at least the early years of the nineteenth century, if not also before.[28] Indeed, many of the large-scale codification exercises from the end of the nineteenth century onwards owe their existence and success to the role of non-governmental bodies such as the *Institut de Droit International* or the International Law Association.[29] Boyle and Chinkin themselves document the critical role played by organisations such as the International Committee of the Red Cross (ICRC) since the mid-nineteenth century, as well as a range of other NGOs and non-State actors in lawmaking in the fields of, for example, humanitarian, human rights and international criminal law.[30]

Of course, as noted in the previous section, the involvement of non-State actors in international lawmaking processes has clearly intensified in recent

27 d'Aspremont, ibid. See also Besson (n 25) 173.

28 Steve Charnovitz accounts for the involvement of private lobbying groups and other non-State actors in a number of intergovernmental lawmaking conferences since the Vienna Conferences of 1814–15. Charnovitz (n 22) 359–62, and developed more extensively in Steve Charnovitz, 'Two Centuries of Participation: NGOs and International Governance' (1997) 18 *Michigan Journal of International Law* 183. Jean d'Aspremont, similarly, notes the continued involvement of NGOs in the formation of key institutions such as the Permanent Court of Arbitration, Permanent Court of International Justice and the League of Nations, to name just a few. See Jean d'Aspremont, 'The Doctrinal Illusion of Heterogeneity of International Lawmaking Processes', in Hélène Ruiz Fabri, Rüdiger Wolfrum and Jana Gogolin (eds), *Select Proceedings of the European Society of International Law* (Hart 2010) 297, at 298–300; and see also Boyle and Chinkin (n 23) 42–43.

29 d'Aspremont (n 26) 299–300.

30 Boyle and Chinkin (n 23) 62–77.

years, but this alone does not in itself undermine the point made about the limited ambit of sources doctrine, at least in terms of the specific ontological function of that doctrine. However, this intensification raises an additional challenge that does not just go to the contribution of non-State actors to the formal sources of international law. The institutionalisation of international law is seen to have helped to add greater 'dimensionality' to the sources of the law themselves. Institutional developments have in this sense introduced degrees of normativity – or 'relative' normativity – into international law.[31] For instance, codification exercises undertaken by the ILC have resulted in treaty and customary recognition of peremptory norms of international law, signalling an emerging normative hierarchy,[32] which in turn has been recognised and tentatively progressed by international courts and tribunals.[33] As Alvarez has noted:

> *Jus cogens* and *erga omnes* obligations are products of the age of IOs [International Organisations] precisely because they made real (or more real than ever before) the idea of a 'community of states as a whole' on which such hierarchical concepts could be built. The articulation of *jus cogens* – in Article 53 of the Vienna Convention on the Law of Treaties – resulted from the kind of 'package deal' that characterizes treaty making in institutionalized global venues involving UN expert bodies . . . and UN-authorized treaty-making conferences . . .[34]

31 For an enthusiastic embrace of the blurring of the normativity threshold in international law in this respect, see Charney (n 20); Dinah Shelton, 'International Law and "Relative Normativity"' in Malcolm Evans (ed.), *International Law*, 3rd edn (OUP 2010) 141–72. For a critical reflection, see the classic work by Prosper Weil, 'Towards Normative Relativity in International Law?' (1983) 77 *American Journal of International Law* 413.

32 On the applicability and effect of *jus cogens* norms, see Articles 53 and 64 of the Vienna Convention on the Law of Treaties 1969; see also, on the particular consequences in terms of the legal responsibility of States for breaches of peremptory norms of international law, and on the possibility of invocation of responsibility by third states for breaches of obligations *erga omnes*, Articles 41–42 and 48, respectively, of the ILC's *Draft articles on Responsibility of States for Internationally Wrongful Acts* (2001) <http://legal.un.org/ilc/texts/instruments/english/commentaries/9_6_2001.pdf> accessed 29 January 2015. Though note that the customary law status of these articles, particularly with regard to third-party enforcement of community interests, remains somewhat controversial.

33 For example, on the *jus cogens* status of the prohibition of unlawful force in international law, see *Military and Paramilitary Activities in and against Nicaragua* (*Nicaragua v United States*), Merits, Judgment of 27 June 1986, ICJ Reports (1986) 14, at 100–101; on the peremptory status of human rights norms as limiting the powers of the UN Security Council, see also the following before the European Court of First Instance: Case T-306/01, *Yusuf and Al Barakaat International Foundation v Council and Commission*, 21 September 2005, [2005] ECR II-3533; Case T-315/01, *Kadi v Council and Commission*, 21 September 2005, [2005] ECR II-3649.

34 Jose Alvarez, 'International Organizations: Then and Now' (2006) 100 *American Journal of International Law* 324, at 327.

As he goes on to note, it is also the UN family of organisations – human rights treaty bodies, the ILC, ICJ, etc. – who have been more likely to cite the peremptory status of particular norms than States themselves, increasing the UN's recognition – among many at least – as a clear centre of normative authority in global lawmaking processes.[35] Within these processes, the 'normative' output of the UNGA itself increasingly acts as evidence of emerging customary international law.[36]

Nevertheless, from the perspective of formal law ascertainment, this recognition does not necessarily – on its own – challenge the sanctity of sources in terms of formal legal rules (though notions such as *jus cogens* clearly modify sources doctrine to some degree). When considering whether State A is bound by customary norm X, and whether customary norm X enjoys peremptory status, a court, international lawyer or other actor wishing to make a persuasive legal argument will still have to make a claim that norm X (and its status as peremptory) is supported by *opinio juris* and State practice, however loosely this is evidenced, or indeed whether or not significant institutional practice in bodies such as the UNGA or other judicial opinion is offered in support of this conclusion. Any such recognition will be accepted or contested on the basis of similar claims that seek to show not merely that the recognition or rejection of such a norm is normatively desirable, but is supported by actual acceptance or rejection in practice, at which point the views of states will again enter the picture as normatively pre-emptive.

What is equally clear, however, is that this relativity is perceived not just to change the status of certain formal norms, but introduces a range of purported legal rules, practices, principles and determinations that fall below the threshold of formal legality as traditionally perceived.[37] Furthermore, the picture of international lawmaking that is represented increasingly in the literature does not just confine itself to the normative output of formally constituted international institutional processes, but encompasses a range of informal and formal international actors, both private and public, all of whom are perceived to be exercising forms of normative authority in a 'postnational' political space (or 'constellation')[38] – spanning the trans-, as much as the supra- and inter-national legal realms. It is clear, for example, that whether or not UN General Assembly resolutions make it to the stage of being recognised as customary international law, they and other products of international institutions give rise not just to different means of international lawmaking, but different kinds of international instrument, norm, decision or standard,

35 Ibid. See also Dinah Shelton, 'Normative Hierarchy in International Law' (2006) 100 *American Journal of International Law* 291.

36 Anthea E. Roberts, 'Traditional and Modern Approaches to Customary International Law: A Reconciliation' (2001) 95 *American Journal of International Law* 757.

37 See, again, Weil (n 29).

38 See, in particular, the Introduction to this volume.

all of which have a significant (though varying) degree of normative impact. It is equally apparent, however, that many of these instruments and practices are increasingly – and crucially, *intentionally* – promulgated outside of the formal sources of international law. In this sense, the critique of the State-centredness – or, better, the one-dimensional nature – of sources doctrine, is not merely concerned to highlight the range of actors involved in international lawmaking processes, but rather the pluralistic nature of those processes. The question, however, is how and in what way a doctrinal perspective can, *or indeed should*, account for all of these processes. This is the question to which I now turn my attention in the following section.

## 3 'Lawmaking' in the shadows of the State

On the basis of the points just raised, it seems doubtful that the range of normative practices, standards, acts and directives, in addition to formal legal rules, which we might draw together under the umbrella of 'postnational rule-making', can be captured, explained and accommodated within international law's formal legal process. At the same time, the status of the actors involved in postnational rule-making will not (and arguably cannot) be determined or demarcated on the basis of formal notions of legal personality. At the postnational level, an actor's ability to influence or shape behaviour, or indeed have any form of regulatory impact, is surely determined more by the semantic authority of their acts, decisions or actions, rather than the formal categorisation of those acts, or indeed of the actor itself.[39] In other words, the form of 'legality' inherent in postnational rule-making is more evaluative than it is formal: in jurisprudential terms, it relates to *content dependence* rather than independence,[40] that is, it is determined by a range of factors including, *inter alia*, institutional autonomy, expertise, legitimacy and coercion, rather than a norm's formal legal pedigree. The trends just accounted for, the challenge of global governance broadly defined, thus suggest that normativity in the postnational constellation should be defined more broadly than a doctrinal approach would permit.

To capture the reality of *all of* these institutional practices, we therefore have to look beyond, even if not yet fully discard, both subjects and sources doctrine as traditionally understood. It is possible to place these practices on a spectrum to include (at one extreme) those that pose little conceptual difficulties for a doctrinal analysis, including what we might term 'law', albeit within specific institutional perspectives. This might include, for example, and most obviously, EU law, as well as the rules of the GATT/WTO, and

39 See generally Ingo Venzke, *How Interpretation Makes International Law: On Semantic Change and Normative Twists* (OUP 2013).

40 On this idea, see Noam Gur, 'Are Legal Rules Content-Independent Reasons' (2011) 5 *Problema* 175.

binding norms of various human rights regimes. We can explain most of this institutional law as forming part of the formal corpus of rules of international law by reference to the treaty itself, a form of *lex specialis*. Of course, in the case of universal organisations such as the United Nations, these kinds of distinctions are somewhat meaningless in practice, with many UN rules also being some of the most fundamental rules of the international legal system itself (e.g. in relation to the use of force).[41] Whatever their functional purport within the broader international legal system, however, we face little if any difficulty accommodating these rules within a formal, doctrinal understanding of international law.

Related to this body of institutional law are those binding determinations (as opposed to general legal rules) that are underpinned by formal legal authority (e.g. decisions of the International Court of Justice, resolutions of the UNSC, the rulings of the WTO Dispute Settlement Body, etc.). Again, it is possible to explain these determinations as legally valid due to the underlying treaty obligation, though, to the extent that some of these determinations seem to have quite considerable 'legislative' purport – e.g. the Security Council mandating an international criminal tribunal,[42] or listing terror suspects,[43] or, more generally, when international courts give precise meaning and normative purport to otherwise fuzzy customary or general legal principles between parties to a dispute – the functional effect comes closer to a kind of general lawmaking power. While it is not impossible to explain these powers and binding determinations in terms of the sources of international law, one must accept that sources doctrine will tell us little about the kind of obligations assumed and their regulatory purport more broadly.[44]

Perhaps more troubling, however, is the regulatory impact and effects of the 'soft' normative output of organs of formally constituted institutions, such as UN General Assembly Resolutions, or the guidelines and codes of conduct of bodies such as the Food and Agriculture Organization (FAO), UN Environment Programme (UNEP), International Labour Organization (ILO), International Maritime Organization (IMO), etc. While most institutional lawmaking within international organisations remains the preserve of states,

41 See in particular, the principles included in Article 2 of the UN Charter.

42 In particular, the International Criminal Tribunal for the Former Yugoslavia (ICTY), established by SC Res. 827 of 25 May 1993, and International Criminal Tribunal for Rwanda (ICTR), established by SC Res. 955 of 8 November 1994. For discussion, see e.g. Wayne Sandholtz, 'Creating Authority by the Council: The International Criminal Tribunals' in Bruce Cronin and Ian Hurd (eds), *The UN Security Council and the Politics of International Authority* (Routledge 2008) 131–153.

43 See series of resolutions beginning with SC Res. 1373 of 28 September 2001, establishing a Counter-Terrorism Committee, and placing a series of general obligations upon states. And see discussion in Eric Rosand, 'Security Council Resolution 1373, the Counter-Terrorism Committee, and the Fight against Terrorism' (2003) 97 *American Journal of International Law* 233.

44 See Venzke (n 39) 6 & *passim*.

a number of programmatic initiatives within institutions, particularly technical organisations such as the ILO or UNEP, stems directly from policymakers, or secretariats. Indeed, the most obvious example of policy initiative in this respect is the UN Secretary General who has the right to propose substantive policy agendas to the organisation's political organs.[45] Furthermore, as Bernstorff notes, the vast majority of rule-making within institutions often occurs at the operational level, where decisions are taken increasingly by secretariats, as well as subordinated intergovernmental panels and bodies with policy initiative – for instance, in institutions such as UNICEF, or the World Bank – but which often have very tangible external normative impacts.[46]

Going further still, one can also analyse the 'soft' normative output of non-treaty or non-governmental organisations (e.g. codifications/reports of bodies such as the ICRC) or indeed policy agreements, guidelines and other instruments produced by informal transnational networks of actors operating below the level of inter-State diplomacy.[47] Even further still along this spectrum, we might also include the 'soft' normative output of 'soft' international actors, which might include private interest groups, multinational corporations, as well as informally constituted meetings of heads of States outside of traditional UN or other IGO diplomacy (the most obvious examples ranging from the high profile summit policy agreed in the context of the G20 or G7/8, or perhaps the more 'shadowy' agreements and understandings reached in the Bilderberg group).[48]

This range of institutional practices raises significant questions of accountability in particular, prompting the question of whether (and if so, how far) international legal doctrine should itself adapt to these developments through some form of strategy of accommodation.[49] From the perspective of subjects doctrine, the issue thus becomes one of how far the doctrine is functionally useful to account for the myriad actors that participate in international legal processes, bearing in mind that subjects doctrine is not merely concerned with sociological prescription, but also constitutive systematisation of international law. As Bianchi notes, for some time the political science language of 'actors' has been adopted to overcome the descriptive

45 See e.g. Jochen von Bernstorff, 'Procedures of Decision-Making and the Role of Law in International Organizations' (2008) 9 *German Law Journal* 1939, at 1952

46 Ibid., at 1955.

47 See principally Anne-Marie Slaughter, *A New World Order* (Princeton University Press 2004)

48 See e.g. Jan Klabbers, 'Institutional Ambivalence by Design: Soft Organizations in International Law' (2001) 70 *Nordic Journal of International Law* 403; Jarna Petman, 'Deformalization of International Organizations Law' in Jan Klabbers and Åsa Wallendahl (eds), *Research Handbook on the Law of International Organizations* (Edward Elgar 2011) 398–430.

49 Armin von Bogdandy, 'Lawmaking by International Organizations: Some Thoughts on Non-Binding Instruments and Democratic Legitimacy' in Rüdiger Wolfrum and Volker Röben (eds), *Developments of International Law in Treaty Making* (Springer 2005) 171.

limitations of subjects doctrine[50] – indeed as it has been in this volume also.[51] Others, such as Higgins, try to move past the intellectual 'prison house' of subjects doctrine to speak instead of 'participants' in international lawmaking processes.[52] In this respect, while himself sceptical of moving to a process-based account of determining legal validity, d'Aspremont recognises:

> . . . the added value of approaching law-making from the angle of participation, for exploring this angle allows legal scholars to liberate themselves from some excessively constraining containers in order to appraise contemporary practice while simultaneously gaining some critical distance. Although participation is certainly not a legal concept, it is of great relevance to international legal scholars, even those who are most interested in the legal product of these processes.[53]

D'Aspremont is surely correct in this respect. It is almost impossible to classify and categorise non-State actor participation in the sense that one could construct a systemic matrix of participation that could be used in a pre- or pro-scriptive way. As we saw above, the formal participatory status of actors as subjects of international law is more often determined merely through acceptance and *ex post facto* endorsement.[54]

Meanwhile, from the perspective of sources doctrine, to the extent that the phenomenon of global governance occurs increasingly through informal – or perhaps deformalised[55] – types of normative instruments, 'the big challenge for international lawyers is . . . to decide when [this normative phenomena] gives rise to international law, and when it does not'.[56] If we take a perspective that sees legal validity as a quality determined by formally accepted criteria, then speaking in gradated terms of softness, or other forms of relative normativity is deeply problematic.[57] It is unsurprising therefore to see a range of perspectives emerge in recent years that have attempted to reformulate sources doctrine to respond to and capture the trends just outlined. Many of these perspectives, motivated by well-meaning concerns for accountability within, as well as systemic integrity of, international law, propose new criteria

50 Andrea Bianchi, 'Looking Ahead: International Law's Main Challenges' in David Armstrong (ed.), *Routledge Handbook of International Law* (Routledge 2009) 392, at 393–94.
51 See here the Introduction to this volume, Section II.
52 Rosalyn Higgins, *Problems and Process: International Law and How We Use It* (Clarendon Press 1995) 12.
53 Jean d'Aspremont, 'Introduction' in d'Aspremont (n 3) 3.
54 Noortmann (n 13).
55 See e.g. Martti Koskenniemi, 'Global Governance and Public International Law' (2004) 37 *Kritische Justiz* 241.
56 Jan Klabbers, *International Law* (CUP 2013) 37.
57 See e.g. criticisms of Jan Klabbers, 'The Redundancy of Soft Law' (1996) 65 *Nordic Journal of International Law* 167.

of validity to capture the normative output of a far greater range of international actors, whether by assessing the effects or 'normative ripples' of institutionalised rule-making,[58] judging the 'publicness' of the acts or purported legitimate authority of a range of formal and informal decision-making bodies,[59] or capturing 'publicness' as part of a modified, more inclusive doctrine of sources, explained in terms of a form of 'Global Administrative Law'.[60] Other, more 'constitutional' perspectives propose similar value-based criteria for assessing the validity of purportedly normative acts and institutional decisions, depending on their conformity with a range of criteria inspired by domestic constitutional protections.[61]

Despite the commendable attempt to plug accountability deficits and desire to enhance the overall legitimacy of postnational rule-making, it is not at all clear that these standards can, or indeed should, be adopted as part of formal criteria of validity. While here I cannot go into all of the potential problems involved with the introduction of new criteria of legal validity that are based on effects, or subjective assessment of values such as 'publicness',[62] the central problem seems to be that if we try to capture new modes of rule-making by reference to older paradigms, we lose anything distinctive about each. There is a benefit to retaining a doctrinal perspective as a mirror against which we can highlight the informal nature of, as well as power imbalances perpetuated by, much of the rule-making that takes place within the postnational constellation of regulatory practice.[63] Furthermore, to introduce subjective determinations of 'publicness' is only to really highlight the fact that those determinations will be made, primarily, by the very same actors

58 Alvarez (n 20).

59 See, most recently, Matthias Goldmann, 'A Matter of Perspective: Global Governance and the Distinction between Public and Private Authority (and Not Law)' (4 November 2013) <http://ssrn.com/abstract=2260293> accessed 6 January 2015, in which legitimate international public authority is identified (at 18) on the basis of whether 'the actor may reasonably claim to act on behalf of a community of which the affected person or entity is a member, or a member of such member'.

60 Benedict Kingsbury, 'The Concept of "Law" in Global Administrative Law' (2009) 20 *European Journal of International Law* 23, at 31–3.

61 See e.g. Anne Peters, 'Compensatory Constitutionalism: The Function and Potential of Fundamental International Norms and Structures' (2006) 19 *Leiden Journal of International Law* 579, at 585. As Dunoff and Trachtman argue, '[a] functionalist approach permits conceptual analysis that is not premised upon a definition setting forth a group of necessary and sufficient conditions which determine whether a given order is constitutional or not'. Jeffrey L. Dunoff and Joel P. Trachtman, 'A Functional Approach to International Constitutionalization', in Jeffrey L. Dunoff and Joel P. Trachtman (eds), *Ruling the World? Constitutionalism, International Law, and Global Governance* (CUP 2009), 3 at 6.

62 In any event, I cover this more comprehensively elsewhere. See Richard Collins, 'The Rule of Law and the Quest for Constitutional Substitutes in International Law' (2014) 83 *Nordic Journal of International Law* 87–127, at 119–124.

63 See on this point, Alexander Somek, 'The Concept of "Law" in Global Administrative Law: A Reply to Benedict Kingsbury' (2010) 20 *European Journal of International Law* 985, at 993–94.

whose behaviour, decisions or actions we might wish to spotlight as problematic. Does this make international law – as a discipline or as a set or system of rules – singularly useless, or irrelevant, as a means of coming to terms with the exercise of normative power in the postnational constellation? Arguably not, as I will now explain.

To the extent that through the formal sources of international law states and other international actors have erected an architecture wherein forms of lawmaking or other less formal normative standard-setting can take place, the option always remains open to revisit and restructure the environment where actors are regulated (or indeed escape regulation). The critical potential to use formal law instruments to restrain normative biases, market forces or other interests represented at the global level still remains, despite the limitations of the *current* international architecture. As I have noted above, there is nothing immutable about the structure of the current system; it merely reflects the legitimacy pulls of a legal order structured between different, and differently constituted, local communities. The point is not to suggest that States and the institutions that they create have a kind of *ipso facto*, preconditioned legitimacy, but rather that little is gained by re-describing or reformulating the institutional structures that are there simply to make them more reflective of the normative forces that are pervasive in the postnational constellation. The stark gap between doctrine and reality in that sense is itself illuminating of certain accountability deficits, potentially sharpening political efforts to restructure and reformulate existing institutional structures, or highlighting the role that States have played in perpetuating practices that escape obvious legal regulation.

The previous points are not at all to suggest that international law is not (or should not be) *concerned with* the kind of phenomena that I have so far been describing, but rather that it is not the point of subjects and sources doctrine to account for all forms of legal participation or normative phenomena occurring in the postnational political space.[64] More than that, however, if much of the concern for international law to reconfigure itself to take account of this normative activity is motivated by a concern for accountability, the necessary adherence to a normative category of subjects and sources may help to ensure an important measure of accountability at the broadest level. I appreciate that this may, at present, sound like a rather vague proposition,

64 Just as in domestic law, there are many forms of 'soft' normativity which have legal implications and impact in a regulatory environment (for example, codes of conduct, circulars, policies, sentencing and other judicial guidelines), but are deliberately intended not to bear the mark of legality. The choice of formal lawmaking versus other forms of regulatory instruments reflects the significant consequences that follow from such a designation. This is not to suggest that the choice of making certain normative instruments non-legal is always or necessarily uncontroversial or benevolent – quite the opposite, in many instances – but if the concept of law were merely to change to absorb all forms of normatively significant regulation, then legal argumentation would seem to lose any critical potential whatsoever.

so in the next and final section let me explain further what I intend in this regard.

## 4 Form and function in postnational rule-making

Many recent accounts of the changes occurring at the international level tell a story of a classic contractual model of international law being slowly replaced by, or at least overlain by both a more value-laden, less State-centric law (perceived positively), as well as an increasingly bureaucratic, regulatory law dispersed through myriad sites of competing formal-institutionalised and informal sites of normative authority (perceived less positively). This is captured well in Joseph Weiler's classic account of the emergence of a 'geological layering' in international law, with a 'regulatory' layer (developed through complex institutional regimes), atop a 'communitarian' layer (the product of a transition away from an individualist, or statist paradigm), itself atop an original base of Westphalian ('transactional') international law.[65]

Weiler's analysis in this respect is sophisticated and insightful, outlining significant legitimacy concerns that come from the pursuit of collective interests and regulatory goals by a system structured, at its base, as a horizontal inter-State agreement. However, his approach also suffers from an over-simplifying tendency. In treating the different geological strata as various, distinct *forms* of international law, and in so doing suggesting that 'transactionalism' finds its justification *only* in an outdated philosophical commitment to State freedom,[66] he overlooks, or perhaps deliberately dismisses, the idea of the transactional layer as playing a necessary constitutive role in a decentralised legal order: it becomes only one (outdated) stratum, existing alongside the others. It is too easy to portray this basal layer here simply as an outmoded philosophical commitment to national interest and unrestrained sovereignty, and in that sense merely an older species of international law, occupying an uneasy space with a more modern, dynamic and, perhaps, more 'public' international law. However, I would argue that this 'transactional' layer plays itself an important legitimising function as part of the continuing structural condition, or *legal form*, of the international legal order within which such developments have taken place. If there remain widely accepted reasons for international law's decentralised structural form, then the 'transactionalism' of Westphalian international law, as Weiler describes it, is not simply one geological stratum, but a necessary, *foundational* base: that which gives authority to all of the subsequent developments (however inadequate this authority might seem as a means of legitimising those developments, or indeed in accounting for their specific nature or function).

65 Joseph H.H. Weiler, 'The Geology of International Law – Governance, Democracy and Legitimacy' (2004) 64 *Zeitschrift für Ausländisches Öffentliches Recht und Völkerrecht* 547, at 549 and *passim*.
66 Ibid., at 552–3.

This is a point better captured in Antonio Cassese's metaphor, where he describes Westphalian international law 'like a human skeleton that can only be seen on an X-ray being covered by flesh and skin and clothes. Though momentarily concealed, it is still very much there, *constituting the framework on which all the rest is based*'.[67] Looking at it this way, as the legal form upon which the more complex edifice of modern international law is constructed, does not in any way prejudice the nature, substance or function of the rules, structures or institutions of this constructed legal order,[68] but it does help us come to terms with a growing tension between this legal form and the entire substantive, regulatory edifice which has been constructed from its basal principles and structures.

We can imagine the implications of this growing *form-function* tension by placing competing legitimacy claims on two linked axes. International law's legitimacy comes from the sense that it is *structured* on a horizontal axis, as a pluralistic order existing between sovereign-equal States, but also, and increasingly (as a result of change in the substance of its normative concerns), to the extent that it penetrates State sovereignty on a vertical axis to protect and enforce community interests, e.g. issues of human rights, human welfare or other 'public goods' that were traditionally conceived to lie within the domestic realm of States.[69] At the risk of distorting Weiler's model, we can see how the competing legitimacy claims sit uneasily one with the other: the intergovernmentalism of the basal layer is what gives legal form and therefore justificatory legitimacy to expressions of collective interest, but which, at the same time, itself appears inadequate as a means of securing collective goods: *hence the development of the regulatory layer*. However, this more efficient regulatory layer – at increasing distance from the intergovernmental – risks always turning out to not represent community interest at all: its legitimacy has to be assessed in more evaluative, effects-based terms – a test that puts it in discrete tension with the kind of formal, source-based authority of the intergovernmental lawyer. In other words, it appears to require another form of legitimisation which not only is the intergovernmental layer itself unable to provide, but which seems to involve exactly the kind of evaluative judgements of 'publicness' or 'justice' that sit uneasily with the legitimating principles of Westphalian international law. In the absence of appeal to some foundational legitimacy, or in the absence of any other, agreed form of mediatory legitimacy (beyond the intergovernmental), pushes on the vertical axis will necessarily therefore invoke counter-pulls on the horizontal axis.[70]

67 Antonio Cassese, *International Law in a Divided World* (Clarendon Press 1986) 32 [emphasis added].

68 For a similar point, though aimed at a slightly different issue, see Klabbers (n 57) 179–81.

69 See e.g. Emmanuelle Jouannet, 'What is the Use of International Law? International Law as a 21st Century Guardian of Welfare' (2008) 28 *Michigan Journal of International Law* 815.

70 As Kratochwil puts this, 'legitimisation deficits will appear in all instances of institutionalized inter-state cooperation that go beyond the classical alliance patterns or ad hoc limited purpose

What I have in mind in this respect is something akin to (though not exactly the same as) the tension explained by Franck in his juxtaposition of two distinct aspects of fairness discourse: one concerned with the conditions of legitimacy giving rise to social order, the other concerned with substantive notions of justice giving rise to legal change.[71] One helps us come to terms with the point of legal structure, *legal form*, the other with its substantives uses or functions. For Franck, these urges may conflict and can only be managed under the discursive rubric of 'fairness' once a legal order has reached a sufficient degree of maturity and is underpinned by a sense of community: a condition he argues now pertains in international relations.[72] Franck's analysis is insightful – even though not concerned directly to address the full complexities of the postnational constellation, and the normative phenomena this entails – in that it locates in the *legal form* of international law an important point of its legitimacy: the formal, procedural requirements of a norm's validity (here, he includes the concepts of 'determinacy', 'symbolic validation', 'coherence' and 'adherence').[73] While space precludes giving Franck's thesis the full consideration it deserves, one can see how these concerns translate into the need for some form of systemic rules against which formal determinations and categorisations can be made.[74] His essential point is not that legality and legitimacy are the same, but part of the requirements of legitimacy within systemic legal orders is an element of legal formality: in the absence of secondary rules and institutional means to secure determinacy, validation, coherence, etc., the law's legitimacy may be brought into question.

My point here is that despite their inherent limits, the formal criteria of subjects and sources reflect the structural conditions of a system for distilling and discerning formal legality at the broadest level of inter-State relations. However, as a structural base, the point of this doctrine is not to provide a descriptive account of all that has been constructed either from within *or outside* of the system, nor does it place any substantive limits on the law that is so created. It is important to realise, as noted above, that this structural legitimacy will form only one element of the overall legitimacy, or legitimate authority, of postnational rule-making. To acknowledge this is to note, first, that the push for accountability, inclusiveness, or other concerns over postnational decision-making, may be better served by seeking alternative

arrangements'. Friedrich Kratochwil, 'Has the "Rule of Law" become a "Rule of Lawyers"? An Inquiry into the Use and Abuse of an Ancient Topos in Contemporary Debates' in Gianluigi Palombella and Neil Walker (eds), *Relocating the Rule of Law* (Hart 2009) 171, at 178.

71 Thomas M. Franck, *Fairness in International Law and Institutions* (Clarendon Press 1995) 22–4.

72 Ibid., 10–13.

73 Ibid., pp. 30–46. These concepts are themselves developed from his early work: Thomas Franck, *The Power of Legitimacy Among Nations* (OUP 1990) 49 *et. seq.*

74 Franck, *Fairness*, ibid., 30; *Legitimacy Among Nations*, ibid., 183–94. Franck himself relates this to Hart's account of legal order as found in H.L.A. Hart, *The Concept of Law* (Clarendon Press 1961).

means of political redress, rather than merely seeking to 'deformalise' formal law-ascertainment (pushing one axis of legitimacy, while pulling on another). Second, and finally, to recognise the limited, but still important structural value of sources and subjects doctrine in maintaining the legal form of international law allows us to see 'deformalised' normative power for what it is: a contestable, revisable and contingent *claim to* authority, rather than any inherently binding aspect of modern international law.

## 5 Conclusion

The forgoing analysis has sought to do two things. The first has been to highlight exactly what a 'doctrinal' international law perspective will reveal in terms of rule-making in the postnational constellation. As I have shown, to the extent that international law structures, categorises and includes/excludes by virtue of the formal categories of sources and subjects, it will reveal very little as to the normative force or legitimate authority of either the actors of postnational rule-making, or indeed the nature of the 'rules' they propagate. The second point of this chapter, however, has been to highlight what this gap between formal doctrine and the actual workings of postnational law nonetheless reveals in terms of the important structural limitations of international law as the basal edifice upon which postnational rule-making takes place. In particular, I have argued that maintaining a limited, formal doctrinal perspective on subjects and sources is not to suggest the immutability or centrality of the State, but instead reflects the best approximation of a systemic construction of legality in a plural international community. This is a community in which other sites of political authority have not yet usurped the State as providing some measure of political accountability and representativeness capable, however indirectly, of holding out any *de jure* legitimacy for the various claims to authority that are made at this level. To that extent, the authority of postnational rules (and the actors who make those rules) will be determined based on evaluative criteria of a kind which are alien to the kind of categorisations which structure the formal sources and subjects of international law. This is not to suggest a fetishism of form over function, but instead an important interrelation and tension between form and function in structuring our understanding of the actors of postnational rule-making.

# 2 The many faces of rule-making in the EU

*Matthias Ruffert*[1]

## 1 Who is the rule-maker in the EU? Two tempting misunderstandings

When facing problems in understanding a very difficult situation, one tends to simplify and may run the risk of oversimplification. Despite all achievements in Treaty reform, rule-making in the EU has become more difficult and complex than ever before. There is a plurality, even a plethora of rule-making actors, most of which are active in the executive but not the legislative field and tend to work in an informal way within their network structures that are partly hybrid, i.e. open to private, societal participants. The legal framework of this plurality, however, is flawed in many instances. But everything could be so easy.

First, we could compare EU rule-making to legislation and its executive environment in Nation States.[2] Without prejudice to existing differences between the EU Member States' various constitutional systems, this would emphasise the prerogative of parliamentary statutes, the categorisation of administrative rule-making that follows from this prerogative, as well as the systematic unity of rule-making as a whole. The outcome would be an obvious deficit of EU rule-making in terms of supremacy of parliamentary legislation, unity of the legal system and institutional coherence. However, this perspective would not only over-idealise rule-making within Nation States where

1 I am very grateful towards my assistant Dr Angela Schwerdtfeger for her valuable comments and towards Christopher P . Hunt for his perfect linguistic support.

2 Comparative assessment by Alessandro Pizzorusso, 'La Loi' in Michel Troper and Dominique Chagnollaud (eds), *Traité International de Droit Constitutionnel*, vol. 1 (Dalloz 2012) 327; Impressive work has been done in the historical-political elaboration of the term 'Gesetz' in German legal scholarship: Fritz Ossenbühl, 'Gesetz und Recht – Die Rechtsquellen im demokratischen Rechtsstaat' in Josef Isensee and Paul Kirchhof (eds), *Handbuch des Staatsrechts*, vol. 5 (3rd edn, C.F.Müller 2007) Ch. 100 para 6ff; as well as in great depth Ernst-Wolfgang Böckenförde, *Gesetz und gesetzgebende Gewalt* (2nd edn, Duncker & Humblot 1981); Gerd Roellecke, *Der Begriff des positiven Gesetzes und das Grundgesetz* (V. Hase & Koehler 1969); Christian Starck, *Der Gesetzesbegriff des Grundgesetzes* (Nomos 1970); Gregor Kirchhof, *Die Allgemeinheit des Gesetzes* (Mohr Siebeck 2009).

phenomena such as informal political negotiation preceding legislation, plurality of actors in federal or regionalised States, as well as influential party politics and interest groups, abound. Above all, such a *Staatsanalogie* would also ignore that the EU is not a State and neither strives for statehood nor is normatively able to achieve it.[3]

A second strategy of (over)simplification lies in claiming that the EU was but an undertaking of the 28 Member States under public international law to use a common institutional framework for cooperative rule-making.[4] According to this view, all EU rule-making would have to be viewed from the sovereignty-based standpoint of classical international law. Clearly, this perspective is at least equally wrong as the State-analogy since it denies the effect more than 60 years of European integration process had on supranational rule – and in doing so, reality.

Consequently, one must not fall back on over-idealisation and misunderstandings. Scholarly efforts in European Union law should not strive to achieve unreachable idealistic goals or deny undisputable developments, but should aim at further developing the theory and doctrine(s) of rule-making in the European legal area in a way that enables EU rule-making to fulfil the requirements of democracy and the rule of law, but that also makes it rational and efficient. There may be many appropriate ways to analyse EU rule-making without falling into one of the traps of oversimplification. Legal scholarship, I submit, should do so by using the basic categories it developed over time and in a way that – more or less – transcends the borders between jurisdictions.[5]

## 2 Actors and rules: treaty and statute, legislation and negotiation

In terms of basic legal categories, there are two options to create the link between 'actors' and 'rules'. The first option is that actors bring forth rules by unilaterally legislating according to a given procedure. This will result in an instrument that may be designated as a statute. What is crucial here is neither the parliamentary origin nor the result, i.e. whether the instrument

3 The term *Staatsanalogie* has been established by the German Bundesverfassungsgericht to describe what the Union is not and should not be: Bundesverfassungsgericht, judgment of the Second Senate of 30 June 2009 – Treaty of Lisbon (available at: http://www.bundesverfassungsgericht.de/entscheidungen/es20090630_2bve000208en.html), paras 264, 272, 278, 376.

4 This is the view of Christian Hillgruber and Wolfgang Durner, 'Review of the Balance of Competences' (2014) 29 *Zeitschrift für Gesetzgebung* 105; and Stefan Haack, 'Demokratie mit Zukunft' (2012) 67 *Juristenzeitung* 753, 756ff. The latter's views are flawed in so many respects that properly dealing with them would need another article.

5 Cf. also the 'public law approach' in international law developed by Armin von Bogdandy, Philipp Dann and Matthias Goldmann, 'Developing the Publicness of Public International Law: Towards a Legal Framework for Global Governance Activities' in Armin von Bogdandy, Rüdiger Wolfrum, Jochen von Bernstorff, Philipp Dann and Matthias Goldmann (eds), *The Exercise of Public Authority by International Institutions* (Springer 2010) 3.

in question is a parliamentary statute/loi/Gesetz or a statutory instrument/règlement/Verordnung that derives its binding force from an order by the executive. It is more important that this type of rule-making originates from a defined legal entity and is created following a fixed procedure. Such rule-making is by no means limited to States alone – evading the State analogy trap – but is also typical for international and supranational organisations.[6]

The second option lies in entering into a contractual relationship following a negotiation process. Treaties under public international law are the archetype of this manner of rule-making.[7] However, contractual relationships also exist within legal entities, e.g. inter-institutional agreements under Article 295, 2nd sentence TFEU.[8] The treaty is the result; the process leading to it is consensual negotiation – combined with controversial bargaining, which has to lead to consensus.

In a nutshell, legislation and statute, on the one hand, negotiation and treaty, on the other hand, are the tools we can apply to gain a sound understanding of current developments in EU rule-making.

## 3 The difficult emancipation of supranationalism

### *3.1 A retrospective view including recent reforms*

In the beginning, European integration was clearly designed to transform the process of rule-making from interstate negotiating and bargaining to supranational legislation.[9] This innovation in rule-making beyond the level of

6 Cf. José E. Alvarez, *International Organisations as Law-makers* (OUP 2005); Jurij D. Aston, *Sekundärgesetzgebung internationaler Organisationen zwischen mitgliedstaatlicher Souveränität und Gemeinschaftsdisziplin* (Duncker & Humblot 2005); *Christian Walter and Matthias Ruffert, Institutionalised International Law* (C.H. Beck/Hart/Nomos 2014) ch 3 paras 85–92.

7 In constitutional law, this has most prominently been elaborated by Carl Schmitt, *Verfassungslehre* (1928, 8th edn, Duncker & Humblot 1993) 62ff.

8 Cf. only (before the Treaty of Lisbon) Florian von Alemann, *Die Handlungsform der interinstitutionellen Vereinbarung* (Springer 2006).

9 Cf. the historical analyses by Tara Una Diedrichsen, 'The System of Legal Acts in the History of Drafts and Proposals of the EC Treaty' in Gerd Winter (ed.), *Sources and Categories of European Union Law* (Nomos 1996) 315, 317–321; and Morten Rasmussen, 'The Origins of a Legal Revolution – The Early History of the European Court of Justice' (2008) 14 *Journal of European Integration History* 77, 89. From the early literature Paul Reuter, 'Aspects de la Communauté Économique Européenne' (1958) 1 *Revue du Marché Commun* 161; Pierre Pescatore, 'Les Aspects Fonctionnels de la Communauté Économique Européenne, Notamment les Sources du Droit' in *Les Aspects Juridiques du Marché Commun* (compte rendu du séminaire organisé à Chaudfontaine les 22, 23 et 24 mai 1958, Commission Droit et vie des affaires, Faculté de droit de Liège 1958) 51, 53; Ulrich Everling, 'Die ersten Rechtsetzungsakte der Organe der Europäischen Gemeinschaften' (1959) 14 *Betriebs-Berater* 52; Hans Joachim Glaesner, 'Übertragung rechtsetzender Gewalt auf internationale Organisationen in der völkerrechtlichen Praxis' (1959) 12 *Die öffentliche Verwaltung* 653, 655; Hans Peter Ipsen, *Europäisches Gemeinschaftsrecht* (Mohr Siebeck 1972) para 19/8; and from a comparative perspective Reinhold Kraushaar, 'Zur Kompetenz der Kommissionen der Europäischen Gemeinschaften zum Erlaß von Verordnungen' (1959) 12 *Die öffentliche Verwaltung* 726.

individual States was less visible under Article 14 ECSC-Treaty, which was oriented towards the management of individual cases and particular companies,[10] but became apparent in Article 189 EEC-Treaty, the predecessor to Article 288 TFEU, even though the Treaty text still uses the term 'Acts' instead of rules, norms or legislation until today.[11] Early writings on European law underline supranationality and do not even reflect the need for unanimity within the Council during the transitional phase as an indication for negotiated (contractual) rule-making.[12] (Mainly) French authors discussed whether Article 189(2) EEC-Treaty was an emanation of a specific type of *pouvoir règlementaire* or whether it was *législation* in a strict sense, while bearing in mind the idea of the *loi* in all its historical comprehensiveness.[13] During the following years, the EU's supranational rule-making power was not seriously called into question as a matter of principle. Regulations as the most pertinent sign of this competence were widely used and not criticised as such.[14] Even the discussions on the transformation of directives and the various consequences their non-transformation may entail ended up in supranational mechanisms being implemented against resistance that was quite strong at times.[15]

The need for reform has been strongly felt since the late 1990s as legal acts for six Member States in certain areas of economic policy are different from legislation in almost every field for now 28 Member States.[16] The reform of EU rule-making, however, did not change the terminology of supranational

10 Cf. Fernand Dehousse, 'Les Aspects Politiques et Institutionnels de la Communauté Économique Européenne' *Les Aspects Juridiques du Marché Commun* (compte rendu du séminaire organisé à Chaudfontaine les 22, 23 et 24 mai 1958, Commission Droit et vie des affaires, Faculté de droit de Liège 1958) 35, 36: 'rôle de réglementation économique'.

11 This is not beyond critique: Matthias Ruffert in Christian Calliess and id (eds), *EUV/AEUV* (4th edn, CH Beck 2011) Art 288 AEUV para 7.

12 Single French authors consier the EEC-Treaty to be a *loi* because of its content, not because of its genesis: Louis Cartou, 'Le Marché Commun et la Technique du Droit Public' (1958) 65 *Revue du Droit Public et de la Science Politique* 186, 189.

13 This was controversial between Pescatore (n 8) 64ff, who objected and Reuter (n 8) 162, who was in favour (similarly Paul Reuter, *La Communauté Européene du Charbon et de l'Acier* (Pichon et Durand-Auzias 1953) para 44; and from a German perspective the first commentary on the EEC-Treaty: Ernst Wohlfahrt in id, Ulrich Everling, Hans Joachim Glaesner and Rudolf Sprung, *Die Europäische Wirtschaftsgemeinschaft: Kommentar zum Vertrag* (Vahlen 1960) Vorb vor Art 189 para 2.

Some draft documents of the EEC-Treaty contain the term *loi/Gesetz* as a matter of course: Article 35 of the draft of the constitutional committee of the ad-hoc-assembly of 29 January 1953 (Doc AA/CC/GT (3) 7) in Reiner Schulze/Thomas Hoeren (eds), *Dokumente zum Europäischen Recht, Band 1, Gründungsverträge* (Springer 1999) 539ff.

14 On the empirical status, cf. already Armin von Bogdandy, Jürgen Bast and Felix Arndt, 'Handlungsformen im Unionsrecht' (2002) 62 *Zeitschrift für ausländisches öffentliches Recht und Völkerrecht* 77, 92ff.

15 Leading monograph: Sacha Prechal, *Directives in EC Law* (2nd edn, OUP 2005).

16 Cf. Herwig Hofmann, *Normenhierarchien im europäischen Gemeinschaftsrecht* (Duncker & Humblot 2000) 43ff, as well as the contributions in Winter (n 8).

legislation. The adaptation of rule-making to legislative reality by use of the words 'laws' and 'framework laws' was given up along with the constitutional project in 2005. The current term 'legislative acts' used in Article 289(3) TFEU is only of limited value for structuring EU legislation, as the terms 'regulation' and 'directive' were retained by the Lisbon reform to eliminate the constitutional horrors from the new text.[17] Further, the reform advanced majority voting in the Council and more intensive participation of the European Parliament, the latter due to the requirements of the principle of representative democracy, Article 10(1) TEU.[18] Only rarely is the European Parliament's role limited to conducting a simple hearing; in most cases, it has far-reaching legislative rights in the ordinary legislative procedure under Article 294 TFEU.[19]

## *3.2 Back to the bargain*

### *3.2.1 Transforming the procedure towards Trilogue*

In the recent past, however, there have been indications for a reinforcement of negotiation processes and contractual relationships. The first of these indications may be detected in the ordinary legislative procedure mentioned above. Inter-institutional arrangements further increase the complexity of this procedure with its three readings, the conciliation procedure after the second reading and the complicated voting rules.[20] This is particularly true for the so-called Trilogue procedure, which was developed from the conciliation procedure and has now been moved from that relatively late stage of the legislative process to before the first reading.[21] It enables the Parliament, the Commission and the Council to unofficially draft their common position. The procedure is weakly regulated by a Common Declaration of these three

17 European Council (Brussels), 21 and 22 June 2007, Presidency Conclusions, Annex I, IGC Mandate, Council Doc D/07/2, No I 3; on this cf. Jonas Bering Liisberg, 'The EU Constitutional Treaty and its Distinction Between Legislative and Non-legislative Acts – Oranges into Apples?' (2006) *Jean Monnet Working Paper* 01/06; Jürgen Bast, 'New Categories of Acts after the Lisbon Reform: Dynamics of Parliamentarization in EU Law' (2012) 49 *CMLRev* 885, 887, 889ff; and Constantin Fabricius, 'Abgeleitete Rechtsetzung nach dem Vertag von Lissabon – Überlegungen zu Delegierten Rechtsakten und Durchführungsrechtsakten' (2011) 14 *Zeitschrift für Europarechtliche Studien* 567, 569.

18 Overview: Matthias Ruffert, 'Parlamentarisierung von Herrschaft im Mehrebenensystem' in Martin Morlok, Utz Schliesky and Dieter Wiefelspütz (eds), *Handbuch des Parlamentsrechts* (forthcoming, Nomos 2014) ch 42 para 12.

19. Cf. only Paul Craig, 'Institutions, Power, and Institutional Balance' in id/Gráinne de Búrca (eds), *The Evolution of EU Law* (OUP 2011) 41, 74ff.

20 Cf. Robert Schütze, *European Constitutional Law* (CUP 2012) 171ff, 175ff on the following.

21 An empirical analysis is provided by: Rik de Ruiter and Christine Neuhold, 'Why Is Fast Track the Way to Go? Justifications for Early Agreement in the Co-Decision Procedure and Their Effects' (2012) 18 *ELJ* 536.

organs.[22] In Parliament, subtle negotiation must anticipate a positive vote, and the Council Presidency must assure there is sufficient Member State backup to reach a qualified majority. If really 70 per cent of legislation is elaborated this way – as the Bundesverfassungsgericht reports in its (first) judgment on the 5 per cent clause[23] – an important negotiation procedure for rule-making has been established beyond the Treaties' rules, even though it is not about negotiation between Member States alone, but includes with strong supranational actors, the European Parliament and the European Commission.

### *3.2.2 Rule-making in the European Council and Ersatz-EU law*

When rule-making is governed by the European Council, these supranational institutions remain in the shadows. Usually, the European Council shall not exercise legislative functions, Article 15(1), 2nd sentence TEU. Some have even considered this prohibition to be superfluous because of its evident character.[24] Recent practice shows, however, that political programming at European Council level generates more and more detailed input for legislation that may trigger ratification situations for the other EU institutions, which is even more disturbing if it is not the European Council that decides, but the Euro Group Summit.[25] The European Council establishes its own working groups to prepare the respective projects and thus tries to share the initiative with the European Commission.[26] Particularly in crisis rule-making, its activity is closely linked to a single Council configuration, the ECOFIN Council, and to the evermore institutionalised Eurogroup.

In this context, the framework of EU law has partly been abandoned and replaced by instruments of public international law. This is done implicitly where Member States 'transpose' a Regulation into national law in a procedure similar to Parliamentary ratification – which indeed happened in the German Bundestag with respect to the 2013 Regulation on Banking Supervision.[27]

22 Joint declaration on practical arrangements for the codecision procedure (article 251 of the EC Treaty) [2007] OJ C145/5 paras 7–9 and 23–25 for the second reading and the conciliation procedure.

23 BVerfGE 129, 300, 333. An English translation is not available. The press release in English (http://www.bundesverfassungsgericht.de/pressemitteilungen/bvg11-070en.html) does not mention this aspect.

24 Cf. e.g. Volker Epping in Christoph Vedder and Wolff Heintschel von Heinegg (eds), *Europäisches Unionsrecht* (Nomos 2012) Article 15 EUV para 4.

25 This holds e.g. for the *Euro-Plus-Pact*: Conclusions of the Heads of State or Government of the Euro Area of 11 March 2011 (without Doc-no) or the Statement by the Euro Area Heads of State or Government of 9 December 2012 (without Doc-no).

26 Final Report by the Task Force 'Economic Governance' of 21 October 2010, Doc 15302/10, as well as the Programme elaborated by the Presidents of the European Council, the European Commission and the ECB 'Towards a Genuine Economic and Monetary Union' of 5 December 2012.

27 *Gesetz zum Vorschlag für eine Verordnung des Rates zur Übertragung besonderer Aufgaben im Zusammenhang mit der Aufsicht über Kreditinstitute auf die Europäische Zentralbank*, BGBl II 2013, 1050; on this statute cf Franz Mayer and Daniel Kollmeyer, 'Sinnlose Gesetzgebung? Die Europäische Bankenunion im Bundestag' (2013) 64 *Deutsches Verwaltungsblatt* 1158.

It is done explicitly when the lack of a EU power leads to concomitant action of the Member States that generates a public international *Ersatz*-EU law (a term invented by Ralph Alexander Lorz and Heiko Sauer),[28] be it in fear of losing the Member States' budgetary sovereignty as in the case of the creation of the European Stability Mechanism (ESM) or be it that consensus between the Member States cannot be achieved, as in the case of the Fiscal Compact.[29] The planned contract management in the framework of macro-economic governance could have a similar rule-making function.[30]

### *3.2.3 Limited hierarchisation and the spectre of comitology*

Astonishingly enough, a similar element of contractual rule-making may be discerned in the results of the rule-making reforms undertaken for the sake of hierarchising EU secondary law.[31] Of course, it can be noted that the Treaty of Lisbon brought about a decisive step in introducing delegated rule-making and highlighting implementation (Articles 290 and 291 TFEU, respectively).[32] Moreover, the ECJ clearly elaborated the difference between legislation and rule-making below the legislative level in interpreting the term 'regulatory act' in a way that it does not mean all regulations under Article 288(2) TFEU, but that it only encompasses general rules without a legislative character, following the wording of Article 263(4) TFEU and its genesis.[33]

The Regulation is: Council Regulation (EC) 1024/2013 conferring specific tasks on the European Central Bank concerning policies relating to the prudential supervision of credit institutions [2013] OJ L287, 63.

28 Ralph Alexander Lorz and Heiko Sauer, 'Ersatzunionsrecht und Grundgesetz' (2012) 65 *Die öffentliche Verwaltung* 573; taken up by Bundesverfassungsgericht judgment of 12 September 2012 (available at: http://www.bverfg.de/entscheidungen/rs20120912_2bvr139012en.html) para 257.

29 Treaty on Stability, Coordination and Governance in the Economic and Monetary Union, http://european-council.europa.eu/media/639235/st00tscg26_en12.pdf (retrieved 3 April 2015).

30 'Towards a Genuine Economic and Monetary Union' (*supra* note 25) 13ff, taken up in the Presidency Conclusions of the European Council of 19 and 20 December 2013 Doc EUCO 217/13, paras 23ff.

31 Cf. only Paul Craig, *EU Administrative Law* (2nd edn, OUP 2012) 124ff.

32 German legal literature tends to use the term 'Tertiärrecht' (tertiary legislation): Thomas Groß, 'Exekutive Vollzugsprogrammierung durch tertiäres Gemeinschaftsrecht' (2004) 57 *Die öffentliche Verwaltung* 20; Wolfgang Weiß, *Der Europäische Verwaltungsverbund* (Duncker & Humblot 2010); Rudolf Streinz, *Europarecht* (9th edn, C.F. Müller 2012) para 560; Sabine Schlacke, 'Komitologie nach dem Vertrag von Lissabon' (2013) 61 *Jahrbuch des Öffentlichen Rechts* (Neue Folge) 293, 305. This should be given up: Gernot Sydow, 'Europäische exekutive Rechtsetzung zwischen Kommission, Komitologieausschüssen, Parlament und Rat' (2012) 62 *Juristenzeitung* 157, 158; Martin Nettesheim, 'Normenhierarchien im EU-Recht' (2006) 41 *Europarecht* 737, 765ff; Ines Härtel, *Handbuch Europäische Rechtsetzung* (Springer 2006) ch 15 para 9.

33 ECJ, Case C-583/11 P *Inuit Tapiriit Kanatami v Parliament and Council*, ECLI:EU:C:2013:625, paras 89ff, confirming GC, Case T-18/10 *Inuit Tapiriit Kanatami v Parliament and Council* [2011] ECR II-5599, paras 38ff. On that case Wolfram Cremer, 'Die Nichtigkeitsklage Privater 50 Jahre nach Plaumann: Der EuGH bleibt sich treu – zum Rechtsmittelurteil vom 3. Oktober 2013 in der Rs. Inuit Tapiriit Kanatam' (2014) 29 *Zeitschrift für Gesetzgebung* 82; Bast (n 16) 898 ff.

Therefore, it cannot be said that hierarchisation of EU law through the reform process was a complete failure. Hierarchy of norms means that the legality and validity of the lower ranking norm depends on the higher ranking ones.[34] This has always applied to secondary law and the Treaties (primary law). Such a hierarchy also exists between legislative acts and delegated rule-making or implementation.[35] Article 290(1) TFEU codifies the ECJ's jurisprudence according to which delegated acts can only amend non-essential elements of legislation and 'essential elements of an area shall be reserved for the legislative act and accordingly shall not be the subject of a delegation of power'.[36] Delegated rule-making will therefore be unlawful where it transgresses this framework. The same applies to rule-making for implementation purposes.

However, the institutional framework established by Articles 290 and 291 TFEU perpetuates and even intensifies the strong influence of negotiation elements within EU rule-making. Subordinate rule-making may take the shape of small 'treaties', contractual relationships between the Member States themselves and the Commission. This is quite obvious with respect to implementation rule-making following Article 291(3) TFEU. In this Article, the Treaty preserves the Member States' participation in subordinate rule-making following the old comitology model.[37] According to section 1 of the Article, implementation – whether in a normative or administrative way[38] –

34 Hans Kelsen, *Reine Rechtslehre* (first published 1934, Matthias Jestaedt ed., Mohr Siebeck 2008) 84ff.

35 Cf. the critical differentiation by Cosima Haselmann, *Delegation und Durchführung gemäß Art. 290 und 291 AEUV* (Duncker & Humblot 2012) 249ff.

36 S. Herwig Hofmann, 'Legislation, Delegation and Implementation under the Treaty of Lisbon: Typology Meets Reality' (2009) 15 *ELJ* 482, 489ff; id and Alexander Türk, 'Die Ausübung übertragener Normsetzungsbefugnisse durch die Europäische Kommission' (2012) 27 *Zeitschrift für Gesetzgebung* 105, 107; Thomas Kröll, 'Delegierte Rechtsetzung und Durchführungsrechtsetzung und das institutionelle Gleichgewicht der Europäischen Union' (2011) 66 *Zeitschrift für öffentliches Recht* 253, 262; in the criterion of essentiality Haselmann (n 34)100ff.
From the Court's case law: ECJ, Case C-133/06 *Parliament v. Council* [2008] ECR I-3189, para 45; Case C-355/10 *Parliament v. Council*, ECLI:EU:C:2012:516, para 64.

37 Herwig Hofmann, Gerard Rowe and Alexander Türk, *Administrative Law and Policy of the European Union* (OUP 2011) 534; Hofmann (n 35) 498; Bast (n 16) 912; Markus Möstl, 'Rechtsetzungen der europäischen und nationalen Verwaltungen' (2011) 62 *Deutsches Verwaltungsblatt* 1081.
On the development of comitology Craig (n 30) 113ff; Hofmann, Rowe and Türk (n 36) 264ff; Jean-Claude Piris, 'La Comitologie: Vers l'Epilogue d'une Longue Saga?' in Chemins d'Europe, *Mélanges en l'Honneur de Jean Paul Jacqué* (Dalloz 2010) 547 ff; as well as Daniele Bianchi, 'La Comitologie est Morte! Vive la Comitologie!' (2012) 48 *Revue trimesterielle de droit européen* 75, 78ff, with a special reference to the CAP.

38 Bast (n 16) 919; Steve Peers and Marios Costa, 'Accountability for Delegated and Implemeting Acts after the Treaty of Lisbon' (2012) 18 *ELJ* 427, 446; Hofmann and Türk (n 36) 112; The opposite view is taken by Ulrich Stelkens, 'Rechtsetzungen der europäischen und nationalen Verwaltungen' (2012) 71 *Veröffentlichungen der Vereinigung der Deutschen Staatsrechtslehrer* 385, and in extenso Art 291 AEUV, das Unionsverwaltungsrecht und die Verwaltungsautonomie der Mitgliedstaaten (2011) FÖV Discussion Papers 68.

is basically within the Member States' powers.[39] If they lose their power of implementation due to the need for uniform implementation of binding EU acts (Article 291(2) TFEU), both procedures established by the relevant 2011 Regulation are designed to compensate for the loss by means of participation in Committees:[40]

- Within the *advisory procedure* –retained from the earlier comitology decisions – the Member States' powers of control are rather weak, as the only obligation of the Commission, when issuing an act of implementation, is: 'taking the utmost account of the conclusions drawn from the discussions within the committee and of the opinion delivered'.[41]
- In the *examination procedure*, however, the committee has a veto right (Article 5(3) Regulation No. 182/2011), and this applies to 'implementing acts of general scope' as well as to acts relating to 'programmes with substantial implications' and in the following fields: the common agricultural and fisheries policies, the environment, security and health safety, the common commercial policy and finally taxation. In some of these fields (taxation, financial services, health protection, multilateral safeguard measures), even silence on the part of the committee prevents the implementing measure from being adopted (Article 5(4)), and this strictness may also be applied to other fields. The complexity of the procedure is further increased by an appeals committee for contentious cases and by the option to take interim measures (Articles 7 and 8 of the Regulation).

The Register to be kept by the Commission under Article 10 of the Regulation currently contains 312 committees on various bases,[42] and

39 Uniform implementation does, however, not imply the power to modify the act to be implemented: Hofmann, Rowe and Türk (n 36) 531; Eckart Bueren, 'Grenzen der Durchführungsrechtsetzung im Unionsrecht' (2012) 23 *Europäische Zeitschrift für Wirtschaftsrecht* 167, 170ff; Thomas Christiansen and Mathias Dobbels, 'Comitology and Delegated Acts after Lisbon: How the European Parliament Lost the Implementation Game' (2012) 16 *European Integration online Papers*, Article 13, 44; a differentiated view is taken by Bast (n 16) 920; Andrea Edenharter, 'Die Komitologie nach dem Vertrag von Lissabon: Verschiebung der Einflußmöglichkeiten zugunsten der EU-Kommission' (2011) 64 *Die öffentliche Verwaltung* 645, 649; as well as – with respect to the genesis of the provisions – Paul Craig, 'Delegated Acts, Implementing Acts and the New Comitology Regulation' (2011) 36 *ELR* 671, 672ff.

40 Regulation (EC) 182/2011 of the European Parliament and of the Council of 16 February 2011 laying down the rules and general principles concerning mechanisms for control by Member States of the Commission's exercise of implementing powers [2011] OJ L55, 13, commented upon by Sydow (n 31) 160ff; Edenharter (n 38) 645; Fabricius (n 16) 596ff; Christiansen and Dobbels (n 38) 47ff; Schlacke (n 31) 313 ff.

41 Exception: Art 2 Abs. 3 Reg 182/11.

42 Available at: http://ec.europa.eu/transparency/regcomitology/index.cfm. Cf as well the standard rules of procedure for committees that were issued by the Commission [2011] OJ L206, 6.

implementation appears to be dominant in relation to delegated rulemaking judging from the legislation database eur-lex.[43]

At first sight, the element of negotiation may appear to be absent from delegated rule-making under Article 290.[44] This impression could be caused by the fact that Article 290 TFEU in a way marks the final point in a long development towards enhanced participation by the European Parliament in subordinate legislation as it transposes the 'regulatory procedure with scrutiny' from the former comitology into Treaty law,[45] whereas in implementation, the competences of Parliament are reduced to the level of mere information (Articles 10(3) and 11 Regulation No. 182/2011). The possibility that the delegating act may vest Parliament with the power to revoke the delegation or to make it subject to Parliamentary approval (Article 290(2) TFEU) needs to be viewed before this backdrop.[46] Although the supranational and Parliamentary element is clearly visible in Article 290, the Member States remain involved in delegated legislation *via* the Council whose rights are formulated parallel to those of Parliament. Furthermore, one cannot overlook the practice that tries to bring in Member State dominance from the comitology experience through the back door by making expert hearings mandatory before the adoption of delegated legislation – and experts are of course Member States' experts.[47] To sum up, Article 290, like Article 291, permits negotiated, contractual rule-making, perhaps with different intensity. If the Commission wants to evade this fettering of its delegated rule-making powers, it may even seek alternatives in informal rule-making ('soft law').

43 The result of the search for 'implementing regulation' is 30 times higher than the one for 'delegated regulation'.

44 Cf. Claude Blumann, 'À la Frontière de la Fonction Législative et de la Fonction Exécutive: les "Nouveaux" Actes Délégués' in *Chemins d'Europe, Mélanges en l'honneur de Jean Paul Jacqué* (Dalloz 2010) 127, 138.

45 Bast (n 16) 916; Hofmann and Türk (n 35) 107; on the consequences for Article 290 TFEU Gregor Schusterschitz, 'Rechtsakte und Rechtsetzungsverfahren' in Waldemar Hummer and Walter Obwexer (eds), Der *Vertrag von Lissabon* (Nomos 2009) 209, 232ff; on the 'regulatory procedure with scrutiny'/'Procédure de réglementation avec contrôle – PRAC': Haselmann (n 34) 39.

46 On the exclusive nature of the powers laid down in Article 290 (2) TFEU and on the relationship of control by the Parliament and the Council cf Peers and Costa (n 37) 444, and Kröll (n 35) 275.

47 Communication from the Commission to the European Parliament and the Council – Implementation of Article 290 of the Treaty on the Functioning of the European Union, Doc [2009] COM 673 final, 7; Common Understanding on EU delegated acts, 3 March 2011, Council Doc 8753/11, no 4; Cf Craig (n 45) 128ff; in detail Fabricius (n 16) 573ff; Christiansen and Dobbels (n 38) 50; and Arne Pilniok, 'Struktur, Funiktionen und Probleme der Expertengruppen der Europischen Kommission: legitime Expertise oder unzulässige Einflußnahme?' (2014) 49 *Europarecht* 62, 76ff.

## *3.3 Pluralising rule-making*

### *3.3.1 The rise of the agencies*

As could be shown, Member States' involvement in EU rule-making increases complexity. The same needs to be said with respect to agencies' participation in rule-making procedures. Until recently, the importance and independence of this particular instrument of EU governance was rather exaggerated in the euphoria of importing a new form of administrative organisation from the US.[48] Meanwhile, the operative influence of agencies has considerably risen.[49] They are involved in rule-making in three ways.[50]

### *3.3.2 Agencies rule-making: three methods*

#### 3.3.2.1 DRAFT RULE-MAKING

Agencies can first of all initiate and draft technical rules that are subsequently transformed into binding instruments by the Commission. This is a rather common method[51] and applies in particular to rule-making in the field of financial markets supervision. The relevant drafting competences are transferred to the European Supervisory Agencies (ESAs), the European Banking Authority (EBA), the European Securities and Markets Authority (ESMA) and the European Insurance and Occupational Pensions Authority (EIOPA).

48 Vgl. Matthias Ruffert, 'Verselbständigte Verwaltungseinheiten: Ein europäischer Megatrend im Vergleich' in Hans-Heinrich Trute, Thomas Groß, Hans Christian Röhl and Christoph Möllers (eds), *Allgemeines Verwaltungsrecht – zur Tragfähigkeit eines Konzepts* (Mohr Siebeck 2008) 431.

49 Writing on agencies is abundant – so just three examples (with many references): Herwig Hofmann and Alessandro Morini, 'Constitutional Aspects of the Pluralisation of the EU Executive through "Agencification"' (2012) 37 *ELR* 37, 41; Steffen Augsberg, 'Europäisches Verwaltungsorganisationsrecht und Vollzugsformen' in Jörg Philipp Terhechte (ed), *Verwaltungsrecht der Europäischen Union* (Nomos 2011) ch 6 para 73ff.

50 Edoardo Chiti, 'European Agencies' Rulemaking: Powers, Procedures and Assessment' (2013) 19 *ELJ* 93, 99, enumerates the first two of them.

51 Examples are the *ENISA* (Art 2 (4) of Regulation (EC) 460/2004 of the European Parliament and of the Council of 10 March 2004 establishing the European Network and Information Security Agency [2014] OJ L77, 1), the *EMSA* (Article 2(a) as formulated in Regulation (EC) 724/2004 of the European Parliament and of the Council of 31 March 2004 amending Regulation (EC) 1406/2002 establishing a European Maritime Safety Agency [2004] OJ L129, 1), the *ACER* (Article 6 (1) of Regulation (EC) 713/2009 of the European Parliament and of the Council of 13 July 2009 establishing an Agency for the Cooperation of Energy Regulators [2009] OJ L211, 1), and the ERA (Regulation (EC) 881/2004 of the European Parliament and of the Council of 29 April 2004 establishing a European Railway Agency (Agency Regulation) [2004] OJ L164, 1). *The examples are drawn from Chiti* (n 49), 97.

According to the common Article 10 ('Regulatory technical standards') of the founding regulations for these agencies, the following applies:[52]

> (1) Where the European Parliament and the Council delegate power to the Commission to adopt regulatory technical standards by means of delegated acts pursuant to Article 290 TFEU . . ., the Authority may develop draft regulatory technical standards. The Authority shall submit its draft standards to the Commission for endorsement.

According to the further provisions of this article, the submission of regulatory technical standards is preceded by public consultation and a thorough cost-benefit analysis. The Commission is given three months to endorse the standards, and there is a complicated procedure for amending the draft if the Commission only wishes to endorse the draft standards subject to modifications. The Commission is even denied its monopoly of initiative (Article 17(2), 1st sentence TEU), as without such a draft it may only act if the authority fails to do so within certain time limits.[53] What is more, the new Single Supervisory Mechanism (SSM) does not affect this rule-making concept, but the standards elaborated by the agencies (in the case of banking, by the EBA) are binding for the ECB's banking supervisory activity.[54]

Who is the rule-maker in these instances? Formally, the Commission remains competent by endorsing the rules, and it can modify them, albeit by a complicated procedure.[55] Substantially, it is the Supervisory Board of the

52 This article is contained in the following regulations: Regulation (EU) 1093/2010 of the European Parliament and of the Council of 24 November 2010 establishing a European Supervisory Authority (European Banking Authority), amending Decision 716/2009/EC and repealing Commission Decision 2009/78/EC [2010] OJ L331, 12 (not modified insofar by Regulation (EU) 1022/2013 [2013] OJ L287, 5; Regulation (EU) 1094/2010 of the European Parliament and of the Council of 24 November 2010 establishing a European Supervisory Authority (European Insurance and Occupational Pensions Authority), amending Decision 716/2009/EC and repealing Commission Decision 2009/79/EC [2010] OJ L331, 48, and Regulation (EU) 1095/2010 of the European Parliament and of the Council of 24 November 2010 establishing a European Supervisory Authority (European Securities and Markets Authority), amending Decision 716/2009/EC and repealing Commission Decision 2009/77/EC [2010] OJ L331, 84.

53 Cf. Madalina Busuioc, 'Rule-Making by the European Financial Supervisory Authorities: Walking a Tight Rope' (2013) 19 *ELJ* 111, 115; furthermore: Niamh Moloney, 'The European Securities and Marktes Authority and Institutional Design for the EU Financial Market – A Tale of Two Competences: Part (1) Rule-Making' (2011) 12 *European Business Organization Law Review* 41, 66ff.

54 Cf. Article 4(3) Reg. 1024/2013 (n 26).

55 Cf. Elaine Fahey, 'Does the Emperor Have Financial Crisis Clothes? Reflections on the Legal Basis of the European Banking Authority' (2011) *MLR* 74 581, 585; Niamh Moloney, 'EU Financial Market Regulation after the Global Financial Crisis: "More Europe" or More Risks?' (2010) *CMLRev* 47 1317, 1347, calls this a 'pragmatic constitutional fix'.

agencies[56] which is composed of the heads of the relevant national supervisory authority plus one non-voting representative each of the Commission, the ECB and the other financial supervisory agency, as well as the (non-voting) chairman. Although in rule-making the Board acts by qualified majority, there is now an element of negotiation between the Member States – to be exact: between the Member States' heads of authorities.[57]

#### 3.3.2.2 INFORMAL RULE-MAKING BY AGENCIES

A second rule-making method is informal rule-making by the agencies. They may issue guidelines, communications or comparable instruments which are not binding under the Treaties or the agency's founding regulation, but which are given quasi-binding force by a mechanism of 'naming and shaming'. Again, one may consider the financial supervisory agencies.[58] They may (under Article 16(1) of the founding regulations)[59] issue recommendations and guidelines '. . . with a view to establishing consistent, efficient and effective supervisory practices . . ., and to ensuring the common, uniform and consistent application of Union law'. Although not binding per se, 'The competent authorities and financial institutions shall make every effort to comply with those guidelines and recommendations', and if they do not intend to comply, this may be published by the agency along with reasons for non-compliance. Albeit non-binding, such 'soft' rules may have far-reaching influence within the respective field.[60]

#### 3.3.2.3 BINDING RULE-MAKING AND ITS LIMITS

The third way of agency rule-making is issuing binding rules. This is a rather new development. An illustrative example for this rule-making method is the ESA's power to 'be able to temporarily prohibit or restrict certain financial activities that threaten the orderly functioning and integrity of financial markets or the stability of the whole or part of the financial system in the Union'.[61] In this context, the ESMA was given the power to '. . . prohibit or

56 Cf. the critical assessment by Busuioc (n 52), 123; on the boards cf also her extensive analysis 'European Agencies and their Boards: Promises and Pitfalls of Accountability Beyond Design' (2012) 19 *Journal of European Public Policy* 719.

57 This is well illustrated by Busuioc (n 52) 121: 'Vessels for a Variety of National Interests'.

58 Other instances could be the *EASA* (Article 18 (c) of Regulation (EC) 216/2008 in the field of aerodromes, air traffic management and air navigation services and repealing Directive 2006/23/EC [2008] OJ L79, 1, as amended by Regulation (EC) 1108/2009 of the European Parliament and of the Council of 21 October 2009 [2009] OJ L309, 51).

59 Cf. n 51.

60 Critically assessed by Busuioc (n 52) 118ff; Moloney (n 52) 65, rightly calls into question their 'softness'.

61 Common Article 9 No 5 of the ESA-Regulations (n 51).

impose conditions on, the entry by natural or legal persons into a short sale' (i.e. 'any sale of the share or debt instrument which the seller does not own at the time of entering into the agreement to sell') by legislative Regulation No. 236/12.[62] In other words: by means of a legislative regulation, rule-making competences are delegated to ESMA in a particular field of financial regulation.

Such delegation obviously raises the question of compatibility with Article 290 TFEU. This article designates the Commission as the sole delegate for rule-making and in doing so does not mention agencies. Is it acceptable that the Union organs use an agency to issue binding rules whose prime institution is a network of the presidents of the national supervising authorities?

We know that the Court – upon an action for annulment brought by the UK – was very generous in accepting this delegation.[63] It used two lines of argument. First, it denied that delegated and implementation powers under Articles 290 and 291 TFEU were exclusively held by the Commission.[64] Although there was no explicit conferral of such powers to a Union body, office or agency, the Treaty presupposed the possibility of such conferral in its Articles 263, 265, 267 and 277, which contained judicial review mechanisms that applied 'to the bodies, offices and agencies established by the EU legislature which were given powers to adopt measures that are legally binding on natural or legal persons in specific areas'.[65] Second, the Court placed an emphasis on the need for rapid intervention in financial markets and for a high degree of professional expertise on the part of the authorities involved.[66]

The weakness of both lines of arguments reveals a series of problems connected to binding rule-making by agencies.[67] Methodically, it is highly questionable to infer a power to issue certain acts from powers to call into question such acts by means of judicial review.[68] Besides, only Article 277

62 Articles 28(1)(b) and 2(1)(b) of Regulation (EU) 236/2012 of the European Parliament and of the Council of 14 March 2012 on short selling and certain aspects of credit default swaps [2012] OJ L86, 1.

63 ECJ, Case C-270/12 judgment of 22 January 2014 *UK v. Parliament and Council*, ECLI:EU:C:2014:18.

64 ECJ (n 62) paras 77ff.

65 ECJ (n 62) paras 65, 80.

66 ECJ (n 62) para 85.

67 Cf. the critical assessment by Natalia Kohtamäki (2014) 49 *Europarecht*, 321, and Christoph Ohler (2014) 69 *Juristenzeitung* 249, 251.

68 The relevant Working Group in the European Convention where the amendments to the articles quoted were adopted was more cautious: 'It is also impossible to state categorically, when an agency is set up, that it will not perform such acts, even if the Regulation establishing it does not give it power to adopt decisions in the formal sense'. (Final report of the discussion circle on the Court of Justice, Doc CONV 636/03, para 25). Cf. also 'Right of Appeal Against Agencies Created by Secondary Legislation' Working Document 09 of 10 March 2003; Communication from the Commission – The operating framework for the European Regulatory Agencies, Doc [2002] COM718 final, 13ff. Ulrich Stelkens in Paul Stelkens, Heinz-Joachim Bonk and Michael Sachs (eds), *Verwaltungsverfahrensgesetz* (8th edn, C.H. Beck 2014) ch 35 para 345ff, explicitely takes the contrary view.

TFEU of the articles enumerated by the Court clearly mentions an '. . . *act of general application* adopted by an institution, body, office or agency of the Union' (emphasis added). Articles 265 and 267 TFEU are only concerned with '. . . acts of bodies, offices or agencies of the Union . . .'; Article 263 TFEU with '. . . acts of bodies, offices or agencies of the Union intended to produce legal effects vis-à-vis third parties'. Indeed, the difference between acts of general application, on the one hand, and decisions in individual cases, on the other hand, is unduly levelled by the Court's first line of argument. This is also shown by the examples the Court mentions: the European Chemicals Agency, the European Medicines Agency, the Office for Harmonisation in the Internal Market (Trade Marks and Designs), the Community Plant Variety Office and the European Aviation Safety Agency are all agencies that have no power to issue binding acts of general application.[69] The second line of argument is even more flawed. The urgency of the need for rapid intervention into the markets and the expertise of the rule-making body cannot in themselves replace a clear conferral of power.[70]

### *3.4 Informal rule-making by the Commission*

Last but not least, to complete the picture of the complexity of EU rule-making, it must be underlined that 'soft' action is by no means restricted to some of the agencies. On the contrary, the Commission has created the undoubtedly most non-transparent body of rules by means of non-binding rule-making beyond Article 288 TFEU (including recommendation and opinion). The scholarly work on that conglomerate of rules rarely goes beyond mere typologies, but they are becoming more and more precise: *communications*, whether related to ECJ jurisprudence, interpretive or concretising, have for a long time been part of the Commission's practice.[71] As their non-binding character is beyond doubt and as judicial review may be exercised concerning the binding acts that implement the non-binding ones, criticism against communications as a means of action is rather limited, although it would have been preferable to integrate them into the Treaty during the Lisbon reform.[72] Criticism is a lot stronger concerning *guidelines*, and rightly so.

69 For the European Medicines Agency cf. Thomas Gehring, 'Deliberative Regulation Through European Union Agencies and other Network Structures?' in Madalina Busioc, Martin Groenleer and Jarle Trondal, *The Agency Phenomenon in the European Union* (Manchester University Press 2012) 105, 113.

70 Kohtamäki (n 66), and similarly (before the Court's decision) Merijn Chamon, 'EU Agencies Between Meroni and Romano or the Devil and the Deep Blue Sea' (2011) 48 *CMLRev* 1055,1074. Cf. also Moloney (n 54) 1370 '. . . the decision-making powers over financial institutions remain muddy . . .'.

71 This typology is taken from Matthias Knauff, *Der Regelungsverbund* (Mohr Siebeck 2010) 325ff; cf. for an alternative typology Fabien Terpan, 'Soft Law in the European Union – The Changing Nature of EU Law', (2015) 21 *ELJ*, 68.

72 On the limits of EU powers and possible transgressions by *soft law* Knauff (n 70) 299.

Guidelines go beyond the internal sphere of the Commission and the EU as they are meant to influence the behaviour of companies or individual economic actors. Regulatory decisions in the fields of telecommunications or energy regulation are partly determined by Commission guidelines;[73] agency guidelines in the field of financial regulation have already been mentioned.[74] Guidelines pose a problem alone for not being, despite their steering effect, anchored in the Treaties other than being mentioned in Articles 156, 168, 173(2) and 183(2) TFEU.[75] What is even more problematic is the question of organisation and powers behind the Commission's practice regarding guidelines. Within the network of the integrated European administration, guidelines may shift powers to the Commission it does not possess under a strict understanding of the principle of conferral. Guidelines of the Commission (and also of the agencies) may convey political decisions, e.g. about sources of energy or risk management without sufficient attribution of legitimacy and accountability and perhaps with a relevant portion of regulatory capture.[76] Who is responsible for soft rule-making – supranational expertise, Member States' negotiation or mixed networks of authorities? The matter becomes even more complicated if soft governance is not undertaken by rules, but by mechanisms of 'new governance' such as coordination, whether under the Treaties or the well-known open method of coordination.[77]

## 4 Bargaining, pluralisation, informality: legal scholarship's answers

### *4.1 EU rule-making and European legal scholarship*

What do we derive from this picture? What follows from the ever-growing influence of bargaining situations, from the proliferation of rule-makers and from the trend to informality? Again, it shall be stressed that a scholarly sound answer does not lie in oversimplifying, idealising or denying the supranational developments of the past decades. What can be done by applying core legal categories is to highlight three overarching structural problems and to provide options for their political solution. These problems are the pluralistic structure of rulemaking (*infra* 2.), the integration of expert advice (*infra* 3.) and the establishment of general rules for rulemaking (*infra* 4.).

73 Jürgen Kühling, 'Telekommunikationsrecht', *Enzyklopädie Europarecht* (2012) vol 5, ch 4 para 76 ff; Markus Ludwigs, 'Energierecht', id., ch 5 para 152ff.

74 Cf. *supra* 3. b) (ii).

75 S. Knauff (n 70) 330.

76 Weiß (n 31) 149ff.

77 Comprehensive assessment by Beate Braams, *Koordinierung als Kompetenzkategorie* (Mohr Siebeck 2013).

### *4.2 The settlement of the pluralistic structure*

First of all, even if we maintain a certain methodological modesty as indicated, there is the strong need to fence in the ever-growing pluralism of rule-making. This does not imply a preference for monolithic, State-oriented models of governance that generally conflict with any inclusion of pluralist interests into the rule-making process. However, one cannot deny that strengthening bargaining by pluralisation entails disadvantages and risks. Bargained solutions tend to be non-transparent as negotiations require confidentiality. Transparency tends to suffer by moving rule-making from an entity established by a Treaty or from the interaction of several such entities to a plurality of actors, and if those actors are themselves sub-structured in a multitude of bargaining processes such as the internal structures of comitology or agencies show, the lack of transparency may multiply.[78] What is more, a deficit of clarity is almost always bound to bring about a deficit in legitimacy and accountability.[79] Who is really acting when Member States' heads of financial supervisory agencies negotiate supervisory standards within one of the ESAs? Is it the EU as such? Is it the relevant agency? Is it the Member States in an international negotiating process, though surely they are probably not willing to be internationally represented by the head of an authority that usually ranks below a minister? Luckily enough, there are means for realigning EU rule-making without falling into the State-analogy trap:

- One of them was depicted in the more consented parts of the ECJ's judgment in Pringle. The Court made clear that even if it was the Member States acting in the field of the Economic and Monetary Union and even if they were entrusting the EU organs with particular tasks in this field, the organs would be within their powers as framed by the aims and targets defined in the Treaties.[80] Rule-making in *Ersatz*-Union law must respect the Union's rule-making framework. Of course, it would be preferable to integrate creations such as the ESM or the institutional arrangements of the Fiscal Compact into the institutional system of the Treaty, but as long as this is highly unlikely in political terms, there is no need to resign since one can follow the Pringle line.
- Furthermore, rule-making by the agencies should be made more institutionally coherent, if not streamlined. This requires additional doctrinal work, as the mere mention of the agencies (together with bodies, offices

78 In this sense, the component parts of rule-making may become more significant than the whole; cf. framework paper [page, at I. (ii)].

79 The classical text for this connection in German legal literature is Gertrude Lübbe-Wolff, 'Europäisches und nationales Verfassungsrecht' (2001) 60 *Veröffentlichungen der Vereinigung der Deutschen Staatsrechtslehrer* 247, 276ff.

80 ECJ, Case C-370/12 judgment of 27 November 2012 *Pringle v. Government of Ireland*, ECLI: EU:C:2012:756, paras 153ff.

and the like) in some Treaty articles, especially on judicial review, is not enough. The agencies need a place in the European legal order, being important actors in the field of rule-making.[81] As developed elsewhere, this may be achieved by establishing the idea of a legal person (*personne morale, juristische Person*) under EU law that is distinct from legal personality under international or domestic law.[82] Such a distinction would allow for a clear attribution of rule-making competences – or not. It could already be shown with reference to the ESMA-judgment that in this respect, the Court is not on the right path. A last step towards institutional coherence could be a supervisory function over the agencies exercised by the Commission, which is particularly important and also viable in the field of rule-making.[83] To date, the issue is still subject to controversy whether this would make necessary a reform at Treaty level or whether the existing Treaty law would allow for such a supervision limited to a scrutiny of legality.[84]

### *4.3 The integration of expert knowledge and its limits*

Second, there is a very strong tendency to shift rule-making to bodies of experts.[85] The integration of neutral, apolitical[86] scientific advice has a strong tradition in EU law. In a way, the Commission (earlier: the High Authority) was designed as an institution for the safeguard of the overall common good of the Union/Community, detached from (party-)political quarrels and particular interests. This is still underlined by Article 17(3) TEU. The same goes for the agencies; Article 298(1) TFEU highlights the independence of EU administration and upholds a similar idea, which is repeated in the founding regulations of many important agencies.[87]

81 Cf. framework paper [page, at II (ii)].

82 Cf. Matthias Ruffert, 'Personality under EU Law: A Conceptual Answer towards the Pluralisation of the EU' [2014] 20 *ELJ* 346.

83 Ruffert (n 81) 361ff.

84 Ohler (n 66) 252. Sceptically Thomas Groß, 'Unabhängige EU-Agenturen – eine Gefahr für die Demokratie?' (2012) 67 *Juristenzeitung* 1087, 1092; on the practical exercise of quasi-supervisory activity Martijn Groenleer, *The Autonomy of European Union Agencies* (Eburon Academic Publishers 2009) 130ff; in general: Madalina Busuioc, *The Accountability of European Agencies* (OUP 2010).

85 Cf. the seminal contribution by Andreas Voßkuhle, 'Sachverständige Beratung des Staates' in Josef Isensee and Paul Kirchhof (eds), *Handbuch des Staatsrechts*, vol. 3 (3rd edn, C.F. Müller 2005) ch 43.

86 Cf. framework paper [page, sub I. (i)].

87 Cf. Christoph Ohler in Rudolf Streinz (ed.), *EUV/AEUV* (2nd edn, C.H. Beck 2012) Article 298 para 8; and in general Matthias Ruffert, 'Die neue Unabhängigkeit: Zur demokratischen Legitimation von Agenturen im europäischen Verwaltungsrecht' in Peter-Christian Müller-Graff, Stefanie Schmahl and Vassilios Skouris (eds), *Europäisches Recht zwischen Bewährung und Wandel, Festschrift für Dieter H. Scheuing* (Nomos 2011) 399, 406.

With regard to rule-making, the rationale behind the creation of expert bodies within agencies is a distinction between strategic and political rules, on the one hand, and technical standards, on the other hand. This becomes most apparent in Article 10(1), 2nd sub-paragraph of the ESA-regulations: 'Regulatory technical standards shall be technical, shall not imply strategic decisions or policy choices and their content shall be delimited by the legislative acts on which they are based'. The delimitation by legislative acts is a matter of course, but the pleonastic beginning of the definition and the definitional elimination of strategy and politics from technics is, with respect, not a very realistic approach, if not to say a rather naïve one. In financial risk assessment and in similarly sensitive fields, there really can be no technicality without strategic or political choice. This implies that rule-making which is objective and science-driven at first sight may become the result of a negotiating process between stakeholders of high expertise. The only way out of this is the realignment of rule-making into the political process and the necessary endorsement of delegated rule-making by the Commission.

### *4.4 General rules on rule-making*

Finally and third, what should be developed is a general law of rule-making – principles and rules that apply to the rule-making activity of the EU. They may be developed by means of theoretical and doctrinal efforts or by codification which is similarly led by scholarly input, as can be observed in the most recent ReNEUAL draft presented by the European Ombudsman.[88]

Such rules and principles should contain some core elements. There should be clarity about a definition of rule-making. Legislative rule-making has been quite intensively regulated in the Treaties throughout the various Treaty reforms, and if one achieved the alignment, if not integration, of public international law that accompanies EU law in the described line of the Pringle judgment, this part of the matter would be settled. As far as non-legislative rule-making is concerned, however, it is submitted that doctrinal differentiations are yet to be advanced. We may start from the Court's jurisprudence on regulatory acts. However, there is no differentiation of such acts by the Commission or by an agency. The clarification of the agencies' position within the EU's legal order needs to be taken into account when addressing rules issued by the agencies; Article 290 TFEU and its limits have to be taken more seriously than in the ECJ's ESMA-jurisprudence. Alongside the question of which issues may be transferred to sub-legislative rule-making and which points must remain in the legislative sphere ('Gesetzesvorbehalt'), a similar, albeit less fundamental, distinction must be made between the Commission and the agencies.[89] Finally, the establishment of principles and rules for

88 Available at: http://www.reneual.eu/.
89 Cf. Henning Rieckhoff, *Der Vorbehalt des Gesetzes im Europarecht* (Mohr Siebeck 2007).

publicity, participation, consultation and control as just recently proposed in the ReNEUAL draft are crucial and important.

## 5 Conclusion

The conclusion drawn from the preceding analysis is therefore the most possible one out of any academic effort: further research is needed. What we also need is an institutional practice that is willing to take into consideration the outcome of scholarly research, which certainly will have repercussions on the content and method of the research performance. It shall be repeated that the use of basic legal concepts may be most useful in this respect, and it may even enhance the legitimacy of the whole construction. The differentiation between treaty/negotiation and statute/legislation is certainly one of those concepts, as could be developed in our workshop's framework of rule-making. Another one might be the distinction between acts of general application and single decision-making – but that is another story.

# 3 International relations and global governance

## The EU and ASEAN as actors in global governance institutions

*Jens-Uwe Wunderlich*

## 1 Introduction

Post-Cold War structural change and globalisation are the driving forces behind a transformation in global governance – away from a predominantly state-centred system to a more complex multilevel governance environment.[1] Rich literatures have emerged in legal scholarship and international relations (IR) exploring the impact of these changes. The discussion around the complexities of postnational rule-making in legal scholarship is mirrored in the global governance literature.[2]

As with globalisation, global governance is a frustrating term to define – it means different things to different people. There is no consensus even at the conceptual level. In the broadest sense, it refers to rules and rule-making in an anarchic environment. As such, global governance has always been at the centre of international relations research in some form or another. Examples include research on international regimes, international society or hegemonic stability.[3] With the spread and intensification of globalisation and its associated problems, global governance seems to have taken on a new dimension as an ever-increasing number of transnational issues require coordination and management on a more transnational or global scale. These include transnational crime, trafficking, migration, financial volatility,

1 See J.A. Scholte, *Globalization: A Critical Introduction* (Basingstoke: Palgrave, 2000); F. Söderbaum and L. van Langenhove, 'Introduction: The EU as a Global Actor and the Role of Interregionalism' (2005) 27(3) *Journal of European Integration* 249–262.

2 See D. Held, A. McGrew, D. Goldblatt and J. Perraton, *Global Transformations: Politics, Economics and Culture* (Cambridge: Polity, 1999); D. Held and A. McGrew (eds), *The Global Transformations Reader: An Introduction* (Cambridge: Polity, 2002); J.N. Rosenau, *Distant Proximities: Dynamics beyond Globalization* (Princeton, NJ: Princeton University Press, 2003); J.N. Rosenau, 'Global Governance as Disaggregated Complexity' (2005) in A.D. Ba and M.J. Hoffmann (eds), *Contending Perspectives on Global Governance – Coherence, Contestation and World Order* (Oxon: Routledge, 2005).

3 See O. Young, *Global Governance: Drawing Insights from the Environmental Experience* (London: MIT Press, 1997); H. Bull, *The Anarchical Society* (New York: Columbia University Press, 1977); R. Gilpin, *War and Change in World Politics* (Cambridge: CUP, 1981).

climate change and pandemics. Global governance here 'refers to collective actions to establish international institutions and norms to cope with the causes and consequences of adverse supranational, transnational, or national problems'.[4]

Another branch of IR literature uses global governance as a new conceptual tool to emphasise the transformation of world politics away from its Westphalian moment.[5] Due to the multifaceted nature of contemporary transnational issues, governance is becoming increasingly decentralised, fragmented and dispersed across multiple levels.[6] This still emerging multilevel global governance system is defined by the overlapping rules, norms, and formal and informal institutional structures of regulatory decision-making and implementation at the subnational, national, regional and global levels.[7] It offers the structure that conditions actors and their behaviour. From this perspective, an emphasis on the state as the only international actor of relevance and central object of analysis in international relations is no longer justifiable. Rather, we ought to broaden the analysis to include a wide range of actors (such as international organisations, non-governmental organisations, multinational enterprises, civil society actors, etc.) and, thereby, expand the issue areas under investigation. Thus, the global governance literature tends to focus much more on rules and rule-making mechanisms as opposed to the emphasis on power and capabilities within traditional international relations theory. It is pushing the boundaries of established international relations theories while, at the same time, pointing to new directions of enquiry. It moves away from the intellectual hegemony of state-centric accounts of world politics and trains the spotlight on the norms and rules that determine actor behaviour and actor interests.

Traditionally dominated by the state as the primary actor in global governance, the international stage is becoming increasingly crowded with diverse actors at various levels of governance engaged in policymaking. This proliferation of transnational actors requires a complete rethinking of the centrality of the state as a unit of analysis. This, however, is not an easy task. To use the words of Alexander Wendt: 'So dominant in contemporary consciousness is the assumption that authority must be centralised that scholars are just beginning to grapple with how decentralised authority might be understood'.[8] This raises the question of who the relevant actors are in

4 R. Väyrynen, *Globalization and Global Governance* (Lanham, MD: Rowman & Littlefield, 1999) p. 25.

5 See J.N. Rosenau and O. Czempiel, *Governance without Government: Order and Change in World Politics* (Cambridge: CUP, 1992) and Held *et al.* (n 2).

6 See D. Held and A. McGrew, 'Introduction' in D. Held and A. McGrew (eds), *Governing Globalization: Power, Authority and Global Governance* (Cambridge: Polity, 2007) pp. 1–21; Scholte (n 1).

7 Held and McGrew (n 6) p. 9.

8 A.E. Wendt, *Social Theory of International Relations* (Cambridge: CUP, 1999) p. 308.

global rule-making processes. Rather than being total, absolute, and dominated by notions of the state and sovereignty, actorness is increasingly becoming functionally dispersed, flexible and dynamic, with contingent legitimacy, access and influence in global governance mechanisms. Regional organisations such as the European Union (EU) and the Association of Southeast Asian Nations (ASEAN) have been widening their brief as member states delegate more authority in order to deal more effectively with transnational issues. As a result, the political and economic influence of these organisations has increased considerably. With economic, political and moral authority resting in different sites in the global governance arena, the EU and ASEAN (and other regional organisations) are able to attain the features of actorness, in particular global governance institutions.

This chapter will explore the concept of actorness within the global governance framework. In particular, it will focus on the actorness of regional organisations, taking the EU and ASEAN as case studies. The chapter proceeds in the following manner. The first section will outline what it means to be an actor within international scholarship. It pays particular attention to the actorness concept that has evolved within the context of the European integration literature. The second part will discuss the issue of regional actorness, i.e. the actorness of regional organisations within the wider global governance framework. The third section applies the actorness concept to the EU and ASEAN to demonstrate two things: (a) regional organisations are indeed emerging as actors in their own right within global governance institutions; and (b) such actorness is no longer restricted to the EU alone.

## 2 Actorness within international relations

There is no consensus on the concept 'actor' within the literature. That is somewhat surprising given the centrality of the concept across disciplines. International law defines actorness with reference to legal personality.[9] Legal actorness in international law is tied to the state and the modern state system. Until recently, only states were subjects of international law. Only states can sign treaties, join international organisations and are recognised as fully-fledged international actors. Conceived in this way, legal actorness confers the right to participate in global governance institutions.[10] The formal and informal recognition rules of global governance institutions have been created with the Westphalian state in mind. As such, they frame and restrict the significance and participation of non-state actors. However, the international legal context is changing and even recognition criteria are being broadened. Increasingly, international organisations have a legal status in

9 See E. Fahey in introductory chapter of this volume.

10 C. Bretherton and J. Vogler, *The European Union as a Global Actor* (London: Routledge, 1999) p. 16.

international law. For example, both ASEAN and the EU have been granted legal personality.

Legal doctrine, with its emphasis on formal criteria such as legal personality, authority to act and institutional autonomy, poses serious constraints on conceptualising actorness in the global governance framework. Its focus on legal status ignores capacity aspects of actorness. It is one thing to be recognised as an international actor by international law; it is quite another to have actual influence or the capacity to participate effectively within global rule-making mechanisms. For example, small and weak states may be fully-fledged actors within the context of the World Trade Organization (WTO) or the United Nations (UN). Their influence, however, may be insignificant, especially when compared to entities such as the EU.

The question of actorness has always played a central role in international relations theory. Actors are conceived as the units constituting the international system. As a discipline, international relations has traditionally focused on analyzing the dynamics of state interaction, concentrating on the state as the primary actor. The realist tradition with its emphasis on power is a typical example. According to Hans Morgenthau, 'international politics, like all politics, is a struggle for power'.[11] As a state is regarded as the biggest concentration of power, it is the only actor of importance in the international system. As a direct consequence, realist scholars tend to analyse global affairs in terms of inter-state relations.[12] States, acting through their governments, are regarded as rational and unitary actors aiming to maximise national interest in a constant competition with other states in an anarchic environment.

Realist scholars do acknowledge non-state actors, but only insofar as they are either arenas for state interaction, such as international organisations, or they are seen as subordinated to the state, such as in the case of economic and civil society actors, and are seen to have little or no impact on global governance or the structure of world politics.[13] This has created a two-tier system in which non-state entities such as intergovernmental organisations and multinational corporations are measured against the state and state capabilities, and found wanting.[14]

This makes sense in a world order based on states where the emphasis of political analysis is on power. From such a perspective, states define the global system and they alone are regarded as key players. The state, referring here to the model of the Westphalian state, rests on a strong connection between territoriality and sovereignty. In order to conceptualise what constitutes a state,

11 H. Morgenthau, *Politics among Nations* (New York: Knopf, 1949) p. 13.

12 J.M. Grieco, 'Anarchy and the Limits of Cooperation: A Realist Critique of the Newest Liberal Institutionalism' (1988) 42 *International Organization* 485–508.

13 K. Waltz, *Theory of International Politics* (Reading, MA: Addison-Wesley, 1979) p. 95.

14 P. Willetts, 'Transnational Actors and International Organizations in Global Politics' in J. Baylis and S. Smith (eds), *The Globalization of World Politics – An Introduction to International Relations* (Oxford: OUP, 2005) pp. 425–445.

and by extension an actor, in world politics, Zürn focuses on three dimensions: *recognition*, *resources* and *realization of governance goals*.[15] Recognition is central to participation in international affairs. In essence, a state becomes a (sovereign) state because it is recognised by others as such.[16] Apart from recognition, states ought to possess material resources to enforce and to defend their authority against domestic and external challenges. And, in order to be internally accepted, states need to deliver certain governance goals such as security and the rule of law, and may also include welfare provision and channels for political participation.

This state-as-the-primary-actor position has not been without its challengers.[17] Keohane and Nye were among the first scholars to recognise the importance of non-state actors in international relations.[18] They stress the relevance of a range of transnational non-state actors such as multinational corporations, churches, scientific networks, revolutionary movements and trade unions.[19] There has also been dissatisfaction with the assumption of the state as a unitary actor and a 'black-box', thereby ignoring, for example, subnational actors (such as political parties) and subnational dynamics (such as party politics) in foreign policymaking.[20] Keohane and Nye draw attention to the inadequacy of the realist tradition to grasp the essentials of contemporary world politics. They question three of the core assumptions of realism by pointing out that states are neither the most important nor are they unitary actors; military force is becoming increasingly inefficient as an instrument of foreign policy; the hierarchy between high and low politics issues has been rendered redundant due to the emergence of a new issue agenda.[21] These pluralistic approaches recognise not only the complexity of international issues, but also acknowledge that not all important dynamics and processes in international relations originate from the action of states. A range of significant actors is being considered with non-state actors not necessarily being subordinated to the state.[22]

Another approach specifies a range of relevant actors – the 'mixed-actor system' – envisaging a scenario in which different types of actors participate

15 M. Zürn, 'The State in the Post-National Constellation: Societal Denationalization and Multi Level Governance', (1999) *ARENA Working Papers* 99/35.
16 This is closely related to the recognition criteria that determine an actor within the legal context.
17 See Willets (n 14) p. 425.
18 R.O. Keohane and J.S. Nye (eds), *Transnational Relations and World Politics* (Cambridge, MA: Harvard University Press, 1971).
19 Ibid. pp. 722–724.
20 See A. Moravcsik 'Preferences and Power in the European Community: A Liberal Intergovernmentalist Approach', (1993) 31(4) *Journal of Common Market Studies* 473–524.
21 R.O Keohane and J. Nye, *Power and Interdependence: World Politics in Transition* (Boston, MA: Little & Brown, 1977).
22 See also E. Aydinli, 'Assessing Violent Nonstate Actorness in Global Politics: a Framework for Analysis', (2013) *Cambridge Review of International Affairs*.

in an increasingly complex international system.[23] Bringing several earlier pluralistic efforts together, James Rosenau argues that the dynamics of global governance are fundamentally changing world politics across the board.[24] Rosenau proposes to break out of the conceptual jail imposed by methodological territorialism 'because the processes of disaggregation so readily span foreign-domestic boundaries, thus making it difficult for states to exercise control over the flows of ideas, money, goods, pollution, crime, drugs, and, terrorists; and they have only slightly greater control over the flow of people'.[25] What has emerged is a bifurcated global structure in which a multi-centric world composed of a great variety of non-state collectivities has come to rival the anarchical state-centric system.[26] This multi-centric world is possible because the significance of actors is less determined by their legal status or references to sovereignty than by their relative capacity to initiate and to sustain action.[27] This is essentially a two-world conception in which non-state and state actors coexist, overlap, cooperate, conflict and compete.[28]

The impact of structuration theory changed the theoretical landscape of the social sciences,[29] supporting the rise of constructivist accounts in international relations theory. Constructivists see structures as intersubjective and not being determined solely in material terms. Alexander Wendt, for example, highlighted the crucial role of norms, interests, ideas and principles in defining international structure.[30] A central concern within social constructivism is agency, denoting the ability to choose between different courses of action, to learn from experience and to initiate change.[31] The form agency takes varies considerably due to the different structures reproduced and shaped by actors, by differing knowledge structures and different access to resources.[32] Actors, therefore, are not only shaping structure, such as global governance institutions; they are also shaped by structure, by the cultural, political, social and economical culture they are embedded in. Who the relevant actors are in world politics and what defines them as actors is subject to continuous revision and change. Constructivism points to a dialectical relationship

23 O. Young, 'The Actors in World Politics', in J.N. Rosenau and M.A. East (eds), *The Analysis of International Politics* (New York: The Free Press, 1972) pp. 125–144.

24 J.N. Rosenau, *Turbulence in World Politics* (New York: Harvester Wheatsheaf, 1990).

25 Rosenau (n 2 2005) p. 135.

26 Rosenau (n 24) p. 247.

27 Ibid. p. 249.

28 Ibid. pp. 246–296.

29 See A. Giddens, *The Constitution of Society: Outline of the Theory of Structuration* (Cambridge: Polity Press, 1984).

30 A.E. Wendt, 'The Agent-Structure Problem in International Relations Theory' (1987) 41 *International Organization* 335–370; Wendt (n 8).

31 K. O'Neill, J. Balsiger and S.D. van Deveer 'Actors, Norms, and Impact: Recent International Cooperation Theory and the Influence of the Agent-Structure Debate' (2004) 7 *Annual Review of Political Science* 155.

32 Ibid. p. 155.

between agency and structure. Agency and structure are mutually constitutive. Actors with casual powers are entities having the capacity to formulate specific goals. 'However, the capacity to act, or actorness is a function both of external opportunities, including those associated with the international legal and institutional framework; and internal capabilities, which include the availability of policy instruments and the capacity and legitimacy of decision making processes.'[33]

There has clearly been a tectonic shift within international relations theory demonstrated by the growing recognition of the importance of non-state actors in international politics.[34] However, there is little agreement as to how to classify non-state actors in world politics. The actorness of international organisations such as the EU and ASEAN (and others) particularly pose problems. On the one hand, they are intergovernmental organisations and as such, their actorness ought to be limited due to the sovereign nature of their respective member states. On the other hand, both ASEAN and the EU are increasingly displaying elements of actorness (albeit in specific areas only). Thus, the definition of regional organisations as international actors creates significant conceptual issues as they are neither purely intergovernmental nor purely supranational or private. In the following section, we take a closer look at the conceptualisation of regional actorness.

## 3 Regional organisations as international actors

An actor in global governance can be defined as 'any organized entity that is composed, at least indirectly, of human beings, is not wholly subordinate to any other actor in the world system in effective terms, and participates in power relationships with other actors'.[35] Thus, any collectivity, including regional organisations, can potentially emerge as actors. What distinguishes an actor from a non-actor has been discussed within the wider actorness literature.[36] Approaches to the actorness of regional organisations can be traced back to the emergence of the European Community (EC) as a foreign policy actor. Today, the EU has undoubtedly emerged as a major economic power, with a number of policy instruments at its disposal, including trade, cooperation and association agreements, as well as instruments related to tariffs, quotas and preferences. It has aid and development policies that include financial, trade, technical and humanitarian instruments. Its capabilities in diplomacy and security issues are growing. It is, therefore, widely accepted now that the

33 Bretherton and Vogler (n 10) p. 29.

34 See R. Mansbach, Y.H. Ferguson and D.E. Lampert, 'Towards a New Conceptualization of Global Politics', in P. Williams, D.M. Goldstein and J.M. Shafritz, J.M. (eds), *Classic Reading and Contemporary Debates in International Relations* (Boston, MA: Wadsworth, 2006) pp. 209–221.

35 Young (n 23) p. 140.

36 See above.

EU is a significant international actor albeit more so in some policy areas than in others.

However, the particularities of the EU, neither purely intergovernmental nor completely supranational, together with the absence of a consensus as to what constitutes an actor in international relations, have made the classification of the EU as an actor difficult. This is mirrored by the complicated legal status of the EU pre-Lisbon: the EC had legal personality and with it the right to represent its members in international negotiations in areas of devolved competences (including the mandate to sign treaties on their behalf). In contrast, the EU itself had no legal personality.

Over the decades, several perspectives emerged to classify first the EC and later the EU within the context of world politics. One is to regard the EU as a subsystem of international affairs and look at the ways in which intra-European affairs are managed.[37] A second possibility is to regard the EU as part of wider global processes and developments.[38] Such a view would regard European integration as a set of institutional responses to particular collective action problems. A third perspective regards the EU as an actor or power in its own right, impacting on contemporary world politics, and shaping the international environment in a multitude of ways.[39] This raises the question as to what kind of actor the EC/EU is or is evolving into. In response, labels such as *superpower in the making*,[40] *soft power*,[41] *civilian power*,[42] *small* and *normative power*[43] have been suggested. Some of these approaches betray an embedded state-centrism (*soft power*, *civilian power*, *emerging state*, *small power*), aiming to fit the EC/EU into a world of states. Others, such as the *normative power* concept, have discarded state-centric assumptions.

Attempts to understand the international persona of the EC/EU have contributed to the development of the concept *actorness*. Actorness goes beyond traditional state-centric IR theory, aiming to better account for the EC/EU's

37 See C. Hill and S. Smith, 'International Relations and the European Union: Themes and Issues', in C. Hill and S. Smith (eds), *International Relations and the European Union* (Oxford: OUP Press 2011) p. 8.

38 Ibid. p. 8.

39 Ibid. p. 8.

40 See J. Galtung, *The European Community: A Superpower in the Making?* (London: Allen & Unwin, 1973); D. Buchan, *Europe: The Strange Superpower* (Aldershot: Dartmouth, 1993); J. McCormick, *The European Superpower* (Basingstoke: Palgrave, 2007).

41 See J. Nye, *Soft Power: The Means to Success in World Politics* (New York: Public Affairs Press, 2004).

42 See F. Duchêne, 'The European Community and the Uncertainties of Interdependence', in M. Kohnstamm, and W. Hager (eds), *A Nation Writ Large? Foreign-Policy Problems before the European Community* (London: Macmillan, 1973); H. Bull, 'Civilian Power Europe: A Contradiction in Terms?' (1982) 21(2) *Journal of Common Market Studies* 149–164; R. Whitman, *From Civilian Power to Superpower? The International Identity of the European Union* (London: Macmillan, 1998).

43 See A. Toje, *The European Union as a Small Power – After the Post-Cold War* (Basingstoke: Palgrave, 2010); I. Manners, 'Normative Power Europe – A Contradiction in Terms?' (2002) 40(2) *Journal of Common Market Studies* 235–258.

distinct role in international affairs.[44] It is largely defined in behavioural terms with an emphasis on actor capacity and capability. The concept was originally developed by Gunnar Sjöstedt back in 1977.[45] Building on Sjöstedt's pioneering work, a whole literature on (EC/EU) actorness has emerged.[46] Sjöstedt defined actorness as the 'capacity to behave actively and deliberately in relation to other actors in the international system',[47] thereby pointing to the complex interplay between actor behaviour and the external environment or structure. He clearly recognised the complexities of the EC's role in the international system, possessing some features of typical international actors (i.e. states), while notoriously lacking others (such as a coherent common foreign and security policy).

The late David Allen and Michael Smith built on this by introducing the concept *presence*.[48] They, too, use a behavioural approach, defining presence as the legitimacy and capacity to act, to mobilise resources, to exert influence and, importantly, the perceptions and expectations of others generated by an actor. Thus, presence focuses on the behavioural impact of the EC/EU in wider politics. For example, simply by existing, the EC/EU leaves economic, political and demographic footprints, thereby creating outside expectations and perceptions. The deepening and widening of the EC/EU has significantly enhanced its presence. However, the relationship between presence and actorness is inevitably complex and uncertain. It is reflected differently and to varying degrees in different policy areas and in respect to different external actors.

Jupille and Caporaso and Bretherton and Vogler combine insights from international relations scholarship with the actorness literature, introducing mildly constructivist approaches to the analysis of EU external behaviour.[49] Jupille and Caporaso propose four factors, including internal and external variables, to assess the EC's capacity to act at the 1992 Rio Earth Summit:

44 R. Ginsberg, 'Conceptualizing the European Union as an International Actor: Narrowing the Theoretical Capability-Expectations Gap' (1999) 37(3) *Journal of Common Market Studies* 447.

45 G. Sjöstedt, *The External Role of the European Community* (Farnborough: Saxon House, 1977).

46 See D. Allen and M. Smith, 'Western Europe's Presence in the Contemporary International Arena', in M. Holland (ed.), *The Future of European Political Cooperation* (New York: St. Martin's Press, 1991); D. Allen and M. Smith, 'The European Union's Security Presence: Barrier, Facilitator or Manager?', in C. Rhodes (ed.), *The European Union in the World Community* (London: Lynne Rienner Publishers, 1998); Ginsberg (n 44); C. Hill, 'The Capability-Expectations Gap, or Conceptualizing Europe's International Role' (1994) 31(3) *Journal of Common Market Studies* 305–328; A. Herrberg, 'The European Union in its International Environment: A Systematic Analysis', in A. Landau and R.C. Whitman (eds), *Rethinking the EU – Institutions, Interests and Identities* (London: Macmillan 1997); Whitman (n 42); J. Jupille and J.A. Caporaso (1998) 'States, Agency and Rules: The EU in Global Environmental Politics', in C. Rhodes (ed.), *The European Union in the World Community* (London: Lynne Rienner, 1998); Bretherton and Vogler (n 10).

47 Sjöstedt (n 45) p. 16.

48 Allen and Smith (1991 n 46).

49 Jupille and Caporaso (n 46); Bretherton and Vogler (n 10).

*recognition*, *authority*, *autonomy* and *cohesion*.[50] Bretherton and Vogler, too, bridge external and internal aspects of actorness. Their approach comprises three key concepts: *presence*, *opportunity* and *capability* (Bretherton and Vogler 1999: 5). *Presence*, as just discussed, refers to the relationship between internal factors and external expectations, i.e. the capacity to generate and shape external expectations and perceptions. *Opportunity* points to the structural factors, the external environment of ideas and institutions (i.e. the wider institutional environment of the global governance complex), enabling or constraining EU actorness.[51]

The opportunity structure can be restrictive for the EU (and other non-state actors) as a direct consequence of the prevailing logic of the state system. At the same time, however, globalisation and structural transformation have created new opportunities for EU actorness in international politics in the areas of trade policy, development and environmental matters. The EU is capable of exerting influence through its enhanced emphasis on human rights, democratic principles, sustainable development and good governance in agreements with third parties.[52] The EU has taken advantage of the new normative and structural international environment and emerged as an actor with its own agenda. The concept *capability* refers to the capacity necessary to respond to opportunities and external expectations. This capacity to act (or actorness) depends on five factors: *shared norms and values*, *the ability to formulate coherent policies*, *the capacity to undertake international negotiations*, *policy instruments* and *legitimacy of decision-making processes*.[53]

As just demonstrated, the literature on EC/EU actorness offers some interesting insights into the internal behavioural aspects of actorness, emphasising the crucial rule of institutions in the construction of international actors. Institutional culture and authority structures are at the core of the EU's particular identity problem in world politics: being a hybrid creature with intergovernmental and supranational features. Much of EU actorness rests on institutional cohesion and consistency (or lack thereof). Indeed, as observed by Antje Herrberg, cohesion is crucial for the effectiveness of EU actorness.[54] For example, EU actor capacity (or *actorness*) appears to be more developed in the area of Common Commercial Policy (CCP), where the Community method of policymaking dominates, than in Common Foreign and Security Policy (CFSP), which even post-Lisbon firmly remains subject to intergovernmental cooperation. Hence, the EU can be a very powerful international actor in trade negotiations within the WTO framework, while lacking cohesion and capability on other foreign policy issues.

50 Jupille and Carporaso (n 46).
51 Bretherton and Vogler (n 10) p. 7.
52 Ibid. p. 8.
53 Ibid.
54 Herrberg (n 46).

Institutional structures, here understood as sets of formal but also informal norms, rules and principles, enhance actor presence and visibility, capacity, cohesion and organisational effectiveness. They forge certain types of behaviour and enshrine particular values and cultures, providing a regional organisation with presence and identity at the international level. The spectrum of institutions ranges from the highly formal and legal, on the one end, to the informal, on the other. The positioning of a collectivity along this spectrum has an impact on its actorness.[55] Informal arrangements based on convention and understanding places restrictions on actor capacity and, thereby, on actorness. Deeper and more formal institutional authority structures enhance capacity, internal cohesion and overall effectiveness.

The second internal feature of actorness is presence. Presence is a variable and multidimensional concept. It goes beyond legal recognition. The presence of an entity may not be consistent across all issue areas.[56] Presence is also linked to institutionalisation: capacity, enhanced by institutionalisation, also enhances presence in international affairs.

Several scholars have also noted the importance of identity as an internal behavioural factor of actorness.[57] Here, identity refers to the normative underpinnings of an organisation, describing a system of norms and principles that sets the rules, procedures, actions and ultimately the self-understanding and institutional culture of a regional organisation.[58]

To summarise at this point, the study of the external persona of the EC/EU has spawned a rich literature on the behavioural determinants of actorness. This has informed scholarship of regional agency outside the European integration context. Björn Hettne, one of the foremost authorities of the new regionalism approach, for example, draws explicitly on Bretherton and Vogler's work in constructing an analytical framework for regional actorship.[59] This is important inasmuch as it suggests that regional actorness is not necessarily specific to the EU, but can be attained by other regional organisations as well.

55 M. Doidge, 'Regional Organizations as Actors in International Relations: Interregionalism and Asymmetric Dialogues', in J. Rüland, G. Schubert, G. Schucher, G and C. Storz (eds), *Asian-European Relations: Building Blocs for Global Governance?* (London: Routledge, 2008) p. 43.

56 Allen and Smith (n 39).

57 See Bretherton and Vogler (n 10); Doidge (n 55); J.-U. Wunderlich, 'The EU as an Actor Sui Generis? A Comparison of EU and ASEAN Actorness' (2012) 50(4) *Journal of Common Market Studies* 653–669.

58 See the notion of 'meta regime' in V.K. Aggarwal and J.T. Chow, 'The Perils of Consensus: How ASEAN's Meta-Regime undermines Economic and Environmental Cooperation' (2010) 17(2) *Review of International Political Economy* pp. 262–290.

59 B. Hettne, 'The European Union as an Emerging Global Actor', in J.-U. Wunderlich and D.J. Bailey (eds), *The European Union and Global Governance – A Handbook* (London: Routledge, 2011); B. Hettne, 'Regional Actorship: A Comparative Approach to Interregionalism', in F. Baert, T. Scaramagli and F. Söderbaum (eds), *Intersecting Interregionalism: Regions, Global Governance and the EU* (London: Springer, 2011).

In this context, the structural environment, providing or denying opportunities for non-state actors to participate in global rule-making, is important. This has been acknowledged by Bretherton and Vogler, as well as by Hettne.[60] Thus, the actorness of regional organisations within the contemporary global governance framework depends on the interplay of structural and behavioural variables. Indeed, new regionalism scholarship maintains that globalisation and structural change trigger regional developments.[61] Regional actorness, therefore, emerges as a response to structural change. The formal and informal rules and procedures of the global governance complex frame the opportunity structure of regional actorness. For instance, by restricting membership to states, the UN Security Council not only curtails the recognition and presence of non-state actors such as regional organisations, but also their participation in global governance and their relevance as international actors.

As suggested above, globalisation and global structural change are creating a more permissive global governance environment. Structural opportunities determine which collective entity is an actor and when. Being an actor is, therefore, context-specific. For example, during the negotiations on a Comprehensive Economic and Trade Agreement (CETA), Canada appeared to be far less coherent as an actor than the EU. The EU, represented by the Commission, made 'the provinces' active participation in the negotiations a condition sine qua non'.[62] This highlights that the state itself is an incoherent collective, masking a variety of often divergent interests and actors. Depending on the issue area and the internal authority structure, these actors will have more or less influence in international relations. It also emphasises the link between the policymaking context and relative actorness within the global governance framework.

## 4 The EU and ASEAN as international actors

It is now widely accepted in the literature that the EU has achieved some form of actorness within the wider global governance framework. However, the EU is no longer the only relevant case in that respect. ASEAN, too, has a long tradition of engaging with the external environment and within global government institutions such as the UN.[63] Regional organisations such as the EU and ASEAN participate in global fora such as the UN or the World

60 Bretherton (n 10) and Hettne (n 59).

61 F. Söderbaum and A. Sbragia, 'EU Studies and the "New Regionalism": What can be Gained from Dialogue' (2010) 32(6) *Journal of European Integration* 563–582.

62 P. Leblond, 'The Canada-EU Comprehensive Economic and Trade Agreement: More to it Than Meets the Eye', *Policy Options*, vol. 31, no. 7, July–August 2010, pp. 74–78.

63 See J.-U. Wunderlich, 'Comparing Regional Organizations in Global Governance Institutions: ASEAN, the EU and the UN', (2012) 10(2–3) *Asia Europe Journal* 127–143.

Trade Organization, establish relations with each other and with other actors, and become important shapers of international norms.[64]

As discussed above, presence is a defining feature of actorness. Presence bridges structural and behavioural factors of actorness. It can be defined as the impact of an actor on transnational activities and the expectations and perception it generates about itself. Thus presence is linked to the institutional dimension of actorness. Presence in the global governance system depends on size, scope of transnational activities, the relative importance of the issue area the actor is involved in, as well as on recognition by external others. This recognition can be conferred in various ways. Legal personality is one way. However, relations with external others and participation in global governance institutions are the most common means for collective entities to be recognised as actors.[65] Both, ASEAN and the EU, are engaged in a complex web of bilateral and multilateral relations. They are also involved with the mechanisms of global governance. For instance, the EU is a full member in its own right of the WTO, the Food and Agricultural Organization (FAO) and has observer status within the UN.[66] The agenda of the WTO itself has been to a great extent influenced by the EU, extending it into new areas of international trade such as public procurement, trade and investment, and social and environmental issues.[67] In other words, the EU has been instrumental in the creation of norms and principles of global governance. ASEAN, too, has a long list of bilateral and multilateral partners. It has also long-standing relations with the UN and its agencies dating back to 1977 when ASEAN became a dialogue partner of the UN Development Programme (UNDP).

Relations between regional organisations, so-called interregionalism, offer an additional level of interaction to the global governance framework.[68] Interregionalism is creating a platform for mutual recognition and reciprocal interaction, thereby directly impacting on the actorness of the participants.

64 Wunderlich (n 57) pp. 660–661.

65 Ibid.

66 Ibid. p. 661. However, the EU's membership in global governance institutions is inconsistent. Gehring *et al.* offer an interesting explanation for this based on actor capability and recognition. See T. Gehring, S. Oberthür and M. Mühleck, 'European Union Actorness in International Institutions: Why the European Union is Recognized as an Actor in Some International Institutions but Not in Others', (2013) 51(5) *Journal of Common Market Studies* 849–865.

67 F. Cameron, 'The European Union as a Global Actor: Far from Pushing its Political Weight Around', (1998) in C. Rhodes (ed.), *The European Union in the World Community* (London: Lynne Rienner, 1998) p. 22.

68 See Söderbaum and van Langenhove (n 1) p. 256; J. Rüland, *ASEAN and the European Union: A Bumpy Interregional Relationship* (2001) Discussion Paper, C95, Bonn: Centre for European Integration Studies; H. Hänggi, R. Roloff and J. Rüland, 'Interregionalism: A new Phenomenon in International Relations' (2006) in H. Hänggi, R. Roloff and J. Rüland (eds), *Interregionalism and International Relations* (London: Routledge, 2006) p. 12.

For the EU, interregional relations have long provided a means of asserting influence and promoting political, economic and security.[69] The EU has a tradition of disseminating its own institutional norms via capacity-building interregional relations.[70] It uses a variety of instruments ranging from socialisation and persuasion to the application of conditionalities and the offer of technical and financial assistance to enhance institutional capacity to induce normative and institutional change in other regions and organisations.[71] What is important here is that the EU is directly influencing the global governance environment and its own recognition as a major international actor through the construction of regional others.[72] Examples include the relations with ASEAN, MERCOSUR, the Andean Community (CAN), SADC, ECOWAS, COMESA, the African Union, SAARC and the Gulf Cooperation Council. ASEAN, too, has established a web of interregional relations. Examples include the links with the Gulf Cooperation Council, the Rio Group, MERCOSUR, the South Pacific Forum and SAARC. Like the EU, ASEAN has had some success in projecting its own normative preferences via such relations. For example, the ASEAN way, with its emphasis on neutrality, sovereignty and non-interference, is the preferred *modus operandi* within the ARF and the ASEAN Plus framework.[73]

However, ASEAN and the EU suffer from an expectations-capability gap.[74] The enhanced presence within global governance institutions has resulted in heightened expectations and perceptions about actorness by outsiders that were simply not matched by capacity and institutional capabilities. In some ways, this bears testimony not only to institutional shortcomings, but, more positively, to the successful creation of international presence by those organisations. In response, the EU and ASEAN have undertaken internal reforms in recent years in order to enhance the behavioural aspects of their

69 See Manner (n 63); T.A. Börzel and T. Risse, *Diffusing (Inter-) Regionalism – The EU as a Model of Regional Integration* (2009) KFG Working Paper no. 7, Kolleg-Forschergruppe 'The Transformative Power of Europe', <http://www.polsoz.fu-berlin.de/en/v/transformeurope/publications/working_paper/WP_07_Boerzel_Risse.pdf> accessed 2 December 2010.

70 See Bretherton and Vogler (n 10); Manners (n 43) and T. Diez, 'Constructing the Self and Changing Others: Problematising the Concept of "Normative Power Europe"', (2005) 33(2) *Millennium: Journal of International Studies* 613–636.

71 See Börzel and Risse (n 69).

72 See J. Gilson, 'New Interregionalism? EU and East Asia', (2005) 27(3) *Journal of European Integration* 307–326; H. Hänggi, 'Interregionalism as a Multifaceted Phenomenon: In Search of a Typology', (2006) in H. Hänggi, R. Roloff and J. Rüland (eds), *Interregionalism and International Relations* (London: Routledge, 2006) pp. 31–62.

73 See R. Stubbs, 'The ASEAN Alternative? Ideas, Institutions and the Challenge of "Global" Governance', (2008) 21(4) *Pacific Affairs* 451–468; J. Dosch, 'Southeast Asia: ASEAN and the Challenge of Regionalism in the Asia Pacific', (2012) in M.K. Connors, R. Davison and J. Dosch (eds), *The New Global Politics of the Asia-Pacific* (Oxon: RoutledgeCurzon, 2012) pp. 121–139.

74 See C. Hill, 'The Capability – Expectations Gap, or Conceptualizing Europe's International Role', (1993) 31(3) *Journal of Common Market Studies* 305–328; Ginsberg (n 47).

international actorness in response to structural changes and new opportunities within the global governance complex.

As stated above, the institutional structures of regional organisations do matter in the construction of regional actorness. Institutions tend to 'lock in' certain norms, values and procedures, thereby creating a certain path-dependency: historical institutional choices determine the direction of contemporary institutionalisation.[75] Thus, institutional choices become self-reinforcing. As a direct consequence of its historical origins, the contemporary EU rests on a complicated compromise between intergovernmental and supranational institutions. In general, EU institutionalisation is characterised by a preference for formal, legal and deep institutionalisation leading to a complex and overlapping web of competing and complementary authority structures.

The external activities of the EU are divided between economic and foreign policies. The Community method dominates policymaking in economic matters while foreign policymaking is by and large the reserve of Union policymaking. The cohesion of the EU as an international actor is further complicated by the fact that EU member states, being sovereign international actors in their own right, continue to pursue their own foreign policy agendas. The EU may on occasion appear to be a single actor within the global governance framework. In reality, however, it hides a diversity of different actors with complementary, competing and conflicting sets of interests within its shadow. They include individual member states, EU institutions (such as the Commission, the Parliament or the Court), as well as lobby groups. As a result, the EU's engagement with global governance institutions is governed by different sets of rules and decision-makers, depending on the policy area.

In response to global structural change, the pressures of globalisation and the more permissible structure of global governance following the end of the Cold War, the EU has undergone a lengthy process of institutional adaptation. The Maastricht, Amsterdam and Nice treaties have all aimed at improving external capability, capacity and consistency of the EU. The Lisbon Treaty is only the latest effort in that respect, trying to address coherence and representation issues. It has conferred a single legal personality upon the EU, enhancing external actorness features such visibility and participation in global governance institutions.[76] Article 21(2) further enhances the EU's actorness by defining eight common external objectives in order to improve consistency and cohesion. Other institutional streamlining measures include

75 This principle of path-dependency is most commonly associated with historical institutionalism. See P. Pierson and T. Skocpol, 'Historical Institutionalism in Contemporary Political Science', (2002) in I. Katznelson H.V. Milner (eds), *Political Science: State of the Discipline* (New York: W.W. Norton, 2002) pp. 693–721.

76 Treaty of Lisbon – Amending the Treaty on European Union and the Treaty Establishing the European Community [2007] OJ C306/01, Art 46.

the creation of the position of a President of the European Council, the setting up of a dedicated External Action Service and the post of High Representative in Foreign and Security Affairs.

ASEAN's approach to institutionalisation is different from that of the EU. To start with, ASEAN has a purely intergovernmental structure. In addition, in contrast to the EU's preference for deep and formal institutionalisation, ASEAN has opted for informal institutionalisation. ASEAN's modus operandi rests on informal agreement, voluntarism and personal relationships to forge out consensual positions before coming to summit meetings. Davidson describes this as a 'relations-based approach'.[77] The contrast between EU and ASEAN institutionalisation can be visualised by comparing the voluminous Treaties of Rome and Paris with the two pages of the 1967 Bangkok Declaration.

ASEAN's low-key institutionalisation has consequences for the behavioural aspects of actorness. Like the EU, ASEAN faces a recognition problem within global governance institutions such as the UN. However, ASEAN's weak organisational capacity further accentuates the issue and limits its actorness. The ASEAN Secretariat is symptomatic of ASEAN's decentralised institutionalisation. Its resources in terms of staff, administration and research support are rather modest when compared to the EU. It does not enjoy executive or legislative functions similar to the Commission. Its financial resources, too, are rather limited with member states contributing $1.4 million per country per annum to the ASEAN Secretariat.[78] The consensus and accommodation procedures make it almost impossible to define 'ASEAN' interests, making it difficult to achieve collective action. There are no formal rules by which ASEAN members must abide and by which non-compliance can be punished.[79] As a result, ASEAN has been unable to deal with several transnational challenges associated with globalisation such as the Asian financial crisis, environmental problems such as the haze, piracy and transnational crime, the spread of pandemics such as SARS or transnational migration.[80]

ASEAN has responded to these issues by attempting to tighten institutional cohesion in order to bolster its international reputation. In doing so, it has looked towards the EU.[81] The Chiang Mai currency swap initiative, for example, was arguably 'stimulated by the system of the EMU in Europe,

77 See P.J. Davidson, 'The Role of Law in Governing Regionalism in Asia', (2009) in N. Thomas (ed.), *Governance and Regionalism in Asia* (London: Routledge, 2009) pp. 224–249.

78 J. Rüland, 'Southeast Asian Regionalism and Global Governance: "Multilateral Utility" or "Hedging Utility"?', (2011) 33(1) *Contemporary Southeast Asia* 100.

79 S. Peou, 'The Subsidiarity Model of Global Governance in the UN-ASEAN Context', (1998) 4(4) *Global Governance* 448.

80 E. Asciutti, 'The ASEAN Charter: An Analysis', (2010) 2(1) *Perspectives on Federalism* 48.

81 Y.L. Hwee, 'EU-ASEAN Relations and Policy Learning', (2008) in R. Balme and B. Bridges (eds), *Europe-Asia Relations: Building Multilateralisms* (Basingstoke: Palgrave, 2008) p. 92.

but framed within non-Western norms'.[82] In 2007, the ASEAN Charter set out the foundations of the ASEAN Community, aiming to ensure the continuing global relevance of ASEAN through institutional consolidation.[83] This Charter mimics EU-style institutionalisation by incorporating elements of the EU structure. Echoing the pre-Lisbon EU structure, the ASEAN Community is made up of a three-pillar structure: the ASEAN Economic Community (with the aim to create a Single Market), the ASEAN Political and Security Community and the ASEAN Cultural Community. The ASEAN Summit structure and the Chairmanship are very similar to the European Council and the Presidency. Article 3 of the ASEAN Charter established ASEAN's legal personality, making it a subject of international law and enhancing its representation within global governance institutions.[84] At the 2010 ASEM meeting, the Secretary General of ASEAN represented the Association alongside ASEAN member states. All of this is pointing to the EU as an institutional template for ASEAN.[85] Furthermore, like the EU, ASEAN has adopted a flag, an anthem and a motto. In short, the ASEAN Charter 'heavily emulates EU concepts and terminology and represents what could have been a lean version of the Constitutional Treaty'.[86] After more than 40 years, ASEAN is moving along the institutional spectrum and is transforming into a more rule-based community. It is doing so by emulating EU institutions and adapting them to fit its own purposes.

Institutions do not only regulate behaviour; they are based on certain cultural and normative priorities. Thus, the core normative structure of an entity determines its institutional culture by setting the parameters or the 'meta-regime', describing a system of norms and principles that shapes the rules, procedures, actions and ultimately the self-understanding of an organisation.[87] At the same time, institutional cultures and norms reinforce constitutive identities.[88] Functions, decision-making structures and capabilities are bounded by institutional cultures. Institutions that define the ability to formulate coherent external positions, goals or policies, the ability to act and interact at the transnational level and the capabilities an actor is able to use are, therefore, defined by internal values and norms.

82 J. Gilson, *Asia Meets Europe – Inter-Regionalism and the Asia-Europe Meeting* (Cheltenham: Edward Elgar, 2002) p. 92.

83 A.D. Ba, 'Regionalism's Multiple Negotiations: ASEAN in East Asia', (2009) 22(3) *Cambridge Review of International Affairs* 362.

84 See ASEAN, *The ASEAN Charter*, (2008) <www.asean.org> accessed 23 October 2014.

85 P. Murray and E. Moxon-Browne, 'The European Union as a Template for Regional Integration? The Case of ASEAN and its Committee of Permanent Representatives', (2013) 51(3) *Journal of Common Market Studies* 523.

86 Börzel and Risse (n 69) p. 13.

87 See Aggarwal and Chow (n 58).

88 See G.M. Thomas, 'Globalization: The Major Players', (2007) in G. Ritzer (ed.), *The Blackwell Companion to Globalization* (Malden, MA: Blackwell, 2007), p. 89.

Ideational and normative structures provide the *raison d'être* for organisations such as the EU and ASEAN. They are much more resistant to change than specific institutions. The normative core of the EU is rooted in the liberal domestic analogy. In other words, to achieve progress at the international level, i.e. to overcome the problem of repeating cycles of warfare between European states, requires the creation and maintenance of a dense network of transnational institutions. This finds its expression in the acceptance of a liberal order based on binding rules and obligations.[89] This political culture is broadly based on a commitment to liberal democracy, some form of free trade, a culture of transnational collaboration and cooperation, transnational law and institutions, and a respect for cosmopolitan human rights norms. This contains elements of a post-Westphalian culture, provides the foundation for the *aqui communautaire* and becomes visible in the negotiations with potential accession countries which have to incorporate the *aqui*. It also finds its reflection in the external policies of the EU, having become part of the actor identity of the EU. The EU sees itself as a normative power, an actor based on a certain normative culture with the explicit mission to export its own values, thereby defining what is considered to be normal within the wider global governance framework through, for example, norm export and promotion, contagion diffusion or simply through living by example.[90]

In contrast to that, ASEAN's normative core is firmly centred on a Westphalian footing. Sovereignty and non-intervention are core values. Given the historical idiosyncrasies of postcolonial Southeast Asia, ASEAN can be regarded as a tool to support the various state-building efforts in the region. Ultimately, ASEAN's purpose was to strengthen sovereignty rather than reining it in.[91] As a result, ASEAN's institutional structure is informal rather than legalised, emphasising sovereignty, non-intervention and loose intergovernmental cooperation instead of supranationalism.[92] The so-called ASEAN way represents the core normative culture of ASEAN.[93] It is centred on a cluster of three principles: the non-use of force in intra-regional disputes, non-interference and regional autonomy.[94] The procedural norms that determine ASEAN's institutional culture includes a preference for consensus-based

89 See T. Risse, 'Social Constructivism and European Integration', (2004) in A. Wiener and T. Dietz (eds), *European Integration Theory* (Oxford: OUP, 2004) p. 163.

90 See Manners (n 43). See also I. Manners, 'Global Europe: Mythology of the European Union in World Politics', (2010) 48(1) *Journal of Common Market Studies* 67–87.

91 K. Bessho, *Identities and Security in East Asia*, (1999) Adelphi Paper 325, IISS, London, p. 41.

92 P. Murray, 'East Asian Regionalism and EU Studies', (2010) 32(6) *Journal of European Integration* 599.

93 L. Jones, 'ASEAN's Unchanged Melody? The Theory and Practice of "Non-Interference" in Southeast Asia', (2010) 23(4) *The Pacific Review* 480.

94 See A. Acharya, *Constructing a Security Community in Southeast Asia – ASEAN and the Problem of Regional Order* (New York: Routledge, 2001); A. Acharya, *Whose Ideas Matter? Agency and Power in Asian Regionalism* (Ithaca, NY: Cornell University Press, 2009); J. Haacke, *ASEAN's Diplomatic and Security Culture – Origins, Development and Prospects* (London: Routledge, 2003).

decision-making, informality and an aversion to formal and highly institutionalised forms of regional cooperation. In many ways, the ASEAN way is the direct result of historical necessities and constructed difference with the EU's institutionalised regionalism.[95] Even today, almost half a century after the signing of the Bangkok Declaration, these norms remain central to the self-understanding of ASEAN: the ASEAN Charter also reaffirms the centrality of sovereignty and non-interference.[96]

## 5 Concluding remarks

The picture emerging from the discussions above is a mixed one. There is evidence that regional organisations are emerging as international actors within the global governance framework. It can also be argued that this phenomenon is no longer restricted to the EU.[97] As highlighted above, ASEAN, too, has enhanced its organisational capacity in recent years and has, indeed, acquired elements of actorness. The EU has played a significant role in the process of actor construction, behaving as a normative power. Norm diffusion has happened in three ways: through a deliberate export and promotions of norms and values, contagion confusion and the 'model-effect'.[98] The EU has directly facilitated capacity-building in ASEAN in order to disseminate its version of regionalism (in line with its own identity), thereby increasing its own presence.[99] It has also directly and indirectly fostered institutional learning and socialisation. In addition, greater institutional cohesion and coordination was forced on ASEAN as the institutionally weaker partner in interregional fora where the EU is present, such as the Asia Europe Meeting (ASEM).

This leads us to question whether ASEAN is indeed emerging as an international actor in its own right or whether it is mimicking EU actorness by creating a hollow mirror image of the EU, a 'Potemkin village'. In many ways, institutional asymmetries remain contrastingly stark between the EU and ASEAN. Even after the ASEAN Charter, ASEAN institutions have limited or no decision-making capabilities. ASEAN's representation in global governance institutions such as the UN, for example, has been marked by its weak organisational capacity, clearly limiting its effectiveness as an actor. The resources of the ASEAN Secretariat remain modest. It still has no executive

95 See Gilson (n 72); S. Lawson, 'Asia/Europe and the Construction of Regional Governance', (2009) in N. Thomas (ed.), *Governance and Regionalism in Asia* (London: Routledge, 2009) pp. 301–320.

96 These principles are outlined in Article 2 of the ASEAN Charter. ASEAN (n 84).

97 For this see also M. Hulse, 'Actorness beyond the European Union: Comparing the International Trade Actorness of SADC and ECOWAS', (2014) 52(3) *Journal of Common Market Studies* 547–565.

98 See Manners (n 43).

99 In this way, the EU is enhancing its own actorness through the creation of regional others. See Gilson (n 82) p. 1.

and legislative powers and remains exclusively a coordinating body. ASEAN's model of regionalism remains decentralised. ASEAN mimics EU norms and institutions because the EU is regarded as the most advanced model of regional actorness. EU-style institutions appear to confer prestige and credibility, especially when dealing with the EU itself. However, EU-style institutions have been crafted on top of ASEAN's ideational underpinnings, which remain sovereignty-centric. To date, it is not clear as to whether the ASEAN Charter signifies structural and institutional change or just institutional mimesis. As Murray and Moxon-Browne state: 'Creating institutions is relatively easy: what matters is the political significance attached to these institutions.'[100]

ASEAN actorness, it appears, is limited by the ideational core of the Association – the ASEAN way based on non-interference. ASEAN members find it very difficult to diverge from this ideational basis.[101] ASEAN member states' ability to control territory, people and resources within national boundaries remains weak. The lack of unconditional political legitimacy further explains the continuing emphasis on sovereignty and non-interference in the region. ASEAN's main purpose remains to support Southeast Asia's state-building projects in the face of the multiple challenges of globalisation and structural change. The ASEAN Community and Charter may have tightened ASEAN's institutional structure but the Charter also enshrines the ASEAN way of consultation and consensus, thus confirming ASEAN's core principles.[102]

However, it ought to be remembered here that the EU itself is far from being a coherent actor. EU actorness, such as it is, has grown historically rather than being the product of some grand design. Consistency problems remain. This is evident in the EU pursuit of interregional relations. Officially, the EU has the ambition to institutionalise relations between regional organisations and to export its own institutional model. Yet for a variety of pragmatic reasons, EU interregionalism displays a bewildering variety defying any simple categorisation.[103] For example, interregional relations can be bilateral or more diverse, they can be issue-specific or multipurpose, and they can involve third states or link to global governance and multilateral structures. This picture is further complicated by the division of external competencies

100 Murray and Moxon-Browne (n 85) p. 525.

101 See Haacke (n 94) pp. 161–182; K. Freistein, 'ASEAN aftet the Bali Summit 2003: From Paralysis to New Life?' (2005) 4(2) *European Journal of East Asian Studies* 182.

102 See Article 20 of the ASEAN Charter. ASEAN (n 84).

103 See F. Baert, T. Scaramagli and F. Söderbaum, 'Introduction: Intersecting Interregionalism', (2014) in F. Baert, T. Scaramagli and F. Söderbaum (eds), *Intersecting Interregionalism: Regions, Global Governance and the EU* (London: Springer, 2014) pp. 1–12; P. De Lombaerde, F. Söderbaum and J.U. Wunderlich, 'Interregionalism', (2015) in K.E. Jørgensen, A.K. Aarstadt, E. Drieskens, K. Laatikainen and B. Tonra (eds), *The Sage Handbook of European Foreign Policy* (London: Sage, 2015).

within the EU between different EU institutions and member states. Far from being anchored to a specific foreign policy doctrine – such as interregionalism – the EU is using whatever type of policy that seems appropriate for a given objective. Thus, it is difficult to discern a common rationale underlying the various interregional contacts. They are based on different foundations, reflecting the nature of the regional states or groupings involved, as well as the interest of the various actors lurking below EU level.

Another problem is that the evaluation of regional actorness remains heavily influenced by the EU model, which in turn is based to a large extent on the desire to enhance the role of the EU in a world dominated by states. Indeed, debates within the regional actorness literature have been substantially shaped by the case of first the EC and now the EU. It should, perhaps, come as no surprise that other regional organisations will fall short as the concept and the various components especially with regard to institutional capacity, may only have limited applicability. By making actorness a function of capability, it also confuses behaviour and being. In addition, the actorness concept demonstrates the same issues that we find in legal scholarship or within traditional state-centric international relations. By focusing on certain institutional criteria, other aspects are being ignored. This includes agents and actors that lurk in the shadow of these institutional structures and heavily influence policy making. Established interest and lobby groups are a good example. The privileged influence of some interest groups on decision-making processes also causes accountability and legitimacy problems that seem to be symptomatic of the wider structure of postnational rule-making. By focusing on institutional actors, these hidden interests and actors remain obscure and their influence is not properly problematised. Instead, it is naturalised. Furthermore, within the EU context other institutions such as the Courts, the Parliament, the Commission and specialised agencies have powers to engage in international relations and, therefore, may be regarded as international actors in their own right.[104] Thus, focusing on the actorness of regional organisations within global governance institutions can be useful under certain circumstances. However, we have to be careful not to exchange one 'black box' for another.

104 Baert *et al.* (n 103) p. 4.

Section II

# New institutional components and systems

## Establishing autonomy in postnational rule-making

# 4 Strained actorness

## The 'new' European Council in theory and practice

*Henri de Waele**

## 1 Introduction

Still today, the European Council (EuCo) remains a relatively understudied institutional actor. To avoid misunderstanding, this statement does not mean to disparage any of the research conducted earlier, but merely point to the richness of the subject for further inquiry, particularly through the lens of postnational rule-making. To be sure, however, the institution's growing political clout has certainly not gone unnoticed, and neither has the progressive enhancement of its position within the Union's legal architecture.[1] After a protracted period of 'floating outside' and 'hovering above' that spanned several decades, the EuCo became more solidly entrenched than ever in 2009, at the entry into force of the Lisbon Treaty. Meanwhile, it has already been alleged that the 'new' European Council can be justifiably perceived as the Union's 'government'.[2] Such assertions may seem overly bold and slightly premature; yet recent developments do testify of a broader momentum that cannot be so easily downplayed – a sterling case of an actor (*en route* towards) cementing its autonomy.

Nowadays, the EuCo unmistakably functions as the 'central venue for directing processes of intensified policy coordination',[3] and with great frequency, the activities it undertakes 'embody determinative policy choices

* This paper builds on selected parts of an earlier publication (co-authored by Hansko Broeksteeg): 'The Semi-Permanent European Council Presidency. Some Reflections on the Law and Early Practice' (2012) 49 *CMLRev* 1039. Dr Broeksteeg's permission to draw on said parts is gratefully acknowledged. Many thanks are also due to Matthijs van Schadewijk for his invaluable research assistance.

1 See e.g. Jan Werts, *The European Council* (John Harper Publishing 2008); Frederic Eggermont, *The Changing Role of the European Council in the Institutional Framework of the European Union* (Intersentia 2012).

2 Tom Eijsbouts and Monica Claes, 'From Confederacy to Convoy: Thoughts about the Finality of the Union and its Member States' (2010) 6 *EUConst* 1. The sentiment has been expressed earlier; see e.g. John Peterson and Elizabeth Bomberg, *Decision-Making in the European Union* (Palgrave Macmillan 1999) 33.

3 Uwe Puetter, 'The European Council – The New Centre of EU Politics' (2013) 16 *SIEPS – European Policy Analysis* 1, 10.

directing the action of the EU institutions and even Member States'.[4] It is equally hard to take issue with the statement that the EuCo currently forms the 'alpha and omega of executive power'.[5] What is more, while it is formally not rendered competent to exercise legislative functions,[6] in reality, its guidance exerts an immediate impact on the legislative process. Consequently, the governance mode that permeates EU decision-making at the present day and time is held to be (neo-)intergovernmentalism.[7]

At the same time, it might be assumed rather too quickly that the 'new' European Council possesses a genuine actorness that enables it to plot the Union's course, either overtly or covertly. To an extent indeed, the rise of intergovernmentalist decision-making in key policy fields may have sidelined the traditional supranational institutions, yet this presents us with one side of the story only. Real-time practices testify of a more subtle, variegated process, and a creeping, surreptitious fragmentation. The latter does not denote the fragmentation of executive power across the Union in a broad sense, but an internalised, incremental and potentially more corrosive development unfolding at the heart of the EuCo's functioning. Lest we forget, the EuCo is not a monolithic actor, perhaps even less so than any of the other EU institutions. In actual fact, it may not so much be the institution itself, but rather a small selection of members, including its President, that has solidified its position most vigorously, and manages to dictate its preferences even when faced by a numerical majority. Hence, for the sake of accuracy, any contemporary assessment needs to take heed of these evermore relevant fracture lines, and the tectonics of the EuCo's component parts. Ultimately, the upshot could not so much be a pattern of increasing intergovernmentalisation of EU governance due to the 'unstoppable advance of the European Council',[8] but in actual fact a state of executive dominance featuring a small set of key players that is effectively capable of forcing the hand of that institution.

With these preliminary admonitions in mind, the present chapter proceeds as follows. It starts off with a brief sketch of the EuCo's early development, taking a mildly unorthodox view of its origin and the motives for its creation (section 2). Next, it proceeds to gauge the institution's modern-day competences, and its position within the wider constitutional framework

4 Editorial Comments, 'An Ever Mighty European Council – Some Recent Institutional Developments' (2009) 46 *CMLRev* 1383, 1391.

5 Deirdre Curtin, *Executive Power of the European Union. Law, Politics and the Living Constitution* (OUP 2009) 71.

6 Article 15(1) TEU.

7 Uwe Puetter, 'Europe's Deliberative Intergovernmentalism – The Role of the Council and European Council in EU Economic Governance' (2012) 19 *JEPP* 161, 166; Uwe Puetter, *The European Council and the Council* (OUP 2014).

8 Jan Werts, 'The Unstoppable Advance of the European Council', in Deirde Curtin, Alfred Kellermann and Steven Blockmans (eds), *The European Constitution: The Best Way Forward?* (TMC Asser Press 2005) 297.

(section 3). Hereafter, the inter-institutional linkages are subjected to review, in an attempt to assess how the Union's other main actors measure up to the revamped EuCo (section 4). After these theoretical reflections, we move on to consider the dynamics in practice, focusing on the three most salient trends from the post-Lisbon period (section 5). The threads are drawn together in the concluding paragraph, presenting a critical appraisal of the EuCo's 'strained actorness' (section 6).

## 2 Origins and early development

While 1974 has gone down in history as the EuCo's official year of birth, it is still all too often overlooked that its true origins date back to the early 1960s. At the inception of the Communities, the erected institutional architecture did not provide for recurrent gatherings of the Heads of State or Government of the Member States. Thus, the first sessions of the embryonic entity, convened in Paris and Bonn in February and July 1961, took place without the Treaties providing legal authorisation for the initiative. These and subsequent conferences were mainly organised for negotiating issues on which the Council of Ministers could not reach agreement, and with an eye to resolving any avoidable stagnation.[9] The organisation of this type of summit reflected a looming desire for institutionalised political cooperation at the highest level, as underscored by the fact that the 1961 meetings quickly received their follow-ups; for already at the dawn of the integration process, in cases of persistent deadlock, none of the existing actors possessed the necessary standing to take decisive action.[10] In retrospect, then, one may say that it was a crescent practical need, more than anything else, that sparked the creation of the 'proto-EuCo'. Correspondingly, the move has been hailed as a classic example of change to accommodate political reality.[11]

The phenomenon was then only formalised (if not canonised) at the 1974 summit in Paris. At that point, the blueprint was agreed for half-yearly conferences under a rotating presidency. The 1975 gathering in Dublin was the first to meet under this new regime. Only in 1987, with the entry into force of the Single European Act, was the existence of the EuCo acknowledged in the EEC Treaty. With the entry into force of the Maastricht Treaty in 1993, its role was elaborated in more detail; Article 4(1) TEU couched its task in familiar terms when it instructed it to 'provide the Union with the necessary impetus for its development and define the general political

9 Werts, *European Council* 3–5; Eggermont, *Changing Role* 3–12. More generally, see Simon Bulmer and Wolfgang Wessels, *The European Council* (Macmillan 1987); Béatrice Taulègne, *Le Conseil européen* (PUF 1993); Philippe de Schoutheete, 'The European Council', in John Peterson and Michael Shackleton (eds), *The Institutions of the European Union* (OUP 2006) ch 3.

10 Werts, *The European Council* 3.

11 Paul Craig and Gráinne de Búrca, *EU Law: Text, Cases and Materials* (OUP 2011) 51.

guidelines thereof'. It was thus designed to take a 'helicopter view', and come up with answers to the paramount questions of European integration.[12]

The pace with which, from then on, the EuCo shaped up from a cuckoo in the nest to a centripetal force remains astounding. In the decades since its creation, no major development could take place without its official blessing, or at least tacit approval.[13] This is all the more remarkable considering that its most regular output, the Conclusions published at the end of every summit, never enjoyed a 'hard law' status.[14] Moreover, the EuCo was only attributed official decision-making powers by the Amsterdam Treaty in 1999.[15]

With the entry into force of the Lisbon Treaty on 1 December 2009, the EuCo's high-speed evolutionary trajectory has reached its provisional apogee. For starters, it was elevated to the rank of an official Union institution, a privilege shared with only six siblings.[16] It was transformed further by being endowed with a plethora of decision-making competences, the installation of a semi-permanent Presidency, and the formal ousting of the Ministers of Foreign Affairs that had hitherto been members.[17] This may, then, with only slight overstatement, be justifiably regarded as the 'new' European Council's genesis.

## 3 Constitutional position

### *3.1 Multiplicity of roles and functions*

Even before it became an official institution, the EuCo has proactively taken up a number of different roles, ranging from that of allocator of budget funds to that of appellate body in case of disputes in or between other institutions, besides getting prominently involved in *inter alia* the shaping of the Common Foreign and Security Policy, the Area of Freedom, Security and Justice, and even typical EC domains such as environmental policy.[18] Legal doctrine offers some fine analyses of the multiplicity of (informal) functions it performs, among which the facilitation of informal exchanges of information and opinions, the fostering of personal understanding between the respective members, acting as supreme arbitrator on delicate problem dossiers, and a constant endeavouring to accommodate divergent national preferences.[19]

12 Werts, *The European Council* 18.

13 See e.g. Tom Eijsbouts, 'Constitutional Sedimentation' (1996) 23 *LIEI* 51, 57.

14 Cf. the contribution of Matthias Ruffert to this volume.

15 (ex) Articles 13 and 15 TEU.

16 Article 15(1) TEU.

17 Article 15(2) TEU; compare (ex) Article 4 TEU. The Lisbon Treaty similarly relegated the Finance Ministers of the Member States, who had hitherto been allowed to attend EuCo meetings when EMU matters were at stake.

18 Puetter, 'European Council' 7.

19 See e.g. Werts, *The European Council* 18–19 and 37–43.

Taking its cue from the additional powers granted in 2009, the EuCo has in the meanwhile managed to expand its role even more, as will be illustrated further below.

### *3.2 Place in the hierarchy*

In terms of hierarchy, the EuCo not only intuitively belongs at the apex of the Union's institutional order; the presumption can be corroborated by pointing to the array of powers that has of late been placed at its disposal. Reference can, for instance, be made to the fact that it takes centre stage in defining the EU's strategic interests and objectives in the field of external relations, as well as in defining the EU's strategic guidelines for action within the AFSJ.[20] Already in this respect, the Council and Commission may be considered to have been placed in a hierarchically inferior position, proceeding as they do on the basis of the EuCo's input. Moreover, the EuCo is to determine the configurations of the Council of Ministers,[21] the composition of the Parliament as regards the allocation of MEPs between Member States,[22] and the tentative rotation system of Commissioners.[23] Even when the Parliament has newly acquired a greater influence, *de facto* if not *de jure*, in its pre-appointment scrutiny of proposed Commissioners, the EuCo maintains the right to definitely appoint the Commission, after the Parliament has approved of the nomination of the envisaged members.[24] In similar vein, at least in the abstract, the President of the Commission and the High Representative for Foreign Affairs and Security Policy could be regarded as hierarchically subservient, since the EuCo possesses the exclusive prerogative to propose the candidates for taking up those offices.[25]

### *3.3 Powers of the Presidency*

Since the entry into force of the Lisbon Treaty, a crucial part is played by the EuCo's Presidency, which has also had a profound bearing on the place of the institution as a whole.[26] As of December 2009, the office of President has obtained a 'stable' or 'semi-permanent' quality, with incumbents being

20 Article 22(1) TEU; Article 68 TFEU. As regards external relations, cf. the contributions of Jens-Uwe Wunderlich and Jan Wouters to this volume.
21 Article 236 TFEU.
22 Article 14(2) TEU.
23 Article 17(5) TEU and Article 244 TEU.
24 Article 17(7) TEU.
25 Article 17(7) respectively 18(1) TEU.
26 Henri de Waele and Hansko Broeksteeg, 'The Semi-Permanent European Council Presidency. Some Reflections on the Law and Early Practice' (2012) 49 *CMLRev* 1039; Spyros Blavoukos, Dimitris Bourantonis, and George Pagoulatos, 'A President for the European Union: A New Actor in Town?' (2007) 45 *JCMS* 231.

expected to occupy the post for a term of 2.5 years (once renewable). The Treaties are conspicuously vague with regard to the content of the function, leaving ample room for diverging interpretations and potentially endless turf-wars.[27] This lack of clarity, as so often, mirrors the inability of the *Herren der Verträge* to reach consensus on a strong definition or delineation. Nevertheless, judging from an appointment-and-dismissal perspective, the President appears to be in a relatively strong legal position: for one thing, he is elected by the EuCo itself, i.e. without the involvement of any other institutions, and if need be by a qualified majority of representatives; in addition, only the EuCo possesses the competence to force him to step down.[28] The President is therefore not accountable to anyone but the EuCo members themselves, so that his position verges on the unassailable.

The foregoing conclusion might seem thoroughly disquieting, yet there would only be true cause for alarm if the office is able to play a substantial part in the EU's lawmaking and policymaking process. In this light, it should be noted that the (few) autonomous powers of the Presidency are largely internal ones, meaning that they relate overwhelmingly to the organisation and management of EuCo meetings. Article 15(5) TEU stipulates that the President chairs the European Council and drive forward its work; that he shall ensure the preparation and continuity of the work of the European Council; that he shall endeavour to facilitate cohesion and consensus within the Council; and that he shall present a report to the European Parliament after each of the meetings of the European Council.[29] The EuCo's Rules of Procedure provide that he is to submit an annotated draft agenda to the General Affairs Council at least four weeks before every ordinary meeting, to prepare draft guidelines for the EuCo conclusions, to draft those conclusions, as well as European Council decisions, which are subsequently to be discussed in the General Affairs Council.[30] The Rules of Procedure moreover state that the EuCo President shall ensure the preparation and continuity of the work of the Council in cooperation with the Commission President, on the basis of the work of the General Affairs Council.[31]

On the basis of these clauses, the constitutional position of the office of EuCo President can nevertheless be characterised as a pivotal one. Crucially,

27 Panos Koutrakos, 'New Links in the Union's Institutional Chain' (2010) 35 *ELRev* 1. See also Peter van Elsuwege, 'EU External Action after the Collapse of the Pillar Structure: In Search of a New Balance between Delimitation and Consistency' (2010) 48 *CMLRev* 987, 992; Jan Rood, 'De EU na het Verdrag van Lissabon: Naar een nieuw politiek en institutioneel evenwicht?' (2008) 56 *SEW* 132, 135.

28 Article 15(5) TEU.

29 On his external representation tasks, see further infra.

30 Article 3(1) of the Annex to European Council Decision of 1 December 2009 adopting its Rules of Procedure [2009] OJ L315/51 (hereinafter: the Rules of Procedure).

31 Ibid., Article 2(1). According to Article 2(2), the latter shall prepare and ensure the follow-up meetings of the European Council, in liaison with the President of the Council and the Commission.

the incumbent chairs all EuCo meetings; this, in combination with his extensive drafting and agenda-setting powers – even when most of these must be exercised in close cooperation with other actors, including the EuCo members themselves – enables him to have a formidable impact indeed.[32] Ultimately, albeit indirectly, the black-letter law competences render him responsible for directing the Union's overall course. The first appointee has, instead, described his tasks in supremely modest terms: to involve everybody, find compromises that respect the interests and sensitivities of each Member State, the prerogatives of the institutions, and the interests of the Union as a whole.[33] As further explored below, though, exploiting his slender array of powers to the max, he has proved capable of leaving a much greater mark in reality than this humble proclamation suggests.

## 4 Inter-institutional relations

The EuCo (and its President) are spun in a complex web of relations with the Union's other main actors. Whereas an exhaustive survey is neither feasible nor intended here, we will in successive paragraphs highlight the ties and linkages between the 'new' European Council and the Council, the Commission, the High Representative and the Parliament. Attention *in obiter* is paid to its position vis-à-vis the Eurogroup, the Euro Summit and national parliaments.

### *4.1 Position vis-à-vis the Council*

As remarked, the EuCo is commonly regarded as hierarchically superior to the Council.[34] This could lead one to think that the relations between the two institutions take a principally asymmetric form, with the latter invariably having to bow to the instructions of the former. Upon closer inspection, however, the picture proves to be rather more complicated. To begin with, when revamping the EuCo and equipping it with a 'stable' Presidency, the

32 Prima facie, this inference is diluted by various stipulations in the Rules of Procedure. While it is laid down there that the President takes the initiative when the European Council adopts a decision and holds a vote, he is required to start a voting procedure on the initiative of a member of the European Council, provided that a majority of the members agrees; also, he may not take part in the vote himself (Article 6(1)). Yet, it needs to be stressed that this provision is only applicable when it truly comes to a vote. In every other situation, the President may considerably steer the decision-making, or even persuade the members not to let the matter come to a vote, so as to maximise his own role. Additionally, he may himself propose to stage a written vote on urgent matters (Article 7).

33 Herman van Rompuy, 'The Discovery of Co-Responsibility: Europe in the Debt Crisis', Speech at Humboldt University, 6 February 2012, EUCO 21/12 5. Cf. Herman Van Rompuy, *Europe in the Storm* (Davidsfonds 2014), 113.

34 See e.g. Deirde Curtin, 'Challenging Executive Dominance in European Democracy' (2013) 77 *MLR* 1, 12.

drafters of the Lisbon Treaty (and the Constitutional Treaty that preceded it) did not decide to disband the revolving Presidency of the Council. The six-month rotation system was left intact, albeit that since 2009, prearranged groups of three Member States operate in close collaboration, following up on one another's activities.[35] Thus, instead of promoting efficiency and transparency, an unhelpful *dédoublement* slid in place.[36] As a result, up to the present day, the role of the rotating Presidency in the governance of the Union can still not be blotted out.[37]

To ensure a smooth interplay between the two institutions, the EuCo's Rules of Procedure have prompted its President to establish a close cooperation and coordination with the Presidency of the Council, in particular by staging regular meetings.[38] The Council Secretariat and its Legal Service, which are nowadays charged with supporting both the EuCo and the Council, represent another significant linkage. From a competence perspective, however, as we have seen, the 'new' EuCo continues to bear responsibility to provide the Union with the necessary impetus for its development, and is expected to define the general political directions and priorities. As Article 15(1) TEU affirms, it does not exercise legislative powers, but it can take legally binding decisions, not least on a number of 'high politics' dossiers (e.g. on the composition of the Parliament and the appointment of the High Representative).[39] On the other hand, the preparation and continuity of the work of the EuCo needs to be ensured by its President, and this is done on the basis of the work of the General Affairs Council.[40] Moreover, the responsibility for the preparation and follow-up to meetings of the EuCo rests equally with the General Affairs Council.[41] Crucially, the European Council President lacks the power to issue

35 See Article 16(9) TEU; Article 236 TFEU; European Council Decision of 1 December 2009 on the exercise of the Presidency of the Council [2009] OJ L315/50; Council Decision of 1 December 2009 laying down measures for the implementation of the European Council Decision on the exercise of the Presidency of the Council, and on the chairmanship of preparatory bodies of the Council [2009] OJ L322/28 (corrigendum in [2009] OJ L344/56).

36 With the Foreign Affairs Council having yet another helmsman in the form of the High Representative for the Common Foreign and Security Policy (see Article 18(3) TEU). However, Article 2(5) of Council Decision 2009/908/EU adds that discussions in the Foreign Affairs Council on Common Commercial Policy issues will be chaired by the six-monthly rotating Presidency. In addition, if the HR is unable to attend a session, he will be replaced by respectively the Commissioner for Enlargement, Development or Humanitarian Aid, who act as his deputies. Finally, it also stipulates that the foreign minister of the Member State holding the rotating Presidency may also step in, should the need arise.

37 In the same vein, Editorial Comments, 'The Post-Lisbon Institutional Package: Do Old Habits Die Hard?' (2010) 47 *CMLRev* 597, 598.

38 Article 2(3) of the Annex to the Rules of Procedure also instructs him to establish such cooperation (and with the President of the Commission).

39 Article 14(2) TEU; Article 18(1) TEU.

40 Article 15(6)(b) TEU, reproduced in Article 2(2) of the Rules of Procedure.

41 Article 16(6) TEU (second sentence of second subparagraph), reproduced in Article 2(1) of the Rules of Procedure.

binding instructions to the members of the Council and/or its Presidency. Thus, the form and function of the different interconnections would on the whole appear to diminish the scope of the powers of the EuCo. To some extent, this may serve to underscore the theorem that there exists a less asymmetric relation between the two institutions than one would initially surmise. All the same, the EuCo does appear to retain a certain primacy for three different reasons. For starters, in providing the aforementioned impetus, it is the European Council and not the Council (nor the latter's Presidency) that determines the general course of the EU.[42] Second, even when it has not been attributed any legislative competences, in actual fact, all decisions taken by the European Council are of a 'high politics' or 'quasi-constitutional' nature.[43] Third and last, the Council is fated to share the bulk of its legislative powers with the Parliament, and in most of the areas where it enjoys those powers, it cannot act autonomously. In some cases of deadlock, it even has to take a step back and refer the dossier to the EuCo.[44] Therefore, a legal-theoretical perspective on their interrelations corroborates as well that the latter institution occupies the more prominent position.

### *4.2 Position vis-à-vis the Commission*

With the Commission, the EuCo has maintained something resembling a classic love-and-hate relationship. Initially, the former was pleased with the establishment of the latter: the Commission regarded the EuCo as an excellent instrument for the revaluation of the Community integration process, which would restore its position as central catalyst.[45] Gradually, however, it came to be overshadowed by the collective of the Heads of State or Government, notwithstanding its President joining their company in 1987. Over time, the EuCo begun to manifest itself with great frequency as agenda-setter, effective coordinator and power-broker between Member States and EU institutions; and in particular by taking on the *de facto* role of initiator of legislation and supervisor on the implementation of EU policies, the EuCo has gradually managed to displace the Commission.[46] One needs to take but a casual glance at the EuCo's most recent annual reports, teeming with decisions on how the EU should proceed, e.g. with regard to the accelerated implementation of the

42 Cf. Eijsbouts, 'Constitutional Sedimentation' 57: 'There is no doubt that the European Council is presently the most powerful body in the Union structure. Its action is crucial to the Union'; De Schoutheete, 'European Council' 57: '[M]anagement of the Union could not be assured without a top-level institution of this type: the European Council has played a fundamental role in European integration and will continue to do so.'

43 Michael Dougan, 'The Treaty of Lisbon 2007: Winning Minds, Not Hearts' (2008) 45 *CMLRev* 617, 627.

44 See e.g. Article 48(b) and Article 82(3) TFEU.

45 Eggermont, *Changing Role* 347.

46 Curtin, 'Challenging Executive Dominance' 8.

Single Market Act, the creation of a Single Research Area, an integrated energy market, or the rolling-out of nuclear stress tests programme.[47] Consequently, the growing importance of the EuCo would appear to have negatively impacted on that of the Commission.[48]

It has nevertheless been contended that the appearance of the EuCo on the political scene has ultimately *not* weakened the Commission, but rather strengthened its role, chiefly by its expansive interpretation of areas of EU competence in which it deemed it appropriate for the Commission to submit proposals.[49] Further, since the EuCo needs the Commission to realise its ambitions in areas where the latter has the exclusive right to submit a proposal, and since the authority of the EuCo is often needed for the Commission to get things through, the two should not be regarded as competitors, and their interaction not as a zero-sum game.[50] Against the common wisdom, one may then indeed go so far as to defend the reverse perspective, arguing that the EuCo has not worked to the detriment of the Commission, but can instead be seen as having enhanced the latter's position.[51] This is all the more remarkable considering that the intent of the *pères-fondateurs* of the EuCo was exactly to hedge in the Commission. While a contrary trend could perhaps be discerned, we should nevertheless take the counterfactual into account, and wonder what would have happened if the EuCo had never come into existence; for it cannot be ruled out that in that scenario, not being bound to work under the former's aegis, the Commission's position would have been even stronger. Moreover, the EuCo inexorably scooped up the role of cardinal instigator, visionary and helmsman, and as regards political clout, the Commission's stature has been on the wane correspondingly. In this respect, a weakening evidently *did* take place, even if novel opportunities to shape the policymaking process were granted in return.

### *4.3 Position vis-à-vis the High Representative*

According to Article 15(2) TEU, the High Representative 'takes part' in the work of the European Council.[52] What this entails is (still) not exactly clear. For one thing, it suggests a more limited involvement, not full and equal rights. Considering the EuCo's powers to define the content and direction of

47 Accessible at <http://www.european-council.europa.eu>.
48 See e.g. Puetter, 'European Council' 10.
49 Eggermont, *Changing Role* 347–350.
50 Similarly Puetter, 'European Council' 10.
51 Eggermont, *Changing Role* 350–351. Cf. the Editorial Comments, 'Ever Mighty European Council' 1383, pointing out how the Delors Commission already started to take initiatives within the EuCo in 1985.
52 Article 18 TEU adds that the HR 'conducts' the Common Foreign and Security Policy, takes initiatives for its further development, chairs the Foreign Affairs Council, and also functions as one of the Commission's vice-presidents.

the Union's Foreign and Security Policy, the HR, expected to proceed on the basis of those instructions, functions to some extent as its delegate or *aide-de-camp*. Moreover, Article 15(6) TEU stipulates that the EuCo President is to ensure the external representation of the Union on issues concerning the CFSP. On the basis of the black-letter law, though, the risk of clashes between his office and that of the High Representative appears minimal.[53] After all, Article 15(6) demands that the President acts 'at his level and in that capacity' and 'without prejudice to the powers of the High Representative'. A different provision instructs the HR to represent the Union for matters relating to the CFSP, conduct political dialogue with third parties on the Union's behalf, and express its position in international organisations and at international conferences.[54] As the Presidency's annual activity reports underscore, Mr Van Rompuy has been pretty active on this front as well, e.g. addressing the UN General Assembly, and attending summits of the NATO and the OSCE.[55] Thereby, he is nevertheless bound to attune the exercise of his external competences to those of the HR; and in actual fact, during his terms in office, Mr Van Rompuy established an excellent *rapport* with Ms Ashton.

With regard to the legal institutional question of 'who controls who', in line with the comments made above, it could overall be posited that the constitutional position of the President is of slightly greater weight than that of the High Representative. To be sure, this conclusion cannot be based on any autonomous powers he enjoys vis-à-vis the HR, for none exist. His position at the head of the new European Council may nevertheless serve as a decisive factor; after all, it is this institution that sets down the objectives and general guidelines for the CFSP, with the Foreign Affairs Council being obligated to frame that policy, and take the decisions necessary for defining and implementing it.[56] As remarked, the High Representative merely 'takes part' in the new EuCo's work, puts the CFSP into effect, and has to carry out all his tasks within the mandate provided by the Council.[57] The EuCo, chaired by the President, has the final say on the priorities for the CFSP, and holds the power to define, alter and limit the mandate of the HR. The EuCo – potentially at the instigation of the President – is also able to dismiss him, and may proceed to do so on an unlimited number of grounds.[58] Theoretically,

53 As regards the European External Action Service, harmony has been imposed by charging it to assist the High Representative, the European Council President, the Commission President as well as the Commission in the exercise of their respective external functions: see Article 2(1) and (2) of Council Decision 2010/427/EU establishing the organization and functioning of the European External Action Service [2010] OJ L201/30.

54 Article 27 TEU.

55 See e.g. 'The European Council in 2010' 12; 'The European Council in 2012' 16; 'The European Council in 2013' 15, all available at <http://www.european-council.europa.eu/the-president/the-ec-in-2013?lang=en>.

56 Article 26(1) and (2) TEU.

57 Article 26(3) TEU; Article 18(2) TEU.

58 Article 18(1) TEU.

then, the President prevails, largely by virtue of the weight and force of the institution he presides.

### *4.4 Position vis-à-vis the Parliament*

Objectionable as it is from a (albeit State-centric) democratic legitimacy perspective, the legal interconnections between the new EuCo and the Parliament are few and far between. Together with the Council, the Parliament frequently gets to approve or is consulted with regard to the legislative proposals that may originally be a product of the imagination of the European Council. Further, the EuCo is bound to propose its candidate for the Presidency of the Commission to the Parliament, taking into account the most recent election results, and ultimately gets to appoint all Commission members upon acquiring the Parliament's consent.[59] That in 2014, the nomination of Mr Jean-Claude Juncker as Commission President was forced upon the EuCo could usher in a whole new era here; yet, the practice is too fresh to pronounce with certainty on its precedential value.[60] At present, the only *direct* legal link that has been created concerns the EuCo President's presenting of a report to the Parliament after every summit.[61] This rule codifies a standing practice which dates back to 1981. The EuCo Rules of Procedure add that the President shall represent the European Council before the Parliament.[62] This 'representation' is, however, essentially noncommittal; it does not entail a formal accountability relationship, for the Parliament has not received any powers of sanctioning vis-à-vis the EuCo, nor in relation to its President. Thus, the latter remain free to ignore any possible negative feedback from MEPs, even if these were to command a parliamentary majority. In fact, the Parliament utterly lacks a guarantee that the President will be attending in person to deliver and elaborate on his report. The fact that Mr Van Rompuy actually decided to do so may be considered a generous favour on his part. The Parliament's President may, conversely, be invited to be heard by the European Council.[63] In reality, such audiences have become a standing practice since 1987.[64] Again, though, nothing more has been granted than a special privilege that can be revoked at any time; the Lisbon Treaty has not transformed the settled practice into a hard and fast rule, so that it continues to depend on the goodwill of the EuCo's members.[65]

59 Article 17(7) TEU.

60 Besides, when duly appointed, the Commission and its President are expected to follow the EuCo's political directions, as before. In this respect also, the '*Spitzenkandidaten*' process does not yet point to a hard break with the past.

61 Article 15(6)(d) TEU, reproduced in Article 5 of the Rules of Procedure (second sentence).

62 Article 5 Rules of Procedure (first sentence).

63 Article TFEU, reproduced in Article 4(2) of the Rules of Procedure. The Rules of Procedure prescribe that this exchange of views is to take place at the start of every meeting, unless, as Article 4(2) of the Rules of Procedure spells out, a different decision is taken by unanimity.

64 Julian Priestley, *Six Battles That Shaped Europe's Parliament* (John Harper Publishing 2008) 27.

65 As attested by the use of the verb 'may'.

On these grounds, the bonds between the Parliament and the European Council may be rightly characterised as weak. The former has no powers to sanction the actions of the latter nor to keep it in check.[66] True reciprocal duties of information do not exist either. In his periodic reporting, the President may restrict himself to elaborating the positions the European Council has adopted, and expounding on matters that have already taken their course; he is not required to defend the relevant policy lines, nor to commit himself to a future course of action. This legal constellation appears to further reinforce the comfortable and relatively carefree position of the EuCo.

At the same time, the absence of any relation of accountability does not mean that the European Council can never be arrested or at least 'hindered' by MEPs when exercising its formal or informal powers. For one thing, the Parliament's power of approval with regard to international treaties has been significantly extended by the Lisbon Treaty, now *inter alia* encompassing the Common Commercial Policy.[67] Marked has also been the influence of individual MEPs, such as those negotiators that succeeded in thwarting the blueprint for the structure of the Single Resolution Fund originally concocted by the EuCo.[68] Similarly, the current President of the Parliament has been known to liaise with prominent EuCo members, and in so doing, successfully obstruct intended changes to the EU Treaties.[69] Therefore, while officially, little or no democratic constraints continue to be placed on the EuCo's exercise of its powers, attempts to stretch these are no longer as successful as before.

### *4.5 Position vis-à-vis the Eurogroup, Euro Summit and national parliaments*

It was already the 'old' European Council that, in 1997, moved to install the 'Eurogroup' collective, consisting of the Ministers of Finance of the Member States participating in the common currency. The Commission's Vice-President for Economic and Monetary Affairs and the President of the European Central Bank participate as well.[70] The EuCo has engaged in close scrutiny of the group's deliberations and decisions ever since.[71] Meanwhile, at the end of 2011, it also decided to create the Euro Summit, bringing

66 With the exception of placing fetters on the allocated financial resources; Eggermont, op. cit. *Changing Role* 34, rightly points to the budgetary powers of the Parliament ex Article 313 *et. seq.* TFEU.

67 Cf. Article 218(6) TFEU and Article 207(2) TFEU.

68 In particular, Ms Elisa Ferreira, Mr Peter Simon and Ms Corien Wortmann-Kool; cf. <http://www.europarl.europa.eu/news/nl/news-room/content/20140217IPR36239/html/Single-resolution-mechanism-and-fund-Key-principles-for-successful-negotiations> and <http://europa.eu/rapid/press-release_STATEMENT-14–119_en.htm>.

69 Cf. Carlos Closa, 'Between a Rock and a Hard Place: The Future of EU Treaty Revisions' (2014) 2 *SIEPS – European Policy Analysis* 1, 4.

70 Protocol 14 on the Euro Group, Article 1.

71 Puetter, 'European Council' 6.

together the Heads of State and Government of the Member States that uphold the common currency. The Eurogroup and the European Commission are even more closely monitored by this forum, and are regularly called upon to carry out its instructions.[72] Potential clashes between the EuCo and Euro Summits have, however, been happily averted by appointing Mr Van Rompuy as its first President, and meetings are often convened in European Council format.[73]

Quite a different set of interlocutors are the national parliaments, the only organs to which the EuCo members are responsible, albeit individually, and only in the domestic *décor*. From the inception of the Euro crisis in particular, the national parliaments' critical feedback has mushroomed. Consequently, the EuCo has to take greater note in advance of the possible difficulties its members may encounter when defending the decisions taken before the national representative assembly.[74] The vaunted democratic safeguards thus appear to have been bolstered here, testifying to the 'compartmented legitimacy' of the Union's executive.[75]

## 5 Shifting practices

As Roscoe Pound reminded us long ago, legal assertions can easily turn out wholly fallacious when the analyst refrains from comparing the law in the books with the law in action. In the past decade, the European Council has functioned in evermore diverse capacities, but already long before the entry into force of the Lisbon Treaty, it played a role and exerted an influence that went far beyond the official place and tasks assigned by the Treaties. Among the novel areas in which it meddles nowadays are economic and financial governance, energy, climate change, and social and employment policy coordination. Thereby, the 'new' EuCo has not shied away from sidelining other institutions and impinging on their prerogatives. According to its first President, in times of crisis, the limits of institutions built on attributed competences are easily reached. New rules then have to be developed, and to his mind, the European Council is the primary *locus* where actions venturing beyond conferred powers can be initiated.[76] A closely related shift, worthy of note, concerns the massive increase in the number of summits. For example, 2011, saw one informal, one extraordinary and five formal meetings, alongside

72 Ibid.

73 Curtin, *Challenging Executive Dominance* 8. The approach is likely to be continued with Mr Van Rompuy's successors; on 30 August 2014, Mr Tusk was simultaneously appointed EuCo and Euro Summit President.

74 David Nederlof, Jan Herman Reestman and Thomas Vandamme, 'The European Council and the National Executives: Segmentation, Consolidation and Legitimation' (2012) 8 *EUConst* 165, 170–171.

75 Ibid.

76 Herman Van Rompuy, 'The Discovery of Co-Responsibility: Europe in the Debt Crisis', Speech at Humboldt University, 6 February 2012, EUCO 21/12 5.

four gatherings of the Euro Summit.[77] Some of these set remarkable duration records.[78]

While a much greater number of salient occurrences could be spotlighted, in recent practice, three major trends can be observed that are likely to cast a particularly long shadow, and therefore deserve special attention. Each of these points to an erosion of the EuCo's homogeneity, which in the long run risk to unhinge it from the position allocated by the Treaties.

## *5.1 Rise of the Presidency*

A first process, unfolding since 2009, pertains to the growing clout of the European Council Presidency. Clearly, the office was intended as a means to improve and maintain cohesion, and designed to drive forward the EuCo's work. We noted before that the President has not been attributed proper decision-making powers; legally, all such competences are exercised by the European Council, leaving him to serve as an arbiter of sorts between the different Heads of State or Government.[79] Moreover, as said, the official autonomous powers he does possess are largely internal ones, meaning that they overwhelmingly pertain to the organisation and management of EuCo meetings. His drafting and agenda-setting powers are certainly significant here, although these must mostly be exercised in close cooperation with other actors, including members of the European Council itself; for instance, the many extraordinary sessions convened during the first stages of the economic and financial crisis sprang from the initiative of the French President and the German Federal Chancellor. Yet, the President functions as a phenomenally important 'totem figure' who is able to have a tremendous impact behind the scenes, e.g. by coordinating policy dossiers, (re-)shuffling priorities, spearheading taskforces, regularly visiting and (pre-)consulting Heads of State or Government – thereby de facto overshadowing other actors and stakeholders.[80]

In deploying his informal powers in practice, the EuCo President's interference has on multiple occasions proved crucial. For instance, it was the European Council, not the Member States autonomously, that agreed on the financial rescue packages for Ireland, Greece and Portugal; and Mr Van Rompuy was responsible for organising and chairing the preparatory high-

77 'The European Council in 2011' 5, <http://www.european-council.europa.eu/media/555285/qcao11001enc.pdf>.

78 Thus, February 2013 witnessed a 24-hour non-stop summit; 'The European Council in 2013' 13, <http://www.consilium.europa.eu/uedocs/cms_data/librairie/PDF/QCAO13001ENC.pdf>.

79 Christian Tomuschat, 'Calling Europe by Phone' (2010) 47 *CMLRev* 1, 4; see also Dougan, 'Treaty of Lisbon' 628–629.

80 Puetter, 'European Council' 3.

level meetings.[81] Similarly, in March 2011, shortly before the session of the UN Security Council where the resolution authorising the use of force in Libya was adopted, the EuCo President decided to convene an extraordinary meeting of the European Council. In the announcement of this special summit, Mr Van Rompuy remarked publicly that he would himself propose the strategic lines of the EU's reaction to the developments in Libya and the Southern Neighbourhood.[82] This served to align the positions of the various Member States, including the permanent (France and the UK) and non-permanent Security Council members (Germany and Portugal). Equally, in early 2013, the EuCo President single-handedly brokered the deal on the EU's budget for the period up to 2020, securing a 40 per cent increase on innovation and competitiveness, immediate measures against unemployment, and the safeguarding of international development aid from cuts.[83]

Mr Van Rompuy has, in addition, been repeatedly appointed as head of ad hoc working groups, established by the EuCo in order to study specific issues and come up with suggestions for their resolution. In March 2010, for example, he was seconded to lead a taskforce entrusted with drafting proposals for stronger economic governance. The taskforce's Final Report, which recommended the establishment of a permanent crisis mechanism, increased fiscal discipline, a broadening of economic surveillance, deeper coordination and stronger institutions, was endorsed at the October 2010 EuCo summit.[84] Next, Mr Van Rompuy was entrusted to explore the possibility and draft a concrete proposal for a limited revision of the Treaties, so as to deliver tighter fiscal discipline and allow for the creation of a permanent bail-out fund for Euro zone countries. He also completed this mission successfully, with the report of this taskforce receiving unanimous backing at the European Council summit in December 2010.[85] A year later, he was mandated to explore the

81 See, respectively, 'Statement of the Heads of State or Government of the Euro Area', 7 May 2010; 'Statement by the Eurogroup and ECOFIN Ministers', 28 November 2010; 'Statement by the Eurogroup and ECOFIN Ministers', 16 May 2011.

82 See 'Herman van Rompuy, President of the European Council, convenes an extraordinary European Council on Friday 11 March 2011', Brussels, 15 December 2010, PCE 055/11.

83 'The European Council in 2013' 13, <http://www.consilium.europa.eu/uedocs/cms_data/librairie/PDF/QCAO13001ENC.pdf>.

84 See, respectively, 'Strengthening economic governance in the EU. Report of the task force to the European Council', Brussels, 21 October 2010, and the Conclusions of the European Council of 28–29 October 2010, EUCO 25/1/10 REV 1.

85 Conclusions of the European Council of 16–17 December 2010, EUCO 30/10. Media reported that the President had carried out 'an enormous amount of preparatory work', which meant that these Conclusions 'were almost entirely agreed in advance' (<euractiv.com/en/future-eu/quiet-summit-could-crown-van-rompuys-mastership-news-500662>). See also 'Invitation letter by President Van Rompuy to the European Council', Brussels, 15 December 2010, PCE 310/10: 'I sent you last week the Conclusions I draw from the consultations held with all Member States, in particular as regards the parameters of such a Treaty change. In the light of this, a draft decision of the European Council has been prepared and circulated to all Member States. We need to reach an agreement on a draft decision at our meeting in order for procedures to

possibilities for a further strengthening of economic convergence and deepening the economic union.[86] This culminated in the December 2012 report 'Towards a Genuine Economic and Monetary Union', besides sparking the adoption of the Treaty on Stability, Coordination and Governance in the EMU.[87]

Mention was made above of Mr Van Rompuy's chairing of the regular gatherings of the countries whose common currency is the Euro – something the Treaties do not make mention of either. Already in August 2011, the French President and the German Federal Chancellor invited Mr Van Rompuy to take up this position structurally. He was designated chair ad interim two months later, and officially appointed Euro Summit President in March 2012.[88] After the European Parliament elections of May 2014, Mr Van Rompuy's office acquired yet another dimension when he was mandated to explore the most suitable options with regard to the appointment of the new European Commission.[89]

Some still believe that the EuCo President merely plays the part of a humble moderator. By now, this view appears overly myopic, and the office's slender array of competences should by no means be considered decisive. In the past five years, the incumbent appears to have succeeded in becoming an influential actor in his own right, through a dutiful exercise of his official powers, tactful dealings with the Union's other institutional players, and clever exploitation of some legal 'grey zones'. Diplomats have given him credit for the resolution of several (major and minor) internal issues.[90] On the external front also,

be launched as fast as possible, both at the EU and national levels, so that this decision can enter into force on 1 January 2013.' The amendment was finalised in European Council Decision of 25 March 2011 amending art 136 TFEU with regard to a stability mechanism for Member States whose currency is the euro [2011] OJ L91/1, subjected to ratification by the Member States, and eventually entered into force on 1 May 2013.

86 Conclusions of the European Council of 23 October 2011, EUCO 52/11 5. See also 'Main results of Euro Summit', Brussels, 26 October 2011 10.

87 'Statement by the Euro area heads of State or Government', Brussels, 9 December 2011; 'Interim Report: Towards A Stronger Economic Union', 6 December 2011; 'Remarks by Herman Van Rompuy, following the first session of the European Council', EUCO 155/11, Brussels, 9 December 2011; Conclusions of the European Council of 1–2 March 2012, EUCO 4/12 1. The Treaty as such was drafted under the auspices of the Eurogroup Working Group (a configuration of the Economic and Financial Committee), chaired by Mr Thomas Wieser.

88 Conclusions of the European Council of 23 October 2011, EUCO 52/11 5; 'Main results of Euro Summit', Brussels, 26 October 2011, 'Ten measures to improve the governance of the Euro area' 11 (Annex 1); 'Herman Van Rompuy re-elected President', EUCO 37/12, Brussels, 1 March 2012. See moreover 'Remarks by President of the European Council Herman Van Rompuy at the European Parliament', EUCO 117/11 4.

89 Henriette Jacobsen and Georgi Gotev, '"No Momentum" For Juncker: EU Leaders Leave Options Open' Euractiv (28 May 2014) <http://www.euractiv.com/sections/eu-elections-2014/no-momentum-juncker-eu-leaders-leave-options-open-302465>.

90 E.g. a spat between the Commission and Poland on pension reform (see <euractiv.com/en/future-eu/quiet-summit-could-crown-van-rompuys-mastership-news-500662>). See also Honor Mahony, 'More Treaty Talk' *EUObserver* (26 October 2011) <blogs.euobserver.com/mahony/2011/

he has functioned as an important figurehead, taking precedence over the High Representative on some eye-catching occasions. Thus, both in theory and in reality, he has proved capable of exerting a more direct and profound influence on EuCo decisions and policies – perhaps even disproportionally so.

### *5.2 New intergovernmentalism*

The advent of what has been labelled 'new intergovernmentalism' constitutes a second discernable trend: the increasing preference of Member States to circumvent the supranational procedures and the main actors therein, resorting instead to other forms of decision-making outside the Treaty framework.[91] This manifestation of a classic tendency stands out for not being accompanied by a general integration fatigue. Moreover, it intends to complement, and not replace, existing activities governed by supranational means and bodies.[92]

A first expression offered the treaty establishing the European Financial Stability Facility (EFSF). In May 2010, representatives of the Member States attending a meeting of the Council of the Ministers of Economy and Finance adopted an executive decision that instantly brought the EFSF to life. The Facility functions as a private company consolidated under Luxembourg law, featuring the Euro countries as its only shareholders. In February 2012, this was followed by the creation of the treaty establishing the European Stability Mechanism (ESM), pursuant to an earlier Euro Summit decision taken in March 2011. The ESM meant to supplant the (temporary) EFSF, and has been designed as a separate entity under international law. Ratification by Euro States holding 90 per cent of the seed capital was required for it to enter into force, which turned out to be the case by November 2012.[93] A third precedent came in the guise of the Treaty on Stability, Coordination and Governance in the EMU, otherwise known as TSCG or 'Fiscal Compact'. The TSCG was adopted by 25 EU countries in December 2011, in face of opposition from the United Kingdom and the Czech Republic. The package tightened the rules agreed before under the 'Euro Plus Pact', 'Six Pack' and (then still

10/26/more-treaty-talk/>, quoting an anonymous diplomatic source: 'There seems to be general agreement that without his attention to detail and fair reflection of all the views in the Council, the rift between the euro ins and outs would be much worse than it actually is. (. . .) [H]e has also been instrumental in making sure that what comes out in European Council Conclusions reflects the balance of the views of Member States and not just those of one or two.' On a similar note, in the further implementation of the Europe2020 agenda, Mr Van Rompuy secured the involvement of the Committee of the Regions, single-handedly adding a phrase to this effect to the European Council Conclusions of March 2011 (see 'Speech by Herman Van Rompuy to the Plenary Session of the Committee of the Regions', PCE 110/11, 11 March 2011 4).

91 Puetter, 'Europe's Deliberative Intergovernmentalism' 166–7; Puetter, *The European Council and the Council* 227–234.

92 Closa, 'Between a Rock and a Hard Place' 3–4.

93 A last-ditch attempt by a member of the Irish parliament to have the mechanism condemned by the CJEU failed in Case C-370/12, *Thomas Pringle v Government of Ireland, Ireland and The Attorney General*, nyr.

forthcoming) 'Two Pack': *inter alia*, limiting annual structural government deficits, providing for an automatic correction mechanism, and obliging parties to anchor a balanced budget rule in their domestic constitutional law. The TSCG, which curiously relies on some Union remedies with regard to its enforcement, was signed off in March 2012, and officially entered into force on 1 January 2013.[94]

This collection of examples illustrates, again, how the European Council is slowly beginning to waver in its exclusive role of taking the Union's lead decisions. Besides the shadowy dealings of its President, smaller groups of countries embark with ever greater regularity on a legal *Sonderweg*, constructing more limited clubs outside the EU cadre. The relevant rules remain principally secondary (and occasionally connected) to the Union mainframe, yet do bind the parties under international law. The practice has been promoted under the 'Union method' sobriquet, favouring 'coordinated action in a spirit of solidarity' above the old *communautaire* approach.[95] Even the EuCo President has showed himself willing to endorse this marked shift, believing that its roots lie in the crisis circumstances, and that it 'confirms the vocation the European Council has had since its foundation'.[96] True, the EU's history is honeycombed with examples that started life outside the Treaty, but were eventually sewn into its fabric. The adage *l'histoire se répète* could be deceptively reassuring, though, in times when the supranational is sidelined to an unparalleled degree.

### *5.3 Germany's rising dominance*

Despite the fact that the European Council proceeds on the basis of equality, the votes of individual countries do not necessarily carry an equal weight. Earlier studies already corroborated that those States that are most advantaged in structural terms also tend to exert the greatest influence in EuCo negotiations. This was chiefly attributed to their broader range of options, the legitimacy of their claim to shape joint decisions, and the resources they are able to commit to an issue. The threat of the veto, the control of the Presidency, and the personalities of chief executives were found to be of secondary importance and mainly mediate the impact of structural power differentials.[97] The European Council also offers much greater leeway for

94 For in-depth reflections, see e.g. Paul Craig, 'The Stability, Coordination and Governance Treaty: Principle, Politics and Pragmatism' (2012) 37 *ELRev* 231.

95 'Speech by Ms Angela Merkel , Chancellor of the Federal Republic of Germany, at the opening of the 2010/2011 academic year at the College of Europe', Bruges campus, 2 November 2010 7, <https://www.coleurope.eu/nl/speeches>.

96 Herman van Rompuy, 'The Discovery of Co-Responsibility: Europe in the Debt Crisis', Speech at Humboldt University, 6 February 2012, EUCO 21/12 6.

97 Jonas Tallberg, 'Bargaining Power in the European Council' *Swedish Institute for European Policy Studies Report* 2007/1 45.

power politics than any other EU institution, and only very limited institutional protection to small and medium-sized Member States. Consequently, those earlier studies found that the preferences of France, Germany and the United Kingdom were most often determinative of the course of EuCo negotiations.[98]

In previous decades, as known, many positive results emerged from the Franco-German tandem. Italy and the Benelux countries often served as *trait d'union*, proffering substantive feedback, or launching new ideas themselves. With the economic decline of France and Italy, the splintering of the Benelux, and the political marginalisation of the UK, the landscape has of late changed drastically – leaving us with Germany as the key protagonist. Of course, in monetary affairs, it is normal for a country that makes the biggest contribution to assume a special role. Globally, the German Federal Republic sports the third-largest GNP after the US, China and Japan – yet this stature also directly informs its bargaining power *within* the EU. For example, the Union's position vis-à-vis Russia is authoritatively determined by Germany, and relayed through Berlin. China ultimately does not pay the price for dumping cheap solar panels on the EU market, not least because the Federal Chancellor advised against it. Germany's response to the crisis continues to be focused on austerity, a strategy not even the Commission has found trouble aligning itself with.[99]

To be sure, not all battles were won by the *Bundeskanzleramt*; for even in today's Union, no country can unremittingly have its cake and eat it. Obviously, to reform or enact officially binding rules, the other actors in either the intergovernmental or the supranational sphere are required to play along. It should be recognised as well that Germany is certainly not basking in its new role, traditionally electing to pursue its foreign policy interests in more covert fashion.[100] It now appears caught in a 'damned if you do, damned if you don't' dilemma: it is criticised when taking the initiative, as well as when refraining from doing so. By at least feigning to engage partners, the coherence of the EuCo may be preserved. Nevertheless, the visible German primacy exposes the fiction of the unanimity principle, and underscores that the Union's governance mode has become ostentatiously hegemonic. That even hegemons are, at times, willing to take a step back is then of small comfort only.

## 6. Conclusion

Before the entry into force of the Lisbon Treaty, there was ample evidence that illustrated how European Council action embodied 'determinative policy

98 Ibid.

99 'Ex-Advisor Criticises Barroso For Siding With Germany' *EUObserver* (7 April 2014) <http://euobserver.com/tickers/123772>.

100 Similarly Ulrich Beck, *German Europe* (London: Polity 2013).

choices that directed the action of the EU institutions, organs, bodies, and even Member States'.[101] Since 2009, the new European Council has made the most of its enhanced status as an official institution, producing evermore weighty output, making effective use of its additional competences, and in some respects, managing to expand their reach. In its inter-institutional relations, it thus acquired an absolute pole position. But one spectacular spin-off effect of this evolution is how the division of tasks and responsibilities within national cabinets and governments has become affected, putting pressure on traditional collegial relations to evolve into more hierarchical structures.[102] In result, we are confronted with a prime illustration of an actor buttressing its new-found autonomy.

At the same time, the idea that we are witnessing a relentless process of intergovernmentalisation, whereby the new European Council has increased the influence of national governments at the expense of the other EU institutions, does not capture the whole picture. Similarly, while it has been asserted before that Union governance is fragmented in that it knows no single, comprehensive and unitary executive, a more surreptitious fragmentation has now taken root as well.[103] Indeed, whereas the EuCo solidified its position at the top of the pecking order, its internal power balance has become heavily skewed. Consequently, in real life it is not so much the institution as a whole, but rather its President and some of its members, that seem to have made the most substantial gains. Formally, the EuCo remains a typical inter-governmental construct operating on the basis of a one-man-one-vote principle, generously allowing every party to block a proposal, in keeping with classic paradigms from the law of international organisations. Behind the scenes, however, the chair has begun to exert a most considerable influence, and a handful of countries with ever-greater regularity succeeds in pre-empting the other 20+ members – leaving room for fine-tuning, but hardly for fundamental discussions and negotiations. In reality, then, the EuCo contains but a small selection of veto players, in close resemblance of the UN Security Council. Thus, the image that arises is less one of an all-powerful monolithic actor, but rather of executive dominance by a select number of key players from within.[104] To an extent, of course, this has always been the case; yet the dynamic seems to have accelerated and intensified due to the Euro crisis. Put differently, the Member States may still be *Herren der Verträge*, but some of these gentlemen are clearly more equal than others; and today, the inequality appears greater than ever. The unravelling of the

101 Editorial Comments, 'Ever Mighty European Council' 1391.

102 Nederlof, Reestman and Vandamme, 'The European Council and The National Executives' 167.

103 Cf. Curtin, 'Challenging Executive Dominance' 6.

104 Garbling the 'intermediate sphere' identified by Luuk van Middelaar, *The Passage to Europe* (Yale University Press 2013).

Franco-German axis has, moreover, laid the notion of shared leadership to rest, so that we must currently wake up to the reality of a neo-hegemonic landscape.

The parallel current shows how the EuCo itself is increasingly being sidestepped under the pretext of a 'Union method', placing further strains on the institution's actorness. Again, therefore, the continuity and stability perceived by some may prove highly deceptive.[105] Different from national cabinets, the institution knows no collective responsibility, and offers ample room for abstentions or deviations. In this light, whereas it makes little sense to reinstate the abolished rotation system, the new semi-permanent Presidency has so far had *too little* impact. Handing the office additional powers in the near future should enable it to function as an effective counterweight; the alternative is to give away completely to the excruciating forces of fragmentation and neo-hegemony. What is more, institutional effectiveness also serves as a catalyst to strengthen the legitimacy of EU governance, even when still plagued by democratic shortcomings.[106] If instead the Union's most powerful institution is left to function as a common organ in the hands of a small selection of States that use it to advance their interests, this would lamentably vindicate the contractual view of international organisations that was supposedly outmoded long ago.[107]

105 Nederlof, Reestman and Vandamme, 'The European Council and The National Executives' 170.

106 Cf. the notion of output legitimacy outlined in Fritz Scharpf, *Governing in Europe: Effective and Democratic?* (OUP 1999). It nicely resounds in Van Rompuy's speech at Humboldt University ('Discovery of Co-Responsibility') 3: 'Legitimacy arises when people see, hear and feel that a political order benefits their prosperity, their freedom and security, that it safeguards their future.'

107 Cf. Carlo Santulli, 'Retour à la theorie de l'organe commun' [2012] *RGDIP* 565; compare also the contribution of Richard Collins to this volume.

# 5 Transnational parliamentarism and global governance

## The new practice of democracy

*Davor Jančić*

## 1 Introduction: the rise of transnational parliamentarism in the global age

The global age of today was born out of the necessity to solve policy problems affecting more than one state in a space that transcends political and legal borders of any such state. This transnational space is fed by globalisation and is constantly expanding thanks to ever-greater politico-economic interdependence between states and citizens. In order to regulate relations within this space, where no centralised enforcement authority exists, global governance was envisaged as a method of rule-making between formal actors in international affairs. As within states, the question of democracy in global governance was raised because the wielding of power by international organisations, institutions and actors was not matched by checks and balances that would ensure oversight over their decisions and thus secure a legitimacy linkage to their addressees.[1] One practical answer was the rise of transnational parliamentarism and thus the parliaments' emergence out of the 'shadows' of postnational rule-making.[2]

Ever since the establishment of the Inter-Parliamentary Union (IPU) in the late nineteenth century, namely in 1889, the idea of parliaments acting beyond the remits of the constitutional orders within which they have been established has grown steadily. The very existence of an 'international organisation of the parliaments of sovereign states', as the IPU Statute describes this body,[3] is quite telling of the rising trend towards drawing domestic parliaments and their members into the global arena. After the end of the Second World War and especially during the Cold War, the world witnessed the proliferation of the so-called international parliamentary institutions

1 Lluís Maria de Puig, *International Parliaments* (Council of Europe Publishing 2008) 17.
2 See the chapter by Fahey in this volume.
3 Article 1(1) thereof. See more on this institution in: Yefime Zarjevski, *The People Have the Floor: A History of the Inter-Parliamentary Union* (Nicholas Albrecht tr, Dartmouth Publishing 1989).

(IPIs).[4] In this period, all major international organisations in Western Europe, such as the Council of Europe (CoE), the European Coal and Steel Community as the precursor of the European Union (EU), the North Atlantic Treaty Organisation (NATO) and the Western European Union, were endowed with a parliamentary component. This wave of the parliamentarisation of intergovernmentalism later spread to the Latin American, African and Asian continents. To date, the literature has recorded the existence of no less than 100 various IPIs.[5] Moreover, many parliamentary bodies maintain bilateral relations, which, as we will see below, can develop within a given region or between regions. The political phenomenon of transnational parliamentarism thus provides a cognitive framework for encompassing all international parliamentary activities under one umbrella.

This chapter argues that, although occurring in the virtual absence of formal powers, the actorness of parliamentarians beyond the confines of the territory covered by their electoral constituencies, unveils new elements of democracy in the twenty-first century. Global governance accentuates the 'diplomatic' facet of parliamentary functions, which can aid the performance of the legislative and controlling tasks of parliaments. Their constitutional link with the citizenry, however, remains an important interest mediation chain, which relies on parliamentarians' representativeness in order to generate the legitimacy of global executive action.

In the following sections, this chapter conceptualises these new manifestations of parliamentary actorness beyond the state. To this end, I discuss the theoretical arguments about the international role of parliaments made by cosmopolitan and postnational variants of democracy and constitutionalism as two key structural devices for guaranteeing freedom, equality and justice in the political sphere. In doing so, legal and political science approaches are blended to furnish an interdisciplinary analysis of the merits of transnational parliamentarism for effecting more legitimate global governance. On that basis, I map out the variety of existing transnational parliamentary bodies by typifying them, examining their structure and operation, highlighting their functions, and probing their credentials for democratising transnational decision-making. This kind of inquiry follows the 'law in context' approach, whereby legal developments are integrated into, rather than insulated from, the perspectives of other related disciplines, including notably political studies

4 Robert Cutler, 'International Parliamentary Institutions as Organisations' (2013) 4 *Journal of International Organisations Studies* 104, 105; Christiane Kraft-Kasack, 'Transnational Parliamentary Assemblies: A Remedy for the Democratic Deficit of International Governance?' (2008) 31 *West European Politics* 534, 535. See also essays in: Olivier Costa *et al.* (eds), *Parliamentary Dimensions of Regionalisation and Globalisation: The Role of Inter-Parliamentary Institutions* (Palgrave Macmillan 2013).

5 Andrea Cofelice and Stelios Stavridis, 'The European Parliament as an International Parliamentary Institution (IPI)' (2014) 19 *European Foreign Affairs Review* 145, 145.

and legal empirical research.[6] The insights gained will permit the conclusion that parliamentarians are gradually piercing the veil of global governance and that this phenomenon changes how public authority is exercised and how institutional autonomy is shaped in the contemporary world.

## 2 Theorising the impact of global governance on the role of parliaments

Several different literature strands approach the issue of transnational parliamentarism insofar as they recognise the problem of ensuring democratic legitimacy in the rapid process of globalisation of public power.[7] This process seeks to address challenges that transcend state borders and that, for this reason, require concerted action by two or more polities to tackle them effectively. In turn, this gives rise to various transnational forms of law, politics and governance, which 'seriously threaten democratic control of foreign policy'.[8] Be it terrorism prevention or environment protection, the necessity of swift policy response to global predicaments by states or entities from different juridico-political and socio-cultural contexts frequently leads to shortcomings in the democratic nature of the mechanisms devised to address them. This is the primary factor that triggers the emergence of international, interregional and intraregional bodies of parliamentarians. The aggregate activity of these bodies forms the core of transnational parliamentarism, which is a facet of the global democratic endeavour.

The debate on the legitimacy of global governance revolves around the ideas of democracy and constitutionalism, which seek to achieve more just and prosperous conditions of life for its addressees by means of interest representation and constraint of public power. I examine below the manner in which theory employs these ideas to conceptualise political organisation and actorness beyond the state. The goal is to determine the role that theoretical models assign to parliaments as bodies whose *raison d'être* is to represent the interests of citizens. This is a question of increasing salience, because many key societal interests – such as trade, economics, international travel, security and environment – are nowadays no longer exclusively decided within the narrow confines of the legal order to which citizens are bound by means of their citizenship.

6 Rob van Gestel and Hans-Wolfgang Micklitz, 'Why Methods Matter in European Legal Scholarship' (2014) 20 *European Law Journal* 292, 314.

7 Michael Zürn, 'Global Governance and Legitimacy Problems' (2004) 39 *Government and Opposition* 260, 262.

8 Karl Kaiser, 'Transnational Relations as a Threat to the Democratic Process' (1971) 25 *International Organization* 706, 706.

### 2.1 Cosmopolitan and deliberative democracy

From the broadest perspective, *cosmopolitan democracy* theorists attach a degree of importance to the role of parliaments in the governance of the world. David Held correctly underlines that whereas state-based accountability was the platform on which the modern polity was built, this paradigm has become insufficient to understand and mould democratic accountability in a global age.[9] In his view, the democratisation of the cosmopolitan polity could be achieved by establishing 'an overarching network of democratic public forums, covering cities, nation-states, regions and the wider transnational order'.[10] This would entail not only the creation of a world assembly representing all states,[11] but also the establishment of regional parliaments and governance structures that would increase the legitimacy of regional and international decisions.[12] Similarly, Daniele Archibugi warns of the democracy problem emphasising that, with the exception of the EU, intergovernmental organisations as a rule do not envisage the participation of citizens in the decision-making process.[13] Ensuring the latter, namely to increase the accountability and transparency of global governance, is indeed a reason why the European Parliament (EP) advocated in 2011 the establishment of a United Nations Parliamentary Assembly.[14]

Yet one ought to bear in mind that participation through the electoral process is not the only way to secure democracy in global governance. As Grant and Keohane stress, focusing merely on democratic accountability neglects various forms of broader accountability effected over transnational power-wielding organisations by states (supervisory accountability) and

9 David Held, 'Democratic Accountability and Political Effectiveness from a Cosmopolitan Perspective' (2004) 39 *Government and Opposition* 364, 364.

10 Held (n 9) 383.

11 See accounts of this idea in: John S. Dryzek, 'Toward a Deliberative Global Citizens' Assembly' (2011) 2 *Global Policy* 33; Jürgen Habermas, 'The Constitutionalisation of International Law and the Legitimation Problems of a Constitution for World Society' (2008) 15 *Constellations* 444; Raffaele Marchetti, 'Global Governance or World Federalism? A Cosmopolitan Dispute on Institutional Models' (2006) 20 *Global Society* 287, 303; Richard Falk and Andrew Strauss, 'Toward Global Parliament' (2001) 80 *Foreign Affairs* 212; Richard Falk and Andrew Strauss, 'On the Creation of a Global Peoples Assembly: Legitimacy and the Power of Popular Sovereignty' (2000) 36 *Stanford Journal of International Law* 191.

12 Held (n 9) 384. See also: Christien van den Anker, 'Institutional Implications of Global Justice as Impartiality: Cosmopolitan Democracy' (2006) 20 *Global Society* 267, 282; Magdalena Bexell *et al.*, 'Democracy in Global Governance: The Promises and Pitfalls of Transnational Actors' (2010) 16 *Global Governance* 81, 87–88.

13 Daniele Archibugi, 'Cosmopolitan Democracy and Its Critics: A Review' (2004) 10 *European Journal of International Relations* 437, 449. One exception, however, is the provision for direct elections of the Mercosur Parliament.

14 Piia-Noora Kauppi *et al.*, *The Case for Global Democracy: Advocating a United Nations Parliamentary Assembly* (2nd ext edn, Committee for a Democratic UN 2010); Daniele Archibugi *et al.*, 'Introduction: Mapping Global Democracy' in Daniele Archibugi *et al.* (eds), *Global Democracy: Normative and Empirical Perspectives* (Cambridge University Press 2012) 1, 2.

money-lending institutions (fiscal accountability).[15] Even so, parliaments provide a valuable source for the democratisation of global affairs. Notably, while a global parliament is virtually impossible, 'enhanced political deliberation'[16] among parliamentarians is not. Indeed, even when they are not directly connected to an international organisation, Charnovitz warns that parliamentary confabulations have 'a political significance beyond typical nongovernmental activism' and carry 'an important potential for helping to improve global governance'.[17] Such processes of communication, information exchange, support, training and assistance between parliamentarians beyond their national electoral mandates, which are aimed at adopting and publicising their common positions on key global challenges, is what Anne-Marie Slaughter refers to as legislative networks.[18] These are a form of global networks operating alongside, and providing a counterweight to, those gathering national government officials and judges.[19]

As Cohen and Sabel argue, the emergence of global rule-making and, consequently, of global politics, requires not the creation of new institutions of electoral accountability based on the principal-agent model but the formation of the public sphere as the core condition for the functioning of democracy.[20] In a similar vein, Marchetti submits that the example of the EP indicates that international democratic institutions could have a 'notable "pedagogic" and civic role' to play in the maturation of a multilayered and heterogeneous global demos.[21] This is a strenuous task, holds Cerny, because global governance is less permeable to democratically grounded values and less capable of generating outcomes desired by the people.[22] This is why

15 Ruth W. Grant and Robert O. Keohane, 'Accountability and Abuses of Power in World Politics' (2005) 99 *American Political Science Review* 29, 37.

16 Patrizia Nanz and Jens Steffek, 'Global Governance, Participation and the Public Sphere' (2004) 39 *Government and Opposition* 314, 318. These two authors use this phrase to undergird the role of expert committees in remedying the legitimacy deficits in international governance, but it can very usefully and adequately be used for interparliamentary cooperation too.

17 Steve Charnovitz, 'Trans-Parliamentary Associations in Global Functional Agencies' (2002) 31 *Transnational Associations* 88, 88.

18 Anne-Marie Slaughter, 'Disaggregated Sovereignty: Towards the Public Accountability of Global Government Networks' (2004) 39 *Government and Opposition* 159, 161. See further in: Anne-Marie Slaughter, *A New World Order* (Princeton University Press 2004) 119 *et. seq.*

19 Slaughter, 'Disaggregated Sovereignty' (n 18) 184.

20 Joshua Cohen and Charles F. Sabel, 'Global Democracy' (2005) 37 *New York University Journal of International Law and Politics* 763, 766.

21 Raffaele Marchetti, 'Models of Global Democracy: In Defence of Cosmo-Federalism' in Daniele Archibugi *et al.* (eds), *Global Democracy: Normative and Empirical Perspectives* (Cambridge University Press 2012) 22, 28.

22 Philip G. Cerny, 'Globalisation and the Erosion of Democracy' (1999) 36 *European Journal of Political Research* 1, 6. There exist a myriad of non-State transnational actors whose actorness may have a bearing on the legitimacy of global governance, such as NGOs, corporations, various social movements, philanthropic foundations and diaspora groups. See essays in: Eva Erman and Anders Uhlin (eds), *Legitimacy beyond the State? Re-Examining the Democratic Credentials of Transnational Actors* (Palgrave Macmillan 2010). See also: Christer Jönsson and Jonas Tallberg (eds), *Transnational Actors in Global Governance: Patterns, Explanations and Implications* (Palgrave Macmillan, 2010).

Scholte is cautious about what he dubs 'suprastate parliaments', i.e. parliaments established beyond the Nation State, and maintains that although they have a role to play in global democracy by ensuring popular participation and control, they are not necessarily a *conditio sine qua non* thereof.[23] In particular, processes of soft regulation and rule-making on the regional and global scale are examples where hierarchical, state-based parliamentarisation has been assessed as a less adequate way of democratisation than open networks that embrace deliberative democratic principles and values.[24] This means that looser relationships between parliamentarians that do not operate according to the principal-agent model, which are indeed mushrooming at the international level, are more suitable for legitimising global governance, where authority is shared and dispersed across multiple executive actors.

Theorists of *deliberative democracy* also furnish a useful doctrinal framework for capturing the gist of transnational parliamentarism and its input into global governance, despite placing principal emphasis on direct citizen involvement in decision-making. Observing the potentialities of democratic deliberation on the global scale, a group of scholars have argued in favour of a systemic approach to democracy, whereby focus is on the interdependence of sites of deliberation rather than on the capability of each individual site to engender democratic rule. They rightly hold that no single deliberative venue possesses the capacity to legitimise most decisions and policies that a polity adopts. Instead, a multitude of mutually interacting forums are more conducive to civic inclusion. However, they tend to oversimplify the role of parliaments when they submit that 'parliamentary deliberation is confined to those forms of deliberation organised by states or subnational units'.[25] In fact, it is not. Transnational parliamentarism is precisely the phenomenon that opens the democratic gates of the Nation State and extends political representation, as the key element of representative democracy, to the world arena. Dryzek's account of transnational democracy equally ignores the role of parliaments in global governance and merely accentuates the functions of transnational civil society.[26] In his own inquiry of the matter, Somek explains that the conspicuous analytical absence of parliaments, elections, parties and voters from the constellation of transnational democracy is not accidental because they are deeply rooted in parliamentary democracy.[27] Similarly,

23 Jan Aart Scholte, 'Reinventing Global Democracy' (2014) 20 *European Journal of International Relations* 3, 12.

24 Ulrika Mörth, 'Soft Regulation and Global Democracy' in Marie-Laure Djelic and Kerstin Sahlin-Andersson (eds), *Transnational Governance: Institutional Dynamics of Regulation* (Cambridge University Press 2006) 119, 133.

25 Jane Mansbridge *et al.*, 'A Systemic Approach to Deliberative Democracy' in John Parkinson and Jane Mansbridge (eds), *Deliberative Systems: Deliberative Democracy at the Large Scale* (Cambridge University Press 2012) 1, 2.

26 John S. Dryzek, 'Transnational Democracy' (1999) 7 *Journal of Political Philosophy* 30, 46.

27 Alexander Somek, 'The Argument from Transnational Effects II: Establishing Transnational Democracy' (2010) 16 *European Law Journal* 375, 391.

Rosenau relies on the territorial unboundedness of the global space to argue that the concepts of representation and accountability are of limited relevance for depicting and constructing global democracy.[28]

Yet, what all of these accounts seem to undervalue is the fact that national parliaments already provide an institutional nexus between the executive branches of government and the citizenry and that this linkage is a crucial aspect of the international role of parliaments and parliamentarians.[29] Because they have a 'privileged', constitutionally guaranteed access to governments, which are the central international actors, parliaments are prime forums for both public and *in camera* deliberation. The international action of parliamentarians in turn feeds into the domestic political process and can be used to make claims in favour or against the global actorness of the executive and thus bolster or question the legitimacy thereof. The robustness and maturity of domestic mechanisms of democratic accountability seriously downplay the necessity to reconstruct electoral accountability on the global stage and exonerate the absence of parallel global mechanisms.

The vivid practice of transnational parliamentarism indeed begs a more nuanced assessment of the role of parliaments in global governance. Parliaments and their members are emphatically an element of transnational democracy and their international actorness evolves on a massive scale encompassing regional or interregional contexts, while a handful of organisations, such as notably the IPU and Parliamentarians for Global Action (PGA), have a universal outreach. It is precisely this international action of parliamentarians that modifies them into a different type of actor. Therefore, it is not that representation and accountability are less relevant in the global sphere, but that parliamentary actorness has taken on a novel form in a more or less organised attempt to counterbalance executive multilateralism and its decision-making opacity. The fact that the mechanics of parliamentary democracy are not watertight in the international realm, but are more diluted and elusive than in the national contexts, does little to discredit the value elected representatives can add to the input legitimacy of global policy-making. Global civil society activism has a different purpose and defends different interests than global parliamentary activism. The two activist camps may utilise similar tools to achieve their goals, but their institutional genetics and representative credentials are fundamentally different. Admittedly, however, the actual influence of transnational parliamentarism on executive decision-making processes may be marginal, yet that is an argument that is exogenous to the question of the nature of non-state transnational actors that act globally.

What transnational democratic theory proponents share is the commitment to the communicative diversification of the democratic process and its

28 James N. Rosenau, 'Governance and Democracy in a Globalising World' in Daniele Archibugi *et al.* (eds), *Re-Imagining Political Community: Studies in Cosmopolitan Democracy* (Stanford University Press 1998) 28, 40.

29 Puig (n 1) 22. See also *infra* text accompanying n 41.

deliberative quality. What they fail to appreciate sufficiently, however, is the fact that political deliberation also occurs within transnational parliamentary bodies, i.e. among elected officials acting outside the remits of their constituencies. In my view, the sum of transnational parliamentary bodies, focusing on a given region or policy field, could be conceived as a decentralised and rudimentary form of global parliamentarism.

## *2.2 Constitutionalism in the postnational global context*

As a concept chiefly aimed at ensuring limited government, constitutionalism is in the state of mutation due to numerous contemporary tendencies that challenge its state-oriented institutional fundament, such as the changing nature of international law, the thickening of global governance, the pluralist imagery of politico-legal authority, and the erosion of Westphalian sovereignty. All of these factors have impacted the role of parliaments. As a corollary, the latter have pierced the veil of the transnational policy-making arena and this aspect of parliamentary actorness deserves adequate scholarly attention.

To begin with, Mattias Kumm's argument that 'constitutionalism does not require the framework of a state to be meaningful'[30] and that therefore constitutionalism can be cosmopolitan despite the differing institutional structures of the state and of global governance provides a fertile analytical parallel for framing the phenomenon of transnational parliamentarism. This phenomenon occurs outside the state and its main protagonists are parliamentarians as actors elected in domestic constitutional settings and for domestic constitutional purposes. Their key competence is thus to perform the roles foreseen by the constitutions, whether formal or material, of their political community. However, for reasons not always spelled out in those constitutions, they engage in a diverse set of international activities and these activities are constitutionally meaningful because parliamentarians enjoy the status of official representatives of citizens. This is where Kumm's argument falters. One of the premises of his cosmopolitan constitutionalist paradigm is that international public authorities need not be subject to electoral accountability for their decisions and actions to be democratically legitimate; compliance with the principles of subsidiarity and good governance suffices.[31] His claim is that, since the legitimating virtues of the electoral process are lacking at the international level, 'central questions are whether, to what extent, and following which procedure the international community

30 Mattias Kumm, 'The Cosmopolitan Turn in Constitutionalism: On the Relationship between Constitutionalism in and beyond the State' in Jeffrey L. Dunoff and and Joel P. Trachtman (eds), *Ruling the World: Constitutionalism, International Law, and Global Governance* (Cambridge University Press 2009) 258, 263.

31 Kumm (n 30) 272, 296 and 301.

ought to have an effective say in decisions of public policy with significant externalities made by states'. While of critical importance, these very questions must be themselves answered through mechanisms that permit citizen involvement at the international level, failing which the involuntary implementation of such international decisions would be undemocratic and illegitimate. Therefore, in trying to export constitutionalism from the state to the global level, Kumm decouples democratic legitimacy from citizen participation and links it to the legitimacy of legal and political action in general and justifies it by the participation of a wide range of other actors. But these other actors, who may have a perfectly justified claim to contribute to the legitimisation of global governance,[32] do not necessarily represent the citizens, or represent only certain citizens, or do so from a perspective that is not aimed at furthering the public good. This cannot be countenanced as sound constitutional modelling because it denies the importance of *democratic* legitimacy understood as 'rule by the people', no matter how fictional or idealistic the principle may be in both national and international legal orders. The electoral process has a distinct purpose, which is rooted in its officiality and embodied in the ballot. No institution or group other than a parliament possesses this quality. This constitutional consideration cannot be ignored, regardless of the level at which decisions are made. Whether it is acceptable to substitute the electoral link with non-electoral arrangements ensuring the transparency and openness of transnational decision-making processes is another, completely different question, which falls outside of the scope of the present discussion.

This chapter subscribes to Gráinne de Búrca's view that 'the fact that a democratic system of the kind developed in the context of the nation state is not realisable for most forms of transnational governance is not a reason for abandoning the values or the language of democracy in the transnational context'.[33] She rightly holds that because people's lives are directly affected by transnational public policy decisions in ways comparable to the way they are affected by state public policy decisions, democracy plays essentially the same role and enjoys the same significance transnationally as it does nationally.[34] This means that the basic values of democracy – such as individual moral autonomy, human dignity, personal freedom, participation and influence over governance processes – function at the international stage all the same.[35] Such an approach enables us to conceive of transnational parliamentarism as a disaggregated apparatus for citizen participation in global governance,[36]

32 See, for instance: Jan Aart Scholte, *Building Global Democracy? Civil Society and Accountable Global Governance* (Cambridge University Press 2011).

33 Gráinne de Búrca, 'Developing Democracy beyond the State' (2008) 46 *Columbia Journal of Transnational Law* 221, 250.

34 Búrca (n 33) 240.

35 Búrca (n 33) 249.

36 See *supra* n 18.

thus securing a measure of democratic legitimacy of the decisions made at the international level, irrespective of the form in which they were adopted. Yet, in assessing the shift from classic international law to international law as governance, Kumm maintains that the national legislature and the national electoral process have ended up being 'the great institutional loser'.[37] He cites various forms of non-state transnational networks as 'significant participants in the international legal process', but completely neglects the fact that the same type of network exists among parliamentarians and that, as Slaughter shows, a burgeoning web of transnational parliamentary bodies deal precisely with the governance dimension of international lawmaking.[38]

When it comes to legitimising international 'legislation', i.e. decisions of international organisations that are binding on the Member States, the crucial role is indeed played by international parliamentary organs (IPOs), i.e. organs composed of elected representatives that belong to these organisations, such as the EP, the Parliamentary Assembly of the CoE, the Mercosur Parliament (Parlasur) or the Pan-African Parliament (PAP), all of which exercise varying degrees of power. These and other, more or less formalised, international networks of legislators, operating alongside governments, have been viewed as 'positive aspects of internationalisation in the sense that they may be able to contribute to the mutual understanding and accommodation between different national jurisdictions, and between the international and the national level'.[39] As Anne Peters submits, global constitutionalism and the production of primary and secondary international law should indeed rest on dual democracy, which is to be accomplished not only through the channel of states, but also by expanding and empowering IPOs. Her caveat that these are 'not parliaments in a constitutionalist sense',[40] for they lack the prerogatives that parliaments typically enjoy under the terms of their constitutions, is pertinent for an adequate understanding of the differing nature of the roles performed by parliamentarians domestically and transnationally. Despite the modest output and impact of IPOs, she underlines that even purely consultative assemblies add democratic value insofar as they mediate political interests, spark public debates and thereby increase the transparency of intergovernmental activity in a way diplomats do not. The dual mandate of parliamentarians, she warns, whereby they are members of both national parliaments and IPOs, is essential for frustrating the scapegoating practices

37 Mattias Kumm, 'The Legitimacy of International Law: A Constitutionalist Framework of Analysis' (2004) 15 *European Journal of International Law* 907, 915.

38 Anne-Marie Slaughter, 'Government Networks: The Heart of the Liberal Democratic Order' in Gregory H. Fox and Brad R. Roth (eds), *Democratic Governance and International Law* (Cambridge University Press 2000) 199, 218–219.

39 Geir Ulfstein, 'Institutions and Competences' in Jan Klabbers *et al.*, *The Constitutionalisation of International Law* (Oxford University Press 2009) 45, 59.

40 Anne Peters, 'Dual Democracy' in Jan Klabbers *et al.*, *The Constitutionalisation of International Law* (Oxford University Press 2009) 263, 322.

of governments by publicising information about their international conduct.[41] The principal-agent link, which lies at the heart of parliamentary democracy, is hence central to this approach.

Nevertheless, as Nico Krisch argues, the postulates of parliamentary democracy, grounded in delegation and control, are less optimal for constructing the accountability of global governance, not least because of the lack of a democratic parliamentary anchor, the growing multiplicity of principals and agents in the international arena, and the consequent fragmentation of the delegation chain.[42] The utensils of domestic constitutionalism are thus merely one aspect of the legitimisation of global governance. In defending his pluralist alternative to postnational constitutionalism, Krisch rightly emphasises that whereas the global polity is incapable of ensuring as thick and effective democratic participation as national polities are, construing democracy beyond and within the state as complementary processes may help reach compromises in achieving global democratic ideals.[43] The pluralist vision thus provides a fruitful cognitive frame for envisioning transnational parliamentarism. It does so inasmuch as it propagates the necessity to limit one's expectations from democratic globalism and acknowledges the benefit of parallel, though structurally and functionally imperfect, transboundary political communication without the pressing need to house ultimate authority in any given institution, polity or level of governance. The admission that 'some of the plurality of decision-making institutions would have to be replicated in the structures designed to hold them accountable'[44] is a generalised ratification of what transnational parliamentarism's core business is: to provide 'lightweight' constraint to intergovernmentalism and secure its democratic accompaniment through the use of a less ambitious participatory toolbox, which is as such adjusted to the global setting in recognition of the little resemblance the latter bears to its domestic counterparts.

David Kennedy's vision of the development of global governance through the diffusion of decision-making to the sites of transnational authority, thus opening new forums for political struggle and heterogeneity,[45] is also consonant with the aggregate consequence of transnational parliamentarism, which is the multiplication of the *loci* of democratic contestation of executive action. More concretely, Neil Walker maintains that even transnational

41 Peters (n 40) 323–324.

42 Nico Krisch, 'Global Administrative Law and the Constitutional Ambition' in Martin Loughlin and Petra Dobner (eds), *The Twilight of Constitutionalism* (Oxford University Press 2010) 245, 248 and 260.

43 Nico Krisch, *Beyond Constitutionalism: The Pluralist Structure of Postnational Law* (Oxford University Press 2010) 86 and 266.

44 Krisch (n 43) 269.

45 David Kennedy, 'The Mystery of Global Governance' in Jeffrey L. Dunoff and and Joel P. Trachtman (eds), *Ruling the World? Constitutionalism, International law, and Global Governance* (Cambridge University Press 2009) 37, 67.

regulatory systems that are remote from the constituency-based methods of legitimisation, which are typical for the Nation State, are capable of nurturing a sense of 'a meta-democratically validated transnational political community'.[46] In particular, he invokes transnational parliamentarism, and especially the emergence of IPOs, as a means of the democratic regeneration of international organisations.[47] As Armin von Bogdandy contends, the EU's dual democratic legitimation, stemming not only from the Member States but also from the EP as an autonomous source, vindicates the argument that transnational parliamentary bodies can be considered to possess the capacity for democratic legitimation even if they do not represent one people or one nation and do not fully embody the principle of electoral equality, as long as they 'operate in a transparent and deliberative way embedded in and responsive to the affected publics'.[48]

In the following sections, I examine the more practical aspects of transnational parliamentarism, such as its typology, structure and practical operation, as well as its functions and impact on the democratisation of global governance.

## 3 The practice of transnational parliamentarism

### *3.1 Typology of transnational parliamentary bodies*

Transnational parliamentarism is a broad phrase that encompasses all manner of activities of parliaments and parliamentarians outside the remits of their constitutional orders. In order to grasp the diversity of transnational parliamentarism, it is necessary to categorise the existing IPIs and the different forms in which they are manifested.[49] The current literature on IPIs distinguishes between essentially three categories thereof: (a) international parliamentary organs, which are mentioned hereinabove as IPOs; (b) international parliamentary associations (IPAs); and (c) interparliamentary GRINGOs (Government Run or Inspired Non-Governmental Organisations).[50]

46 Neil Walker, 'Postnational Constitutionalism and Postnational Public Law: A Tale of Two Neologisms' (2012) 3 *Transnational Legal Theory* 61, 79.

47 Walker (n 46) 80.

48 Armin von Bogdandy, 'The European Lesson for International Democracy: The Significance of Articles 9–12 EU Treaty for International Organisations' (2012) 23 *European Journal of International Law* 315, 326 and 328.

49 See more in: Special Issue 'Parliamentary Diplomacy Uncovered: European and Global Perspectives' *The Hague Journal of Diplomacy*, Stelios Stavridis and Davor Jančić (eds), forthcoming in 2015.

50 Zlatko Šabič, 'Building Democratic and Responsible Global Governance: The Role of International Parliamentary Institutions' (2008) 61 *Parliamentary Affairs* 255, 258; Cofelice and Stavridis (n 5) 149; Claudia Kissling, *The Legal and Political Status of International Parliamentary Institutions* (Committee for a Democratic UN 2011).

The *first category*, IPOs, can be divided into two sub-categories. On the one hand, there are classic IPOs, which belong to an international or regional intergovernmental organisation. They cover virtually all continents, and examples include the Parliamentary Assembly of the CoE (1949), the EP (1951), the Nordic Council (1952), OSCE Parliamentary Assembly (1992), ECOWAS Parliament (2000), East African Legislative Assembly (EALA) (2001), PAP (2004), Andean Parliament (Parlandino) (1984), Parlasur (1994), Parliamentary Assembly of the Black Sea Economic Cooperation (1993), and the Arab Parliament (2010). One the other hand, there exist more novel IPOs, which belong to multilateral forms of cooperation that do not constitute international organisations as such. Here, we can admit the ACP (Africa-Caribbean-Pacific)-EU Joint Parliamentary Assembly (1963), the Parliamentary Assembly of the Union for the Mediterranean (1998), the Euro-Latin American Parliamentary Assembly (EuroLat) (2006), and the EURONEST Parliamentary Assembly (2009).

The *second category*, IPAs, encompasses independent, self-constituted IPIs that do not officially belong to any international organisation. Within this category, too, one can discern two sub-categories. One sub-category includes those IPIs whose operation is tightly linked to an international organisation or a mutilateral form of cooperation without being an official organ thereof. They therefore resemble IPOs but are not IPOs. One author dubs them 'parliamentary specialised agencies' to underline this specificity.[51] Notable examples are the NATO Parliamentary Assembly (1955), the ASEAN Inter-parliamentary Assembly (1977), the Baltic Assembly (1991), and the SADC Southern African Development Community Parliamentary Forum (1997). The other sub-category refers to IPIs that are entirely autonomous from any other organisation, such as the aforesaid IPU (1889), the Latin American Parliament (Parlatino) (1964), the Amazonian Parliament (1969), and the Parliamentary Confederation of the Americas (1997).

The *third category*, interparliamentary GRINGOs, is composed of more loosely organised IPIs that gather national parliamentarians who act in a private capacity in pursuit of independent initiatives with the aim of realising certain political and economic objectives by lobbying and cooperating with state or international institutions.[52] This is what makes them akin to NGOs. Interparliamentary GRINGOs can be area-related or issue-related. Examples of area-related interparliamentary GRINGOs are the Commonwealth Parliamentary Association (1911), Interparliamentary Forum of the Americas (2001), Asia Pacific Parliamentary Forum (1993) and various speakers' conferences, such as those related to the G8 (2002), the Council of Europe (1988), the EU (1963) or West Africa (1999). Issue-related interparliamentary GRINGOs, for instance, include: the aforesaid PGA (1978), which

51 Kissling (n 50) 26.
52 Kissling (n 50) 13.

concentrates on the work of the United Nations and promotes peace, democracy, human rights and the rule of law; the Association of European Parliamentarians with Africa (1984), which focuses on the eradication of poverty and development on that continent; the International Medical Parliamentarians Organisation (1994), which cooperates with the World Health Organisation, has regional subdivisions and addresses matters of health and medical care; the Global Organisation of Parliamentarians Against Corruption (2000), which was initiated and is sponsored by the World Bank and has no less than 13 regional branches; the Parliamentary Network on the World Bank (2000); the International Parliamentarians' Association for Agriculture and Fisheries (2000), which focuses on influencing the World Trade Organisation; the Global Legislators Organisation for a Balanced Environment (1989); and Parliamentarians for Nuclear Non-Proliferation and Disarmament (2001).[53]

One other classification is pertinent for the present purposes. Robert Cutler very usefully typifies IPIs according to their stage of development and the powers they enjoy. His 'epigenetic' scheme holds that IPIs come in the form a congress, assembly, parliament and legislature. A *congress* occurs at the very beginning of the life cycle of an IPI as the initial gathering of parliamentarians intent on establishing a more permanent structure with very few powers. Following in these footsteps, an *assembly* represents a first regularised form of transnational parliamentary body which possesses its own secretariat and, with time, acquires powers to create rules and perform advisory oversight over its own functioning and, at a later phase, over other organisations. An assembly grows into a *parliament* when its supervisory competence starts having a deterrent effect on the international or regional organisation to which it is affiliated or on another relevant intergovernmental centre of public authority. As the most advanced form of transnational parliamentary body, a *legislature* comes into being when it becomes empowered to exercise full-blown legislative authority within an international or other relevant organisation.[54]

### *3.2 Structure and operation of transnational parliamentary bodies*

The IPIs presented and classified above, particularly IPOs and IPAs, are the most important agents of transnational parliamentarism due to their structural characteristics, which, albeit to a variable extent, guarantee their competences, longevity and visibility. However, besides IPIs as multilateral forms of interparliamentary collaboration, the political praxis bears witness to multifarious bilateral forms of transnational parliamentarism that carry out important policy-oriented tasks intraregionally, i.e. within a given region,

53 See Tables 1 and 2 in: Kissling (n 50) 54–67.
54 Cutler (n 4) 112.

or interregionally, i.e. between two or more regions. Saliently, not only do national parliamentarians engage in bilateral transnational relations, members of supranational or regional integration parliaments do too.

These bilateral interparliamentary relations beyond the state unravel between domestic parliaments themselves, as well as between domestic parliaments, on the one hand, and transnational parliamentary bodies, on the other. The case of EU integration is of particular significance here because, reflecting the 'many faces of rulemaking' within its midst,[55] it hosts the most developed form of transnational parliamentarism and exhibits a wealth of such bilateral relations.[56] These include relations: (a) between national parliaments themselves (e.g. Franco-German parliamentary liaison); (b) between national parliaments and the EP (e.g. a whole array of joint parliamentary or committee meetings and interparliamentary conferences on the Common Foreign and Security Policy and the Common Security and Defence Policy, on Economic and Financial Governance of the EU, and COSAC which gathers members of the European affairs committees of national parliaments and MEPs); (c) between EU national parliaments and non-EU national parliaments or transnational parliamentary bodies (e.g. relations between the Spanish *Cortes Generales* and certain Latin American parliaments); (d) between the EP and non-EU national parliaments (e.g. the EP-US Congress relations in the form of the Transatlantic Legislators' Dialogue[57] or the EP-Brazilian National Congress relations); and (e) between the EP and other IPIs, such as relations between the EP and Parlasur or between the EP and Parlatino. The last type is specific because it represents relations between two IPIs, which also exist in the multilateral form, such as, for instance, EuroLat.

These bilateral frameworks are institutionalised forms of parliamentarism beyond the state and can represent important channels for interparliamentary discussion and communication on global, regional or domestic policy making. This militates their placement on the world map of transnational parliamentarism.

55 See the chapter by Ruffert in this volume.

56 See various aspects thereof in: Christina Bengtson, 'Interparliamentary Cooperation within Europe' in John O'Brennan and Tapio Raunio (eds), *National Parliaments Within the Enlarged European Union: From Victims of Integration to Competitive Actors?* (Routledge 2007) 46; Cristina Fasone, 'Interparliamentary Cooperation and Democratic Representation in the European Union' in Sandra Kröger and Dawid Friedrich (eds), *The Challenge of Democratic Representation in the European Union* (Palgrave Macmillan 2012) 41; Donatella M. Viola, 'Interparliamentary Cooperation in the European Union: Towards Multilevel Governance' in G.P.E. Walzenbach (ed.), *European Governance: Policy Making between Politicisation and Control* (Ashgate 2006) 165.

57 Davor Jančić, 'The European Parliament and EU-US Relations: Revamping Institutional Cooperation' in Elaine Fahey and Deirdre Curtin (eds), *A Transatlantic Community of Law: Legal Perspectives on the Relationship between the EU and US Legal Orders* (Cambridge University Press 2014) 35; Davor Jančić, 'The Transatlantic Connection: Democratising Euro-American Relations Through Parliamentary Liaison' in Stelios Stavridis and Daniela Irrera (eds), *The European Parliament and its International Relations* (Routledge 2015) 183.

As concerns the actual operation of transnational parliamentarism, it is crucial to note that it develops not only within the abovementioned IPIs as isolated forums as presented above, but also in multiple layers across various bilateral and multilateral forums whenever the same parliaments are represented in more than one forum devoted to the same region. As I demonstrate elsewhere, interparliamentary relations between the EU and Brazil and the broader Latin American parliamentary outcry against the EU's enactment of the Returns Directive in 2008 was exemplary of the way in which the same parliamentary institutions act within different forums to maximise their goals. In this particular case, the Brazilian National Congress and the EP have engaged in political dialogue on the substance of this Directive not only bilaterally, but also multilaterally through pronouncements by Parlatino, Parlasur and EuroLat.[58]

## 4 Functions and impact of transnational parliamentarism on the democratisation of global governance

Transnational parliamentarism is one of the key institutional responses to the effect that globalisation and global governance have had on domestic democratic practices. As many constitutive acts of IPIs reveal,[59] it represents a concerted attempt by elected officials to address the problem of democratic legitimacy of global governance.

This chapter argues that the externalisation of rule-making beyond the state brings sociological, non-constitutional functions of parliaments to the fore. This is because parliaments acting within states enjoy constitutionally guaranteed and enforceable rights of participation in the governing of the polity that they do not enjoy outside the confines of the state framework. Reviews by a number of scholars document this state of affairs. A 2014 survey of the formal powers of the EP, CoE Parliamentary Assembly, EALA and the ASEAN Interparliamentary Assembly concludes that, apart from the EP as the clear leader of the ranking, IPIs on the whole score fairly low on matters

58 Davor Jančić, 'Multilayered International Parliamentarism: The Case of EU-Brazil Relations' (2014) *LSE Law, Economy and Society Working Paper 17/2014*, <www.lse.ac.uk/collections/law/wps/WPS2014–17_Jancic.pdf> accessed 18 November 2014.

59 For instance, the EuroLat Constitutive Act (Article 5(a) thereof) states that it is a forum for 'parliamentary debate, control and review of all questions relating to the Biregional European Union-Latin American and Caribbean Strategic Partnership, as the parliamentary institution of the Partnership'. The NATO Parliamentary Assembly's mission statement shows that its goal is to 'discuss and influence decisions on Alliance security' and 'support national parliamentary oversight over defence and security'. See <www.nato-pa.int/default.asp?SHORTCUT=1> accessed 18 November 2014. Even the IPU Statute (Article 1(b)–(c) thereof) states that the purposes of this IPI are *inter alia* to 'consider questions of international interest and express its views on such issues with the aim of bringing about action by parliaments and their members' and to 'contribute to the defence and promotion of human rights, which are universal in scope and respect for which is an essential factor of parliamentary democracy and development'.

of accountability, legislative powers, transparency and democracy support.[60] The key impediment for their further empowerment, the study finds, is the reluctance of governmental actors to submit themselves to further layers of scrutiny. Another collaborative study, published in 2013, assessed the role of IPIs in the regionalisation and globalisation processes. Based on the analysis of the EP and the major regional integration parliaments in Latin America, Africa, Asia, the Afro-Carribean-Pacific region, the Mediterranean region, and the Baltic Sea region, the authors concluded that the EP's constant rise in power is indeed an anomaly compared to other IPIs.[61] Many other smaller-scale appraisals share the finding that transnational parliamentarism suffers from more or less severe authoritative incapacity.[62]

At the global level, therefore, transnational parliamentary bodies act in pursuit of goals that do not mirror those pursued within their domestic legal orders. Accent is no longer on legislating and controlling as purely constitutional functions as prescribed by domestic law, but on deliberation and communication as political and sociological determinants of democratic legitimacy. Hence, once parliaments step outside of their legal orders, they exercise different functions. Most of them exercise few or no binding powers. Most of them meet infrequently. Yet arguing that transnational parliamentarism is superfluous because of the diminished authoritative powers of IPIs in world affairs misses the point that functions that are exercised transnationally are not the same. On the world stage, parliamentarians are different actors. They are diplomats, not legislators. They are public tribunes, not controllers. However, thanks to the parliamentarians' electoral and representative pedigree, their transnational functions are significant for the politicisation and democratisation of global governance despite the restricted arsenal of powers that they exercise directly at the international level.[63]

From a broader point of view, just as 'the absence of a single world constitutional order [. . .] should not blind us to the ever-increasing relevance of international cooperation and concomitant legal regulation for individual

60 Georgios Papanagnou *et al.*, *Democracy Building in the Regional Context: Insights from the European Parliament and Beyond* (International IDEA and UNU-CRIS 2014) 38–39.

61 Olivier Costa *et al.*, 'Conclusions' in Olivier Costa *et al.* (eds), *Parliamentary Dimensions of Regionalisation and Globalisation: The Role of Inter-parliamentary Institutions* (Palgrave Macmillan 2013) 231, 239.

62 See, for example, the assesssment that PAP has 'no contraining power' but has 'a large consultative and advisory role'. Julien Navarro, 'The Creation and Transformation of Regional Parliamentary Assemblies: Lessons from the Pan-African Parliament' (2010) 16 *Journal of Legislative Studies* 195, 202.

63 For instance, the competences of the ACP-EU Joint Parliamentary Assembly are limited to those of a 'consultative body that cannot exercise control over the budgets or the executives', but it has succeeded in exerting 'a certain degree of influence' thanks to the domestic prerogatives of its members. See: Sarah Delputte, 'The ACP-EU Joint Parliamentary Assembly Seen by Its Members: Empowering the Voice of People's Representatives' (2012) 17 *European Foreign Affairs Review* 241, 245.

human beings',[64] such as placing individuals on international terrorist lists, so the absence of a global government, global demos and global constituency should not blind us to the growing importance of transnational parliamentarism. The latter lies in ensuring the openness, transparency and fairness of international cooperation through interparliamentary dialogue and political evaluation of the desirability of policy approaches taken by the global and regional executive actors.

The primary functions of transnational parliamentarism complement those that form the basis of statal constitutionalist principles of limited and representative government. IPIs generate the greatest benefits for global governance and rulemaking through activities that have variously been described as advocacy,[65] institutional pressure, deliberation, communication, socialisation, networking, lobbying,[66] norm entrepreneurship, value promotion, diplomacy, prevention and arbitration of conflicts, capacity and confidence-building. These are all elements of the principle of democracy *lato sensu* insofar as they indirectly underpin and support the untrammeled functioning of constitutionalism. These functions are primordial inasmuch as they are secondary to those of making law and holding exponents of the public authority to account. This is not surprising if one flips the coin and inquires whether the authority of global governance is as high as to necessitate state-like structures for guaranteeing the achievement of democratic policy outcomes, because this question, in my opinion, must be answered in the negative. Organisations and mechanisms of governance still do not possess the level of autonomy from the Nation State that would warrant the institution of state-like channels of constitutionalism at the global level. Whether or not the current state of development of transnational parliamentarism is sufficient, adequate or appropriate is a matter for a different discussion.

## 5 Concluding remarks

The legal and political science approaches to the democratisation of global governance surveyed in this chapter pay no more than marginal attention to the transnational parliamentary evolution and, as a result, they tend to overlook the democratic advantages that such evolution may carry. One of

64 Andreas L. Paulus, 'The International Legal System as a Constitution' in Jeffrey L. Dunoff and and Joel P. Trachtman (eds), *Ruling the World? Constitutionalism, International Law, and Global Governance* (Cambridge University Press 2009) 69, 70.

65 In functional terms, one may also conceive of international parliamentarism in the context of transnational advocacy networks because transnational parliamentary bodies frequently resort to advocacy techniques to achieve their goals. See: Margaret E. Keck and Kathryn Sikkink, *Activists Beyond Borders: Advocacy Networks in International Politics* (Cornell University Press 1998) 9.

66 See on non-parliamentary lobbying the chapter by Korkea-aho in this volume.

the focal divergences between the two approaches is the importance they attach to the electoral dimension of democracy, which is the nuclear component of domestic parliamentarism and constitutionalism. It is through elections that citizens give their assent to be governed by rules adopted by the representatives they elect in a fair procedure. While the advocates of cosmopolitan democracy view the legitimation of global governance as preferably stemming from a single overarching source, systemic deliberative democracy adherents stress the importance of the 'democratic' spread across sites and forums. Constitutionalist models also differ as to the centrality of elections for legitimising global governance. While cosmopolitan constitutionalism rejects the significance of elections in this respect, a number of postnational constitutionalists, implicitly or explicitly, regard them as the cornerstone of global democracy. In my view, electoral legitimacy and accountability are paramount ingredients for democratising global governance. Electoral processes matter not necessarily as a method of constituting a transnational parliamentary body, but as a tool for proffering to global governance a constitutionally relevant linkage to the citizens, domestic public spheres and domestic politics.

In structural terms, transnational parliamentarism is inspired by national parliamentarism insofar as both aspire to ensure popular representativeness. In functional terms, there is a gaping discrepancy between the prerogatives of national and transnational parliaments, with the latter considerably lagging behind. Supranational parliamentarism, epitomised by the EP as the world's most advanced transnational parliamentary body, provides influential agency in the transnational domain. Not only does the EP exhibit leadership in establishing novel forms of transnational parliamentarism, it provides a model for the incremental evolution of it. Institutional mimicry is indeed widely acknowledged as one of the principal effects that the EP has had on generative parliamentary endeavours beyond the state in many regions of the world.[67] The development of transnational parliamentary activities and the sheer variety of the shapes they take are a consequence of the globalisation of policy making and the relocation of a portion of public authority away from the state. Transnational parliamentarism helps to strengthen the loosened link between the domestic and global exercise of public power.

Due to the proliferation of the transnational action of parliamentarians, their functions are in flux. They may be deemed to be at an early stage of transition from being purely 'internal' players of their polities to being 'mixed' players of the global polity. Parliamentary action beyond borders moreover illustrates the porousness and utility of domestic constitutionalism, as well as the transformation of the Nation State. The totality of transnational parliamentary action is a composite way to provide a form of democratic check

67 See further: Clarissa Dri, 'Limits of the Institutional Mimesis of the European Union: The Case of the Mercosur Parliament' (2010) 1 *Latin American Policy* 52.

on global governance. It steers parliamentarians towards deliberative and 'diplomatic' aspects of their democratic capacity. It also affects the notion of parliamentary democracy to the extent that parliaments are no longer solely a governance tool for the use within the Nation State, but also beyond it. Yet mechanisms of parliamentary democracy, whereby the government of the day depends on parliamentary support to remain in power, are weaker in the transnational domain. Still, they are not inexistent. Although it is difficult to measure the influence of transnational parliamentary bodies on international affairs, they constitute important mediums for civic inclusion and participation, political contestation and pluralism, and generally, for the prevention of the democratic alienation of executive actors. Whether this will bring about 'a profound change in parliamentarianism as we have known it', as a former President of the CoE Parliamentary Assembly seems to suggest, remains to be seen.[68]

68 Puig (n 1) 8.

# 6 Interaction as a site of postnational rule-making

## A case study of the Inter-American system of human rights

*Rene Urueña*

One central characteristic of postnational governance is the decline of formal intergovernmental organisations as the preferred sites of rule-making. Keohane *et al.* report that growth rate in IGO creation has declined in 20 per cent since the beginning of the twenty-first century; moreover, the increase in the total number of multilateral agreements in force between 2002 and 2012 was only 36 per cent, down from 146 per cent in the 1990s.[1] At the same time, other forms of governance have emerged: regulatory networks (such as the Basel Committee on Banking Supervision),[2] public-private entities (such as the International Organization for Standardization (ISO)),[3] and purely private entities (such as the Fédération Internationale de Football Association (FIFA))[4] or privatised public utilities at the transnational level,[5] among many others, have become crucial players in determining the distribution of global regulatory power today.

These transformations have revealed important blind spots in the notion of 'actor' that underlies legal scholarship, particularly the body of work concerned with the practice and experience of law beyond the Nation State. As Elaine Fahey's introduction suggests, as postnational legal practices increase, the notion of actor in rule-making increasingly needs to strike a difficult balance between formalism and flexibility: not every act or practice that has a cross-border effect can be deemed relevant for postnational rule-making, but the narrow concept of international law's international legal

1 Kenneth W. Abbott, Jessica F. Green, and Robert O. Keohane, 'Organizational Ecology and Organizational Strategies in World Politics', *Harvard Kennedy School of Government Discussion Papers* 13–57 (2013).

2 See Anne-Marie Slaughter and David Zaring, "Networking Goes International: An Update', *Annual Review of Law and Social Science* 2, no. 1 (December 2006): 211–229.

3 See Jan Klabbers, 'Reflections on Soft International Law in a Privatized World', *Finnish Yearbook of International Law* 16 (2005): (exploring soft law regulation by the ISO).

4 See L. Casini, *Il diritto globale dello sport* (Milano: Giuffrè, 2010).

5 See Bronwen Morgan, *Water on Tap: Rights and Regulation in the Transnational Governance of Urban Water Services* (Cambridge: Cambridge University Press, 2011).

personality seems unhelpful.[6] While the changing political landscape of global governance seems to require a more flexible approach to 'actorness', a normative (or 'formalist', in Fahey's terms) threshold is still needed to assess which 'actors' *should* be allowed to contribute to international norms, formal or informal. To refer to two well-known examples of new 'actors' in global governance: while it makes intuitive sense to accept that non-governmental organisations promote labelling standards that protect the environment and which may, in practice, end up having the effect of a global norm,[7] it seems less intuitive to accept that mining corporations define the environmental and human rights norms under which their behaviour is assessed.[8] While the notion of 'actorness' needs to be flexible enough to register non-State rule-makers, it still cannot accept as rule-makers all those who happen to have the power or influence to push their particular agenda under the effigy of informal norms.

Part of the challenge with striking this delicate balance is the way the 'action' is understood. Two ways of framing the issue stand out. On the one hand, much work has been produced in international relations (IR), where a central focus has been *whose* actions count (or should count) in terms of world politics. The key question there is what how to identify the actor, and the standard realist answer is that State actions count, which makes states central 'actors'. But others may count as well: individuals, networks of activists or regulators, and so on. All these, then, are 'actors' whose behaviour matter in terms of description of the dynamics of power.[9] In contrast, legal scholarship, particularly the most innovative work in international and transnational law, has focused on identifying *what* actions count as a matter of rule-making. Thus, legal scholars have strived to propose external normative criteria, of a legal character, that would help identify the behaviour that should count towards building transnational norm – for example, the international public authority project,[10] and some of the more theoretical work on global administrative law,[11] among others. Instead of characterizing the actor, as IR

6 See generally, Janne Elisabeth Nijman, *The Concept of International Legal Personality: An Inquiry into the History and Theory of International Law* (The Hague; New York: T.M.C. Asser Press, 2004).

7 See Samir R. Gandhi, 'Voluntary Environmental Standards: The Interplay Between Private Initiatives, Trade Rules and the Global Decision-Making Processes', in 3rd Global Administrative Law Seminar (Viterbo, Italy: IRPA, 2007), http://iilj.org/gal/documents/Ghandienvironment.pdf.

8 See John Gerard Ruggie, *Just Business: Multinational Corporations and Human Rights* (New York: W.W. Norton & Company, 2013), pp. 37–80.

9 For a useful summary of the IR debate on state-centrism and the possibility of other actos, see John M. Hobson, *The State and International Relations* (Cambridge; New York: Cambridge University Press, 2000), pp. 1–10.

10 Armin von Bogdandy, 'General Principles of International Public Authority: Sketching a Research Field', in *The Exercise of Public Authority by International Institutions*, ed. Armin von Bogdandy *et al.* (Heidelberg: Springer, 2010), pp. 727–760.

11 Benedict Kingsbury, 'The Concept of "Law" in Global Administrative Law', *European Journal of International Law* 20, no. 1 (2009): 23–57.

theories do, these efforts provide an indirect answer to the question of 'actorness' in postnational rule-making: the actor is the player who fulfils the normative criteria that each framework proposes, regardless of whether they are private or public, national or international, formal or informal.

This chapter builds on these latter contributions, but suggests that the problem with their way of reading the issue is that they assume that the 'actor' that participates in postnational rule-making exists in a vacuum, undertaking 'actions' that are discrete events unrelated to other 'actions'. From this perspective, the role of the scholar is to isolate the action that is being studied (for example, an investment tribunal award, or a terrorist list adopted by the Security Council), and then classify it according to a pre-established normative criterion, in order to draw conclusion of its 'actorness'.

Against this view, this chapter suggests that such a way of framing the issue obscures the important dynamics of interaction. 'Actors' in global governance are not discrete entities that exist independently from each other, but are rather part of a wider landscape that defines their 'actorness'. Quite on the contrary, they are expressions, and form part of a changing global regulatory space, in which they interact. Thinking in terms of interaction, I suggest, provides the basis for a different conceptualisation of the architecture of postnational rule-making. This general landscape, though, is not useful in the abstract. We need to understand, in practice, the trajectories of institutions as they influence each other. Beyond the appeal of the general narrative of interaction, it seems important to look to specific instances of interaction.

There are different possibilities to research this constant: one way is to investigate the interaction of international institutions, and map the different modes of interaction (cooperation, competition, etc.).[12] A different approach has been to use the metaphor of an 'ecosystem', and think of the interaction between institutions as a problem of evolution and competition for scarce resources.[13] Others, in turn, have tried to make sense of regime complexity.[14] The choice made here is to look at specific dynamics of interaction in a case study in Latin America. This paper will explore rule-making in the context of the Inter-American system of human rights, and contrasts two readings of rule-making in that context. On the one hand, the dominant narrative, according to which human rights rule-making in Latin America is a constitutional process, with the Inter-American Court of Human Rights

12 For example, *Regime Interaction in International Law: Facing Fragmentation*, ed. Margaret Young (Cambridge: Cambridge University Press, 2012). For a summary of similar efforts outside international law, see Oberthür and Gehring, 'Institutional Interaction: Ten Years of Scholarly Development'.

13 Abbott, Green, and Keohane, 'Organizational Ecology and Organizational Strategies in World Politics'.

14 Karen J. Alter and Sophie Meunier, 'The Politics of International Regime Complexity', *Perspectives on Politics* 7, no. 1 (2009): 13–24.

(IACtHR) at the top. This view, defended by the Court itself and by most scholars in the region, is then contrasted with a reading based on interaction among institutions that occur in a global regulatory space, in particular the interaction between the IACtHR and domestic courts.

Thinking in terms of a regulatory space as a site of rule-making, this chapter argues, allows us to better appreciate the complex dynamics of postnational lawmaking, and the important political stakes of interaction. In particular, this chapter argues that 'actors' enter a populated regulatory space, where they *adapt* to the other actors that exist in that space. Rule-making is, therefore, not only the product of the will of an actor, but also of a subtle process of adaptation to the other players in the field. This means, moreover, that institutions have less 'tunnel vision'[15] than one might expect: against the view that regimes and institutions have a 'structural bias'[16] and push it as hard as they can, we observe a process of change in the institution's internal rationale.

This chapter proceeds in the following way. The next section introduces the constitutional reading of international rule-making, and describes its two pillars: 'control de convencionalidad' (control of conventionality), and the domestic constitutional provisions that integrate the Inter-American Convention to several legal systems in the region. Then, section 2 points out some of the challenges of this constitutional reading, and proposes a different approach: rule-making interaction, which allows us to see some of the dynamics of power and change that remain obscure in the constitutional reading. This approach, though, also features certain challenges, which are also explored in section 3. Section 4 concludes.

## 1 The Inter-American Court's constitutional reading of international rule-making

As was hinted above, the dominant reading of Inter-American human rights rule-making is that of a constitutional system. According to this reading, favored by the Court itself, the law is made by one actor (the IACtHR) and is then applied and enforced by domestic courts and other domestic institutions. This section will present in detail the doctrinal components of this reading, in order to set the scene for the alternative reading, focused on interaction, proposed below.

The Inter-American Court of Human Rights (IACtHR) is a regional human rights tribunal effectively operating since 1979. It is an independent tribunal based in San José (Costa Rica) belonging to the Inter-American system of human rights, together with the Inter-American Commission of Human

15 Teubner and Fischer-Lescano, 'Regime-Collisions: The Vain Search for Legal Unity in the Fragmentation of Global Law'.

16 Martti Koskenniemi, *From Apology to Utopia: The Structure of International Legal Argument*, 2nd ed. (Cambridge: Cambridge University Press, 2005).

Rights, that based in Washington, DC. Both the Court and the Commission have the power to interpret and enforce the American Convention of Human Rights of 1969 (IACHR).[17] The Court was created by the 1969 Convention, while the Commission was established 10 years earlier, in 1959, as an organ of the Organization of American States (OAS).

The IACtHR has fairly traditional competences in its contentious jurisdiction, common to all regional human rights tribunals. However, it has been quite innovative in the exercise of its jurisdiction and its interpretation of the Convention.[18] It has understood the system as a wholly integrated regime of human rights, where the Court places itself as an Inter-American Constitutional Court, with the power of striking down domestic legislation; the competence of requiring domestic courts not to apply domestic law that is contrary to the Convention and, as importantly, to the Court's own interpretation of the Convention. Ultimately, the Court's vision is one of a constitutional regime with two complementary venues of enforcement: domestic courts and the IACtHR. This vision is built on two pillars: (1) the notion of 'control de convencionalidad' (control of conventionality); and (2) the constitutional provisions that integrate the Inter-American Convention to domestic legal systems in several States in the region.

### *1.1 Norm-makers: 'control de convencionalidad' and the making of Inter-American constitutionalism*

The IACtHR has become the centre of normative production concerning human rights in the Latin American region. As with many other tribunals, the Court has developed expansive case law that has made it a veritable 'rule-making' institution.[19] However, the Court has gone beyond that point, as it has placed itself at the apex of a judicial review system that controls domestic legal acts. Such a system ultimately makes the Court a formal source of hierarchically higher norms with direct effect in States. This move has been performed through two complementary mechanisms: the doctrine of 'control de convencionalidad', and the Court's interpretation of the exhaustion of local remedies requirement.

The concept of 'conventionality control' ('control de convencionalidad') is the Court's approach to complementing constitutional review by domestic

17 American Convention on Human Rights, 22 November 1969, O.A.S.T.S. No. 36 (entered into force 27 August 1978)

18 See generally, David Harris, 'Regional Protection of Human of Human Rights: The Inter American Achievement', in *The Inter-American System of Human Rights*, ed. David Harris and Stephen Livingstone (Oxford: Oxford University Press, 1998), pp. 1–30.

19 On lawmaking by international tribunals, see Armin von Bogdandy and Ingo Venzke, 'Beyond Dispute: International Judicial Institutions as Lawmakers', in *International Judicial Lawmaking: On Public Authority and Democratic Legitimation in Global Governance*, ed. Armin Bogdandy and Ingo Venzke (Heidelberg: Springer, 2012), pp. 3–34.

judiciaries. The idea is that just as domestic courts perform judicial review of domestic norms on the basis of the Constitution (a 'constitutionality control' – 'control de constitucionalidad'), the Inter-American system gives the power to both domestic and the IACtHR to perform judicial review of domestic norms on the basis of the Convention (a 'conventionality control' – 'control de convencionalidad').[20] This doctrine has strengthened the integrated vision of the Inter-American system, making national courts the enforcers of international human rights provisions.

The 'conventionality control' works simultaneously in references to a horizontal (national) and a vertical (Inter-American) axis. On the horizontal axis, domestic courts have the obligation to guarantee that national legal systems are in accordance to Inter-American standards.[21] Domestic courts are, therefore, required not to apply domestic norms that violate the Convention. This system is completely decentralized, as each domestic court decides whether to apply or not the domestic norm it is assessing. For the IACtHR, 'the judiciary must exercise a sort of "conventionality control" between the domestic legal provisions which are applied to specific cases and the American Convention on Human Rights. To perform this task, the judiciary has to take into account not only the treaty, but also the interpretation thereof made by the Inter-American Court, which is the ultimate interpreter of the American Convention'.[22] Such control should be exercised *ex-officio* by national courts,[23] and should be performed considering not only the actual text of the Convention, but also the case law of the IACtHR, which is 'the ultimate interpreter of the American Convention'.[24]

On the vertical axis, the IACtHR has played the role of a veritable constitutional tribunal, by expressly holding that domestic laws that violate

20 To the extent of my knowledge, in the context of the IACtHR, the notion was first used in 2003 by Sergio García Ramírez in his concurring opinion in *Myrna Mack Chang v. Guatemala* (see IACtHR, *Myrna Mack Chang v. Guatemala*, Decision of 25 November 2003 (Merits, Reparations and Costs) para. 27). A year later, Garcia Ramirez elaborated the analogy between domestic constitutional control and 'control de convencionalidad' presented above, in his concurring opinion in IACtHR, *Tibi v. Ecuador*, Decision of 7 September 2004 (Preliminary Objections, Merits, Reparations and Costs), para. 3. The concept is also present in his concurring opinions in ICtHR, *López Alvarez v. Honduras*, Decision of 1 February 2006 (Merits, Reparations and Costs), para. 30, and in IACtHR, *Vargas Areco v. Paraguay*, Decision of 26 September 2006 (Merits, Reparations and Costs) paras. 6–7.

21 Víctor Bazan, 'La Corte Interamericana de Derechos Humanos y las cortes nacionales: acerca del control de convencionalidad y la necesidad de un diálogo interjurisdiccional sustentable'. Ponencia presentada en el VIII Congreso Mundial de la Asociación Internacional de Derecho Constitucional 'Constituciones y Principios'. México 6 a 10 de diciembre de 2010. At 5.

22 IACtHR, *Almonacid-Arellano et al v. Chile*, Decision of 26 September 2006 (Preliminary Objections, Merits, Reparations and Costs), para. 124.

23 See IACtHR, *Trabajadores Cesados del Congreso (Aguado-Alfaro et al) v. Peru*, Decision of November 24, 2006 (Preliminary Objections, Merits, Reparations and Costs). Par. 128.

24 IACtHR, *Almonacid-Arellano et al v. Chile*, at 124.

the Convention 'lack legal effects', and have never produced them.[25] While the Court has not used the expression 'control de convencionalidad' to label this exercise of jurisdiction, it is clear that the same principle applies: the IACtHR reviews the legality of domestic acts on using the Convention as the standard. For the Court, its decisions are 'ipso iure part of domestic legal systems', and are 'wholly incorporated' in them.[26] This is an astonishing move and, to some commenters, a first of its kind in international law.[27] And it has very clear effects in domestic politics: in 2008, based on the very decision being discussed here, Peruvian domestic courts sentenced General Julio Salazar Monroe, head of the Peruvian National Intelligence Service (SIN) under ex-President Alberto Fujimori, to 35 years in prison for the kidnapping and murder of students and faculty at the University of La Cantuta.[28] Perhaps mindful of this fact, the Court has used this doctrine sparingly. While present in its most extreme form in cases dealing with amnesties and transitional justice,[29] the judicial control by the IACtHR of domestic law has sometimes led to an order to change national norms in a 'reasonable period of time'.[30] Such orders to change domestic law may even concern the national Constitution, as was the case of Chile and its Constitutional provision that allowed for prior censorship.[31]

For the IACtHR, international rule-making making is, ultimately, a process centralised in its own jurisdiction, complemented by both centralised and decentralised mechanisms of enforcement. This exercise of power on behalf of the Court, though, is not deemed to be an unconsented intervention in the domestic legal systems of the region, as the IACtHR can only exercise its jurisdiction if domestic remedies for the violation of the Convention have been exhausted, or are insufficient. This requisite often takes the procedural form of a preliminary objection to jurisdiction: States object to the Court's jurisdiction, arguing that the victim has failed to exhaust local remedies, and

25 See IACtHR, *La Cantuta v. Peru*, Decision of 29 November 2006 (Merits, Reparations and Costs), para. 189. In his separate opinion to this decision, Segio García Ramírez argues that domestic laws that violate the Convention are 'basically invalid' (paras. 4–5).

26 IACtHR, *La Cantuta v. Peru*, para. 186.

27 Antonio Cassese, 'Y-a-t-il un conflit insurmontable entre souveraineté des États et justice pénale internationale?' in Antonio Cassese and Mireille Delmas-Marty (eds), *Crimes Internationaux et Juridictions Internationales* (2002) 13 at 16, quoted in Binder, 'The Prohibition of Amnesties by the Inter-American Court of Human Rights', at 1212.

28 See Human Rights Watch, 'Boletín Informativo Human Right Watch', 10 April 2008. Available at: http://www.hrw.org/doc/?t=spanish&c=peru.

29 See, for example, IACtHR, *La Cantuta v. Peru*. See also: ICtHR, *Barrios Altos v. Peru*, Decision of 14 March 2001 (Merits).

30 For example, IACtHR, *Suarez Rosero*, Decision of 12 November 1997 (Merits); ICtHR *Castillo Petruzzi el al v. Perú*, Decision of 30 May 1999 (Merits); IACtHR *Fermín Ramírez v. Guatemala*, Decision of 20 June 2005 (Merits).

31 See IACtHR *'La Última Tentación de Cristo' (Olmedo Bustos y otros) v. Chile*, Decision of 5 February 2001 (Merits and Reparations).

the IACtHR established that a State presenting such objection had the burden of proving, not only which were the local remedies that failed to be exhausted by the victim, but also why those remedies were effective and adequate.[32]

This assessment of adequateness and effectiveness provides two valuable tools for the Court's own constitutional reading of international rule-making: first, it reinforces the notion that the Court has the power to decide whether domestic law and its application comply or not with the Convention;[33] and, second, it provides a rhetorical shield against criticism for expansive use of its powers of the IACtHR, as it establishes the narrative of a reluctant international tribunal that steps in when domestic law is failed or inadequate.

The doctrine of 'control de convencionalidad', in both its horizontal and vertical axis, sets the first pillar for the Court's constitutional reading of internal rule-making. On the one hand, it identifies a single centre of international norm-production, and gives an international Court the power to enforce such legal regime – including the formal power to annul domestic norms (even the Constitution). The Court's reading is, in this sense, a perfect fit to the 'constitutional mindset'[34] of global governance, where power is exercised in a top-down fashion, on the basis of legal norms adopted in the name of humanity.[35]

The Inter-American regime, though, has one further aspect to it: it recruits the domestic courts in the construction of this constitutional framework. Through the horizontal (national) axis of 'control de convencionalidad', Inter-American constitutional standards are not only enforced by an international tribunal, but also by domestic courts, which are required to follow the case law of the international tribunal. In this second aspect, the Inter-American regime is an example of much of the literature being produced on 'international law in domestic courts'. The work of André Nollkaemper is a case in point. For Nollkaemper, the rule of law requires 'accountability' (in the sense that public powers that contravene their legal obligations, whether international or national, are accountable on the basis of the law).[36] This accountability may be provided by international and by domestic courts. However, States are reluctant to subject themselves to international justice. So, 'in some states

32 IACtHR, *Velásquez-Rodríguez v. Honduras*. Decision of July 29, 1988. (Merits) paras. 59–63.

33 For instance, see IACtHR, *Godínez-Cruz v. Honduras*. Decision of June 26, 1987 (Preliminary Objections), para. 93; also: IACtHR, *Genie-Lacayo v. Nicaragua*. Decision of January 29, 1997 (Merits, Reparations and Costs) para. 77.

34 Martti Koskenniemi, 'Constitutionalism as Mindset: Reflections on Kantian Themes About International Law and Globalization', *Theoretical Inquiries in Law* 1 (2007): 9–36. Also: Martti Koskenniemi, 'The Fate of Public International Law: Between Technique and Politics', *Modern Law Review* 70, no. 1 (2007): 1–30, at 19.

35 For a map of global constitutionalism and global administrative law as two species of a distinctively liberal mindset trying to infuse legal regulation back into global governance, see Rene Uruena, *No Citizens Here: Global Subjects and Participation in International Law* (Leiden/Boston, MA: Martinus Nijhoff Publishers, 2012) at 128–139.

36 André Nollkaemper, *National Courts and the International Rule of Law* (Oxford: Oxford University Press, 2011) at 5.

and under some conditions, national courts can fill the missing link in the international rule of law by providing relief when public powers act in contravention of their international obligations'.[37] Such would be the role of domestic courts in Latin America. For this to happen, one needs to let go of 'dualist' reveries and realise that international and domestic law are complementary – this, of course, requiring that international law holds supremacy over domestic law,[38] as is the case in the Inter-American system.

### *1.2 Norm-takers: Inter-American constitutionalism and comparative international law in Latin America*

The second pillar upon which the IACtHR rests its constitutional reading of international rule-making is domestic constitutions. Indeed, one salient aspect of Latin American constitutionalism in the late twentieth century was its consistent openness to international human rights law. Emerging from the hardships of dictatorship and civil wars, most States in the region adopted new constitutions in a couple of decades: Argentina (1994), Bolivia (1994 and 2009), Brazil (1988), Colombia (1991), Dominican Republic (1994, 2002 and 2010), Ecuador (1996, 1998 and 2008), Nicaragua (1987), Paraguay (1992), Peru (1993) and Venezuela (1999). Most of these constitutions recognise international human rights law as an important aspect of their respective domestic systems, and they do so along a spectrum that finds in the doctrine of 'bloque de constitucionalidad' ('constitutional bloc') the most intense form of integration between domestic and international law.

The notion of 'bloque de constitucionalidad' has its inspiration in French law[39] and travelled via the Spanish Constitutional Tribunal[40] to the case law

37 Ibid., at 6.

38 See André Nollkaemper, 'Rethinking the Supremacy of International Law', *Zeitschrift Für Öffentliches Recht* 65, no. 1 (2010): 65–85 at 65–67 (elaborating on the implication of the principle of supremacy of international law over domestic systems).

39 The notion is traditionally traced back to the 1971 decision of the Conseil Constitutionnel (Decision 71-44 DC, 16 July 1971, Liberté d'association, Rec. 29) where it held that the Preamble to the French 1958 Constitution (which in turn refers back to the Preamble to the 1946 Constitution and to the Déclaration des Droits de l'Homme et du Citoyen) was part of the French constitutional canon. This meant that constitutional review by the Conseil would be undertaken not solely on the basis of the 1958 Constitution, but also on other texts of constitutional standing. The compound of such plurality of texts would form a 'bloc de constitutionnalité' – an expression originally coined by in 1970 Claude Emeri (Claude Emeri, 'Chronique Constitutionnelle Et Parlementaire Française – Vie Et Droit Parlementaire', *Revue Du Droit Public Et De La Science Politique En France Et à L'étranger* 3 (1970): 678). The expression was then used often by Louis Favoreu, who gave it its current use (see Louis Favoreu, 'Bloc De Constitutionnalité', in *Dictionnaire Constitutionnel*, ed. Olivier Duhamel and Yves Meny (Paris: P.U.F, 1992), 87–89). On the history of the notion in France, see Charlotte Denizeau, *Existe-t-il Un Bloc De Constitutionnalité?* (Paris: L.G.D.J., 1997) at 7–28.

40 The Spanish Constitutional Tribunal first referred to the notion in 1982, in decision STC 10/82. See Francisco Rubio Llorente, 'El Bloque De Constitucionalidad', *Revista Española De Derecho Constitucional* 9, no. 27 (n.d.): 9–37 at 23–32.

of several Latin American Constitutional Tribunals, starting in the 1990s. The notion generally refers to an expanded constitutional canon that includes norms not featured in the immediate text of the written Constitution. As such, the notion falls into the debate of the so-called 'unwritten Constitution', which has interested US constitutional scholars for some time now.[41] In Latin America, though, the issue became inextricably linked with the domestic application of international human rights instruments, as these instruments were consistently brought by Constitutional Tribunals in the region to bear on their own expanded constitutional canon, that is, on each system's 'constitutional block'.

Thus, 'bloque de constitucionalidad' became shorthand in the region for giving constitutional status to international human rights law in domestic systems. For example, in Argentina, Article 75(22) of the 1994 Constitution recognises constitutional status to several human rights treaties, expressly named in the text. For the last decade, this provision has been understood by the Supreme Court as creating a 'constitutional block'.[42] Similarly, Article 410 of the 2009 Bolivian Constitution refers to human rights treaties as part of the 'constitutional block'. In Colombia, Article 93 of the Constitution also provides that human rights and international humanitarian law instruments, among others, are part of the domestic order.[43] This article, which has been interpreted by the Constitutional Court as creating a 'constitutional block',[44] includes rights that are not expressly recognised in the Constitution, such as the right to prior consultation embodied in the International Labor Organization (ILO) Convention 169.[45] Another example is Ecuador,[46] whose 2008 Constitution provides in Article 11(3) for the direct effect of human rights contained in international instruments. In principle, human rights instruments have a lower hierarchy than the Ecuadorian Constitution; however,

41 See Jed Rubenfeld, 'The New Unwritten Constitution', *Duke Law Journal* 51 (2001): 289–305 at 392–300.

42 See, for example, Supreme Court of Argentina, *Verbitsky, Horacio s/ habeas corpus*, V. 856. XXXVIII, 9 February 2004, paras. 5, 13, 39 and 57; Llerena, Horacio Luis s/ abuso de armas y lesiones arts. 104 y 89 del Código Penal -causa N° 3221-, L. 486. XXXVI, 17 May 2005, paras. 7, 22, and 28; Dieser, María Graciela y Fraticelli,Carlos Andrés s/ homicidio calificado por el vínculo y por alevosía -causa N° 120/02-, D. 81. XLI. 6 August 2006, opinión del Procurador, at 5.

43 See generally Rodrigo Uprimny, 'El Bloque De Constitucionalidad En Colombia: Un Análisis Jurisprudencial y Un Ensayo De Sistematización Doctrinal', in *Compilación De Jurisprudencia y Doctrina Nacional e Internacional*, ed. Oficina del Alto Comisionado de Naciones Unidas Para los Derechos Humanos, 2001.

44 Constitutional Court of Colombia, Decision C-488 de 2009, drafted by Jorge Iván Palacio Palacio.

45 Constitutional Court of Colombia, Decision SU-039 de 1997, drafted by Antonio Barrera Carbonell.

46 On the Ecuadorian case law under the 1998 Constituion, see Juan Carlos Riofrio Martinez-Villalba, 'El Bloque De Constitucionalidad Pergeñado Por El Tribunal Constitucional', *Foro – Revista De Derecho* 6 (2006): 227–244.

under Article 424, human rights treaties that provide for more favourable rights than the Constitution will prevail in the domestic order, over 'any other legal norm or act of public power'. Thus, under Article 417, domestic law is forbidden from restricting international human rights.

Peru's 1979 Constitution established in Article 105 that international human rights treaties had constitutional status. And, while this norm was excluded from the 1993 Constitution, the later text did establish in Article 55 that all treaties (not only human rights instruments) are part of national law. On that basis, and invoking also the Constitution's Fourth Transitory Disposition (which states that domestic rights must be construed in accordance with international human rights), the Constitutional Tribunal of Peru has held that international human rights have constitutional status,[47] even expressly referring to a 'constitutional block' when referring to ILO Convention 169.[48]

Elsewhere in the region, though, the doctrine of 'bloque de constitucionalidad' is less useful as an analytical category, because international human rights treaties have no constitutional status. Such is the case in Brazil, where Article 5(2) of the 1988 Constitution provides that the recognition of domestic rights does not hinder other rights from arising from international human rights law and, while there was debate over a 'bloco de constitucionalidade',[49] the Supreme Federal Tribunal considered that human rights treaties had infra-constitutional status.[50] However, in 2004, a Constitutional amendment added one section to Article 5, according to which human rights treaties approved by a more demanding procedure in Congress would be equivalent to a constitutional amendment. Under this new amendment, the Supreme Federal

47 Constitutional Tribunal of Peru, Decision 0047–2004-AI/TC (José Claver Nina-Quispe Hernández, en representación del Gobierno Regional de San Martín), par. 22; Decision Case 5854–2005-AA/TC (Pedro Andrés Lizana Puelles), at par. 23; Decision 00007–2007-PI/TC (Colegio de Abogados del Callao), paras. 12–17.

48 Constitutional Tribunal of Peru, Decision 05427–2009-PC/TC (Asociación Interétnica de Desarrollo de la Selva), para. 9

49 See Valério de Oliveira Mazzuoli, 'Os Tratados Internacionais De Direitos Humanos Como Fonte Do Sistema Constitucional De Proteção De Direitos', *Revista CEJ* 6, no. 18 (2002): 120–124.

50 Supreme Federal Tribunal of Brazil, Ação Direta De Inconstitucionalidade 1.480, 03/09/1997 (drafted by Celso de Mello), which reviewed ILO Convention 158. For the Tribunal, 'in the Brazilian legal system, international conventions or treaties are hierarchically subordinated to the normative authority of the Constitution. Consequently, international treaties will have no legal value, if after being incorporated to the system of national positive law they transgress, in its form or subject, the text of the Charter Policy. (. . .) Once the international treaties and conventions have been incorporated to the domestic legal system, they are located in the same level of validity, effectiveness and authority than the ordinary laws, thus, having towards the latter a relationship of parity. (. . .) The prevalence of the international treaties or conventions over the ordinary laws is only justified in the case of an antinomy that is resolved through the application of the chronological ("lex posterior derogat priori") or the specialty criteria.' In the same sense, see Recurso Extraordinário 206.482–3, 27/05/1998 (drafted by Maurício Corrêa). The Tribunal thus confirmed its pre-1988 precedent; see, for example, Supreme Federal Tribunal of Brazil, Recurso Extraordinário nº 80.004, 01/06/1977 (drafted by Xavier de Albuquerque).

Tribunal changed its approach and, following the lead of Judge Gilmar Mendes, held that human rights treaties had supra-legal and infra-constitutional status.[51] The minority, represented by the opinion of Judge Celso de Mello in the same case,[52] considered that human rights treaties have constitutional status in Brazil, and invoke the work of Antônio Cançado Trindade to that effect.[53]

The integration of international law by domestic legal systems provides the second pillar of Inter-American constitutionalism. The IACtHR is able to create a direct link between its decisions and domestic constituencies. Despite the fact that the court has traditional powers and judges States, the IACtHR is able to directly influence through this second pillar the law and politics of States in the region and, most importantly, the actual life of individuals. Through this structure, the IACtHR is able to bypass executive branches in the region (who are often among its most keen contradictors) and have a direct influence in the distribution of power and resources among domestic groups.

## 2 Beyond Inter-American constitutionalism: rule-making interaction

The constitutional reading of human rights rule-making reading obscures three dynamics of power. First, it assumes that the Inter-American Court enters a human rights vacuum in domestic settings, where only norm-takers or norm-enforcers exist. Second, it assumes that all 'actors' (mainly, the IACtHR and domestic courts) are static, and that their behaviour remains unchanged, independently of the signals sent by other actors. Finally, it assumes that the only relevant information in terms of rule-making is the formal decision of the court, as represented in formal decision. All these assumptions are wrong: the IACtHR enters very populated contexts, where other institutions are already regulating (in one way or another) human rights issues. As a result, all the actors end up adapting their strategies and behaviour to the actions and expectations of other actors, which are communicated and stabilised not only through formal judicial decision, but also through shared common senses of those operating in this environment. Rule-making is the result of this process of interaction, in which domestic law is transformed by international law, which is in turn transformed by the former, in a never-ending

51 See Supreme Federal Tribunal of Brazil, Recurso Extraordinário 466.343–1, 03/12/2008 (drafted by Cezar Peluso).

52 Supreme Federal Tribunal of Brazil, Recurso Extraordinário 466.343–1, 03/12/2008, at 129. A few weeks after this decision, Judge Celso de Mello would draft an extensive analysis on the existence of a constitutional block in Brazilian law (see Supreme Federal Tribunal of Brazil, Ação Direta De Inconstitucionalidade 514, 24/03/2008).

53 Ibid.

loop. This process is completely lost in the Court's constitutional reading. What remains of this paper is an exploration of this other reading of human rights rule-making in Latin America.

In order to think in terms of creative interaction, the starting point is not the strict division between national and international implicit in Article 38 of the ICJ's Statute, and neither is it the vertical structure of Inter-American constitutionalism. Rather, the challenges to postnational rule-making can better be understood if the analytical unit is the *space* where interaction between institutions takes place. In this space, institutions are dynamic, as they change and adapt to their interactions. Human rights norms do not enter a regulatory vacuum when they are implemented locally. A national ecosystem of institutions and actors is already in place when international human rights norms enter the domestic system, and there already is some sort of human rights regulation that needs to be transformed or replaced by the Inter-American norms. The IACtHR enter as actors in a space where regulation is *already* being adopted, discussed, implemented and rejected. Of course, as time passes by, the IACtHR may become the main player in this regulatory field, which has been the experience in the decision regarding amnesties in Peru and Uruguay. However, they do not completely crowd-out the regulatory space: there is a regulatory space that exists outside the IACtHR, where these agencies interact with other relevant actors.

What is the specific added value of thinking in terms of a 'space', and not of a hierarchical order or norms? In domestic administrative law, the notion of a 'regulatory space' was suggested as reaction to the narrow reading of the regulatory process in terms of a conflict between public authority and private interests. Against this view, the regulatory process can be better understood as a 'space', where it becomes possible to explore the 'complex and shifting relationships between and within organizations at the heart of economic regulation'.[54] The key is to 'to understand the nature of this shared space: the rules of admission, the relations between occupants, and the variations introduced by differences in markets and issue arenas'.[55]

Despite Hancher and Moran's early insight on the importance of thinking rule-making as a problem of *space*, the interplay within regulatory spaces has been mostly overlooked by administrative law scholarship, which has focused on individual agencies, and their procedures. Recently, some US scholarship has explored interaction,[56] focusing on inter-agency interaction

54 Leigh Hancher and Michael Moran, 'Organizing Regulatory Space', in *Capitalism, Culture, and Economic Regulation*, eds Leigh Hancher and Michael Moran (Oxford; New York: Clarendon Press, 1989), 271.

55 Ibid.

56 Keith Bradley, 'The Design of Agency Interactions', *Columbia Law Review* 111, no. 4 (2011): 745–794. Jody Freeman and Jim Rossi, 'Agency Coordination in Shared Regulatory Space', *Harvard Law Review* 125 (2012, 2011): 1131.

and coordination as a problem of overlapping legislative delegation.[57] That has not been the case in global governance scholarship, where the concept of an emergent 'global administrative space' has become influential, understood as 'a space, distinct from the space of inter-state relations governed by international law and the domestic regulatory space governed by domestic administrative law, although encompassing elements of each'.[58]

The notion of a space is useful to think about the way in which human rights rule-making occurs in Latin America. Indeed, the image of a 'regulatory space' aptly captures some of the dynamic interactions between norms and institutions that charaterise global governance. Most important for our purposes, it is also useful to think differently about postnational rule-making. To do so, we must engage in a thought experiment. Let us imagine for a minute that norms and institutions exist in the global regulatory space, much like planets and other great masses exist in the actual physical space. To be sure, we can think of each planet independently; we often do, and such is our usual practice. However, many of the realities that affect our daily life are not just the mere product of our independent planet, but are rather a function of *other* planets and masses in space. For instance, think of seasons, or sea tides: Earth spins in one way and not another, at a certain angle and the other, not only because of events that happen on Earth, but rather due to the relative equilibrium of gravitational forces around it, which include, of course, its own mass and gravitational force.

This is just an image. My argument is not that the global regulatory space is an actual space with actual forces.[59] It is useful, though, to illustrate the kind of dynamics triggered by institutional interaction in the global regulatory space, and its impact on our idea of rule-making. Norms and institutions (for instance, the IACtHR and other institutions acting in Latin America) seem to have a 'mass' that exerts a certain pull towards them.

### *2.1 Postnational rule-making and communities of practice*

In contrast with a hierarchical order of norms, the global regulatory space needs constant development, which requires an actual community of people constantly contributing to its construction. In the absence of a constitutional, top-down, rule-making process, such a process of development is bound to be incoherent. This process has been often read through the prism of fragmentation of international law, i.e. the emergence of specialised and relatively autonomous rules or rule-complexes, legal institutions and spheres

57 Jacob E. Gersen, "Overlapping and Underlapping Jurisdiction in Administrative Law," *The Supreme Court Review* 2006, no. 1 (2006): 201–247.

58 Benedict Kingsbury, Richard B. Stewart, and Niko Krisch, 'The Emergence of Global Administrative Law', *Law and Contemporary Problems* 68 (2005): 15–61.

59 But see Donald T. Hornstein, 'Complexity Theory, Adaptation, and Administrative Law', *Duke Law Journal* 54, no. 4 (2005): 913–960.

of legal practice at the international level.[60] It is well documented that international law has been suffering from 'fragmentation anxiety', and that such an issue has stirred one of the central debates taking place in contemporary legal scholarship.[61] To be sure, human rights law and, in particular, the Inter-American regime of human rights, are examples of such specialised areas, where a set of rules and institutions have emerged in relatively autonomy. However, the scholarship that recognises such fragmentation seems focused on considering them as discrete actors that compete, cooperate or dominate each other – a dynamic that has been observed in international relations,[62] transnational business governance,[63] environmental governance,[64] and domestic regulation.[65] Even critical work that underscores the importance hegemony still depicts each regime as a self-standing unit eager to dominate other self-standing regimes.[66]

This way of thinking, though, seems to overlook the actual people involved in rule-making. 'Regimes' are rather a group of people that interact, on the basis of the rules contained in the Inter-American Convention of Human Rights, to push their own agendas and fulfil their mandates. They constitute a community of practice,[67] composed by different actors: transnational NGOs that bring cases before the IACtHR, grass-roots organisations that protect victims on the ground, clinics at law schools that file amicus briefs, domestic

60 International Law Commission. Fragmentation of International Law: Difficulties arising from the Diversification and Expansion of International Law (Finalized by Martti Koskenniemi) UN Doc. A/CN.4/L.682 (2006), par. 8.

61 See Uruena, *No Citizens Here: Global Subjects and Participation in International Law* at 36–43 and accompanying footnotes.

62 Abbott, Green, and Keohane, 'Organizational Ecology and Organizational Strategies in World Politics'.

63 Burkard Eberlein *et al.*, 'Transnational Business Governance Interactions: Conceptualization and Framework for Analysis', *Regulation & Governance* 8, no. 1 (1 March 2014): 1–21.

64 Sebastian Oberthür and Thomas Gehring, 'Institutional Interaction: Ten Years of Scholarly Development', in *Managing Institutional Complexity: Regime Interplay and Global Environmental Change*, ed. Sebastian Oberthür and Olav Schram Stokke (Cambridge, MA: MIT Press, 2011), 25–58.

65 Rene Uruena, 'The Rise of the Constitutional Regulatory State in Colombia: The Case of Water Governance', *Regulation & Governance* 6, no. 3 (2012): 282–299.

66 Martti Koskenniemi, 'Hegemonic Regimes', in *Regime Interaction in International Law: Facing Fragmentation*, ed. Margaret Young (Cambridge: Cambridge University Press, 2012), 305–323.

67 Emanuel Adler, *Communitarian International Relations: The Epistemic Foundations of International Relations* (London and New York: Routledge, 2005) at 11. The following use of the notion of community of practice, as well as the idea of shared understandings, is influenced by the enlightening approach proposed in Stephen J. Toope and Jutta Brunnée, *Legitimacy and Legality in International Law: An Interactional Account* (Cambridge: Cambridge University Press, 2010). Brunné and Toope's argument, though, seeks to unpack the notion of international legal obligation through a reinterpretation of the Fullerian criteria of inner morality of law. My interest is not in legal obligation, nor in compliance with international law; for that reason, I focus solely on their description of interactional international rule-making, and not in their effort to provide a normative basis for that process.

courts that interpret and apply the Convention and IACtHR case law, civil servants that work on human rights for domestic governments, scholars writing and teaching Inter-American human rights law, and, of course, the IACtHR, among others.

To be sure, all these actors have different, even conflicting, views of human rights: that matters not. The community of practice is not constituted around a single goal, but rather a shared common understanding of what they are doing and why.[68] The Inter-American human rights community of practice shares collectively held background knowledge: its institutions, its participants, its challenges, and its realities. In this framework, each actor proposes its view of Inter-American human rights, and through continuous interaction with other actors, the international norm is settled – and may be unsettled later again – by further interaction. From this perspective, the hierarchical mindset of a top-down constitutional layout, with the Court at the top, on the other, stops making sense. The community of practice includes both domestic and international actors: national courts, the IACtHR, domestic administrative agencies, scholars – in other words, all those who belong to the community of practice contribute the interaction that creates norms.

This is not to say, though, that hierarchy disappears from the equation. While the idea of a community of practice allows us to think of rule-making as an interactional process, the Court's own reading of its jurisdiction injects hierarchy back to the process. When the Inter-American regime is involved, the idea of dialogue stops, and hierarchy steps in: due to the domestic legal architecture that is predominant in the region, domestic courts are bound by Inter-American legal standards and, more concretely, by the IACtHR's interpretation of such standards. Examples of this move abound in the case law of the region: in Argentina,[69] Bolivia,[70] Brazil,[71] Colombia,[72]

68 Emanuel Adler, *Communitarian International Relations: The Epistemic Foundations of International Relations*, at 22.

69 Supreme Court of Argentina, Mazzeo, Julio Lilo y otros s/ recurso de casación e inconstitucionalidad, M 2333 XLII. 13 July 2007 (holding that 'the integration of those principles recognized by the international community for the protection of those rights inherent to the human person to the national punitive system, was one of the basic guidelines for the construction of the institutional framework which prompted the Constituent Convention of 1994 to incorporate the international treaties in the same order as the National Constitution (. . .).' In effect they stated that the objective was to 'establish a constitutional policy base on the universalization of human rights, the recognition of the supra-national organs of dispute settlement, such as the Inter-American Commission of Human Rights and the Inter-American Court of Human Rights, and the promotion of the advisory opinions of the Inter-American Court', par. 18).

70 Tribunal Constitucional de Bolivia, Decision 0110/2010-R , 10 May 2010.

71 Supreme Federal Tribunal of Brazil, Recurso Extraordinário nº 511.961, 17/06/2009, interpreting the right of freedom of expression in accordance with article 13.1 of the American Convention on Human Rights.

72 Constitutional Court of Colombia, Decisions C-067 of 2003, drafted by Marco Gerardo Monroy Cabra (holding that human rights treaties are an interpretative tool to study the constitutionality

and Peru.[73] In this sense, domestic courts play the role of receptors of international legal standards: instead of participating in the making of international law, domestic courts perceive the Inter-American regime as a source of univocal norms which are to be applied by them, never questioned.[74] In fact, the system leaves very little space for differing approaches to Inter-American standards by domestic courts. In sharp contrast with recent literature that explores the possibility of a legitimate variety of domestic approaches to international legal norms[75] (just as prior work by Richard Falk[76] and William Butler[77] did decades ago), the Inter-American regime is based on the idea that there is a single correct interpretation of international norms (that of the IACtHR), and that domestic courts should converge towards it – or else be flatly wrong. From the perspective of the IACtHR, Inter-American constitutionalism is less an exercise of 'comparative international law' than an integrated hierarchical system of norms that is enforced by both international and domestic tribunals.

## *2.2 Iterative contacts and adaptation*

Despite these limitations, focusing on global regulatory space and the communities of practice that populate them allows us to better appreciate

of domestic legal norms); C-578 de 1995, drafted by Eduardo Cifuentes Muñoz (striking down domestic laws on the basis of international human rights and international humanitarian law standards), C-155 de 2007, drafted by Álvaro Tafur Gálvis (holding that, 'in case of conflict between the national legislation and a international treaty or convention that regulates the same subject, the [domestic] authorities shall apply an interpretation directed to harmonize them and to respect Colombia`s international commitments').

73 Constitutional Tribunal of Peru, Decision 309-2002-HC/TC (incorporating to Peruvian law the right to be judged in a reasonable period of time embodied in article 9 (3) of the International Covenant on Civil and Political Rights and article 7(3) of the ACHR); 1277-99-AC/TC (applying article 14 of the ICCPR to solve a dispute regarding the existence of compensations in the case of a judicial error, and holding that 'if the applicants have sued base on the International Covenant on Civil and Political Rights and not the Political Constitution, is not only because the former has more explicit dispositions regarding the subject of compensation, but also because the content of each fundamental right (as compensation is in the facts of this case) shall be interpreted in accordance with the internal human rights norms (para. 10).'

74 Against this view, some scholars have argued that in other regions, a kind of Habermasian dialogue may exist between international, supranational and domestic human rights tribunals; see, for example, Aida Torres Perez, *Conflicts of Rights in the European Union: A Theory of Supranational Adjudication* (Oxford: Oxford University Press, 2009), at 104–106, 112, 115, 126, 131.

75 For example, Boris N. Mamlyuk and Ugo Mattei, 'Comparative International Law', *Brooklyn Journal of International Law* 36 (2011, 2010): 385. Also: Anthea Roberts, 'Comparative International Law? The Role of National Courts in Creating and Enforcing International Law', *International and Comparative Law Quarterly* 60, no. 01 (2011): 57–92.

76 Richard A. Falk, *The Role of Domestic Courts in the International Legal Order* (Syracuse, NY: Syracuse University Press, 1964).

77 William Butler, 'Comparative Approaches to International Law', in *Academy of International Law at The Hague, Recueil Des Cours*, vol. 190 (Leiden: Martinus Nijhoff Publishers, 1985), 9.

the process of dynamic adaptation in postnational rule-making. Indeed, part of the problem with the Inter-American constitutional mindset is its conception of time, as it conceives human rights rule-making as a matter of discrete utterances that happen once and will never happen again. This problem is well known in game theory, where the difference between single (isolated) and iterated games has been studied extensively,[78] an idea that has gained some traction in international law as well.[79] Iteration creates an interaction that is qualitatively different from that of discrete contacts. Time is, as they say, of the essence. As we have seen, civil society has grown to have expectations of the IACtHR. There is no reason to think that other participants of the community of practice (even the Court itself) have not developed similar expectations on the basis of their continuous encounters. Unlike the mindset of Inter-American constitutionalism, the interaction approach presumes that the actors interact with expectation towards an unknown number of interactions.

Iteration in this case changes not only the strategies, but the game itself – in game-theory parlance, the norm-making interaction of the Inter-American human rights community of practice is a dynamic evolution game.[80] This idea has been explored by constructivist international relations as well: the interaction between agents transforms the structure, which in turn also triggers transformations in the interests and strategies of the agents.[81] In sharp contrast, Inter-American constitutionalism believes that the structure is immutable, and all that agents can do is simply adapt to it, trying to get whatever benefits they can reap from an all-powerful centralised centre of norm production. Against this view, the norm-making interaction approach suggests that the interests of the actors are not static, but rather merge into each other endlessly, and in turn transform the legal structure that frames their interaction. Instead of reifying each actor or legal order (national/international)

78 See Larry Samuelson and George Joseph Mailath, *Repeated Games and Reputations: Long-run Relationships* (Oxford: Oxford University Press, 2006), at 1–14 (introducing the basics if iterated games).

79 See John Setear, 'An Iterative Perspective on Treaties: A Synthesis of International Relations Theory and International Law', *Harvard International Law Journal* 37, no. 1 (1996): 139–230 (arguing that the law of treaties is can be understood as promoting 'formally delineated series of structured interactions between parties ("iterations")', and that such a design promotes cooperation). John K. Setear, 'Treaties, Custom, Iteration, and Public Choice', *Chicago Journal of International Law* 5, no. 2 (2005): 715 (arguing that, from this iterative perspective, leaders are more likely to choose treaties as the legal from of their international obligations, instead of customary law).

80 'In an evolving game, the game structure evolves as it iterates due to internal changes resulting from the operation of institutions responding to external events, such as new scientific or technological findings, that cause the underlying game structure to change.' Brett Frischmann, 'A Dynamic Institutional Theory of International Law', *Buffalo Law Review* 53, no. 3 (2003): 679–809 at 682.

81 See Alexander Wendt, 'The Agent-Structure Problem in International Relations' (1987) 41 *International Organization* 335; Adler, *Communitarian International Relations*, at 5–6.

and presenting them as machines that collide or coexist, repel or impose over each other, interaction in the community of practice transforms the terms of engagement; in other words, the game evolves. Human rights law that results of the interaction is not causally triggered by dominant strategies of participants in the community, but should be rather understood on its own, in the context of the regulatory space that is defined by the specialised regime created by the Pact of San José.

This dimension of time and constant change implies that creative interaction is not a matter of regulation/non-regulation. Scholars, practitioners and activists who work from an Inter-American constitutional mindset act as if the world was being created every time that a domestic court applies an Inter-American standard, as if there was somehow a legal lacuna that is then filled by international law. The exact opposite is true: this interaction occurs in a dense environment of laws and regulation, based on the expectation of an unknown number of interactions. Therefore, the rule-making interaction approach implies that new human rights law is created when the participants of the community of practice interact, and also when they fail to do so. This lack of interaction has to be read as a choice that was made, and not a fortuitously occurring event. Lack of interaction in the Inter-American human rights community is also a matter of norm-making interaction – if a domestic court decides that no international law is relevant in a case, or when an international court sees domestic law as a mere 'fact', all of this is new regulation, choices that can be contested and resisted.

Thinking in terms of interaction allows us to think dynamically of incremental change in global rule-making. This is particularly important, because traditional international legal thinking features a view of change according to which, ultimately, there is really *no change* in international law. That is to say, international law approaches norms and institutions as though they had always been there. Once change occurs, it approaches new (or changed) norms and institutions as if *those* norms had always been there. The underlying idea is that international norms and institutions are discrete events that occur linearly over time, and can be thought of not as a continuum, but rather as a collection of discrete points in time that have little interaction with what happened earlier or later. According to this view, change is the sudden and complete replacement of the old by the new, which in turn implies the complete disappearance of the old, or the coexistence of the old with the new as two timeless artefacts. As a result of this view of change, then, all looks as if nothing had ever changed: the norms and institutions that we have now look permanent, and completely unconnected to what came before them. Ultimately, international law's theory of change is one of a constant present.

In contrast, the idea of a global regulatory space where international norms and institutions exercise different gravitational forces is useful to conceptualise change and temporariness in international law differently. To do so, consider the relative 'weights' of the different norms and institutions that interact, which in turn will determine their own pull, and ability to resist the pull of other norms or institutions. Relative differences in weight, and the dynamics of the 'gravitational' pull, imply that the possibility of permanence in international law stops making sense. The global regulatory space is dynamic: each and all norms and institutions are exerting their pull over the others. Each norm and institution is always 'moving' towards others, or is remaining still because it is resisting the pull of others. The point is that the principle of the global regulatory space is movement and change; there is nothing static, only constant movement. The idea of permanence becomes, in that context, difficult to maintain. Even the most permanent of institutions (say, the United Nations) is exerting its pull; thus moving, or resisting moving, in dynamic terms. Note, however, that the impossibility of permanence is not related to the idea of the long term as a time horizon. The argument is not that nothing is permanent because in the long term all will be gone. The argument here is that institutions that right now seem permanent are actually moving, and thus cannot be thought of as permanent in any significant sense.

Moreover, this strategy also allows us to think about interaction when collusions occur, and also when collusions are not occurring. Most of legal scholarship that factors in the challenges of the multiplicity of legal orders in international law seems to be biased towards focusing on events of conflict, that is, when two international norms provide conflicting solutions to similar cases, or when two institutions collide when exercising their powers.[82] It assumes that the principle is non-interaction, and the exception is interaction, which triggers collision and incoherence. This bias is understandable, as instances of collision are clearer, and seem more politically important. But the opposite is true: international norms and institutions are *all the time* in interaction with each other. While collisions do exist, they tell us little of the day-to-day workings of postnational rule-making. In contrast, thinking in terms of a global regulatory space allows us to consider the interactions that result not in conflict, but rather in the practice of global governance.

These dynamics can be observed in the practice of the IACtHR and of domestic Constitutional Courts in the region. The IACtHR is increasingly called to adjudicate on human rights issues that concern structural problems of Latin American societies, which have an important impact on the way in which scare resources are distributed within each State – and it has stepped in hesitantly as a reaction to the behaviour of other actors. Perhaps the best example of this transformation is the IACtHR's approach towards social and economic rights. In the last decade, the IACtHR has decided cases that could impact in a structural fashion the distribution of resources in a State, as is the case with social security and retirement pensions. For instance, in the case of the *Five Pensioners*,[83] the Court got involved in a complex conflict related

82 See, for example, Joost Pauwelyn, *Conflict of Norms in Public International Law: How WTO Law Relates to Other Rules of International Law* (Cambridge: Cambridge University Press, 2003).

83 IACtHR, *Cinco Pensionistas v. Peru*. Decision of 28 February 2003 (Merits, Reparations and Costs).

to dual and overlapping retirement schemes in Peru, and found that, by changing the amount of the pension received by the complainants, Peru was in violation of their right to property.[84]

While much has been said about the justiciability of social and economic right in the Inter-American system,[85] what is interesting for our purposes here is the approach adopted by the IACtHR vis-à-vis domestic courts and its self-image as being at the centre of an Inter-American Constitutional regime. The Court seems to be adapting its own strategy. This is not the expansive Court of the amnesty decisions that declared 'without legal effects' domestic norms. Rather, this is a much more cautious Court, which shows deference toward the Peruvian Constitutional Tribunal and cites it as an authority on the domestic Constitution.[86] In fact, when called to decide whether, through its treatment of the five pensioners, Peru had structurally violated its duty to progressively develop social and economic rights under Article 26 of the Convention,[87] the Court held: 'economic, social and cultural rights have both an individual and a collective dimension. Their progressive development [. . .] should be measured [. . .] in reference to the growing coverage of economic, social and cultural rights in general, and to the right to social security and to a pension in particular, of the entire population, bearing in mind the imperatives of social equity, and not in reference to the circumstances of a very limited group of pensioners, who do not necessarily represent the prevailing situation'.[88] The Court therefore declined to decide on the issue[89] – a decision that was celebrated in the concurring vote of Judge De Roux Rengifo, as 'it is evident that the controversies that emerged or may emerge from the (substance of the case) can only be resolved by domestic courts'.[90]

This approach was confirmed six years later, when the court faced another important case dealing with pensions in Peru. In Acevedo Buendía,[91] the Court again declined to rule on the violation of Article 26 of the Convention, as it

84 IACtHR, *Cinco Pensionistas v. Peru*, paras. 93–121.

85 See Pilar Arcidácono, Nicolas Espejo and César Rodríguez Garavito (eds), *Derechos Sociales: Justicia, Política y Economía en América Latina* (Bogotá: Siglo del Hombre Editores/LAEHR, 2010); Malcolm Langford (ed.), *Social Rights Jurisprudence: Emerging Trends in International and Comparative Law* (Cambridge: Cambridge University Press, 2008).

86 IACtHR, *Cinco Pensionistas v. Peru*, paras. 98–100.

87 Under Article 26, 'the States Parties undertake to adopt measures, both internally and through international cooperation, especially those of an economic and technical nature, with a view to achieving progressively, by legislation or other appropriate means, the full realization of the rights implicit in the economic, social, educational, scientific, and cultural standards set forth in the Charter of the Organization of American States as amended by the Protocol of Buenos Aires'.

88 IACtHR, *Cinco Pensionistas v. Peru*, para. 147.

89 IACtHR, *Cinco Pensionistas v. Peru*, para. 147.

90 IACtHR, *Cinco Pensionistas v. Peru*, Concurring opinion by De Roux Rengifo, p. 1.

91 IACtHR, *Acevedo Buendía et al. v. Peru*. Decision of July 1 2009 (Preliminary Objection, Merits, Reparations and Costs).

considered that the issue was whether a decision adopted by the Peruvian Constitutional Tribunal was being complied with or not.[92] And what about the enforcement of social and economic rights? The Court accepts that a 'flexible' approach is needed, as each State will follow its own particular path, depending on its 'economic and financial resources'.[93] Even when the Court holds that measures that would affect the progressive development of social rights in region would be in violation of the Convention, it still accepts that such norms should not be understood as a prohibition to take measures that restrict the exercise of those rights: 'any deliberately retrogressive measures in that regard would require the most careful consideration and would need to be fully justified by reference to the totality of the rights of the [International] Covenant [on Economic, Social and Cultural Right] and in the context of the full use of the maximum available resources [of the State]'.[94]

It is important to underscore that there is no inherent legal limit preventing the IACtHR from adopting an astonishing decision in one of these cases, along the lines of what it did in the amnesty decisions. In a pure Inter-American Constitutional mindset, the Court could have engaged in a 'conventionality control' of the Peruvian pension system, and argue that, since it violated the right to property, it should be left 'without legal effect' – even *ab-initio*, as was the case with the Barrios Altos amnesty decision (also affecting Peru). The Peruvian government then would have had to reimburse the pensioners, or create a fund for transition between pension regimes, etc.

However, the Court reacted to other incentives, and declined to do so. This fact changes the interaction between the IACtHR and domestic courts. Whereas, as we have seen, Inter-American Constitutionalism is based on the idea domestic courts are essentially enforcers of a single correct interpretation of international norms (that of the IACtHR), in this new context domestic courts are perceived as having better information on domestic issues and power disputes – a 'political margin of appreciation', in one wills.[95] The IACtHR seems to be looking less for enforcers than for partners in the further development of the Inter-American regime.

Domestic courts, in turn, find themselves in a moment of transition as well. As the IACtHR is called to adjudicate on issues of redistribution or on issues of gender or identity politics (such as gay rights[96] or the protection of women),[97] domestic courts find it less plausible to outsource to the Inter-

92 IACtHR, *Acevedo Buendía et al. v. Peru*, para 106.

93 IACtHR, *Acevedo Buendía et al. v. Peru*, para 102.

94 IACtHR, *Acevedo Buendía et al. v. Peru*, para 103.

95 Interestingly, the notion of 'margin of appreciation' has recently started to be pitched around in dissenting votes in the IACtHR. See, for example, IACtHR, *Attala Riffo y niñas v. Chile*, Decision of 24 February 2012 (merits) dissenting vote of Judge Perez Perez, paras. 16 and 23.

96 See IACtHR, *Attala Riffo y niñas v. Chile*, Decision of 24 Febrary 2012 (merits).

97 See IACtHR, *Claudia Ivette González, Esmeralda Herrera Monreal y Laura Berenice Ramos Monárrez v. México*, Decision of 16 November 2009 (merits).

American regime the legitimacy of their own domestic decision regarding these matters. Ultimately, it becomes less plausible for domestic courts to use the Inter-American regime in order to bolster their independence, when the IACtHR is perceived as one more player in a complex political process with several reasonable positions. Consequently, strong hierarchical arguments of the sort found in the Inter-American constitutional mindset become less frequent, and other forms of interaction start to emerge: for example, domestic courts start seeing Inter-American institutions as partners in the enforcement of their own domestic decisions.[98]

## 3 Risks of the rule-making interaction approach

The analytical unit of the rule-making interaction approach is specialised regimes; in this case, the Inter-American regimes of human rights. This choice carries some costs that need to be discussed. Perhaps the two main challenges refer to: (a) the issue of normative standards of rule-making; and (b) the issue of 'tunnel vision'.[99] In what remains of this chapter, I will briefly discuss each of them.

Let us begin with the problem of normativity. The challenge can be summarised in the following way: while it makes sense to think about rule-making by interaction in the context of the Inter-American system of human rights, one is left unable to distinguish between law and non-law. That is, if all the options brought to the table by participants of the community of practice have rule-making potential, then how are we to identify the *real* Inter-American human rights law that results of the interaction?

This challenge resonates much with the balance between flexibility and formalism that Elaine Fahey's introduction to this volume presented. In the context of the IACtHR, it presupposes that there is a point of view that is external to the community of practice, which would allow an external observer to apply a threshold of legality, thus defining what is law and what is not. In fact, the opposite is true: Inter-American human rights law is what the community of practice says it is. The IACtHR is part of the community,

98 For example, the Colombian Constitutional Court has begun to heavily on the Inter-American Commission of Human Rights for monitoring the compliance of its decisions on internally displaced population. See for, example, Constitutional Court of Colombia, Decision T-025 of 2004 (drafted by Manuel Jose Cepeda), and Auto 092 of 2008. The Court has also relied in part on the Commission for the development of indicators to monitor compliance with its decisions, see: Rene Uruena, 'Internally Displaced Population in Colombia: A Case Study on the Domestic Aspects of Indicators as Technologies of Global Governance', in *Governance by Indicators: Global Power Through Quantification and Rankings*, ed. Benedict Kingsbury *et al.* (Oxford: Oxford University Press, 2012), 249–280.

99 For an introduction of the problem of 'tunnel vision', see Gunther Teubner and Peter Korth, 'Two Kind of Legal Pluralism: Collision of Transnational in the Double Fragmentation of the World Society', in *Regime Interaction in International Law: Facing Fragmentation*, ed. Margaret Young (Cambridge: Cambridge University Press, 2012), 23–54 at 37.

then it will have an important say in the rule-making. But also domestic courts are participants, and transnational networks of activism. They are all parts of the interaction that creates Inter-American human rights law. The line between rule-making and law-applying has to collapse. The search for an external criterion to define legality can be hardly reconciled with the idea of rule-making through interaction – which may be read as one of the main challenges to Brunneé and Toope's interactional approach.[100]

Moreover, the approach I propose risks perpetuating the status quo. When thinking about the pull that one norm or institution exerts over others, one is simply describing such movement. However, this view provides no vocabulary to perform a critique of the reasons behind such a powerful pull, or a normative standard to discuss whether the fact that one institution or norm carries so much weight is appropriate or not. In this sense, the description that is proposed here could be subject to critique in terms of ideology, understood as 'the ways in which meaning serves to establish and sustain relations of domination'.[101] Thus understood, ideology is part of the legal consciousness of a given time or, more precisely, the legal consciousness of a given time uses ideology to perpetuate the status quo it represents. In our case, the idea of incremental change could sustain an unequal distribution of power by occluding the normative dimensions of the 'gravitational pull'.

Specifically, the main challenge is the issue of 'tunnel vision'.[102] Each institution and norm acting in the global regulatory space has a particular mandate, or exists in order to regulate a certain area of global politics or production; that is, they are only concerned with that specific issue, and not necessarily with wider societal concerns. The climate change regime will be concerned with climate change and not with, say, the rights of women. And the Inter-American human rights regime is not concerned with, say, economic development, or the environment. Using specialised regimes as an analytical unit risks losing sight of an overarching narrative of a 'good' society. Each of these institutions may talk in terms of 'common good'; however, when these norms and institutions 'pull' towards them, they pull towards their own structural bias[103] – leaving the common good to be sorted out by the competition among norms and institutions in the global regulatory space. Talking in terms of a 'gravitational force' creates the risk of losing sight of an overarching narrative of a 'good' society.

Moreover, specialised regimes are not static objects. Instead, they are put together in order to achieve a goal that is not given by the specialised regime

100 See Martti Koskenniemi, 'The Mystery of Legal Obligation', *International Theory* 3, no. 2 (2011): 319–325.

101 J. Thomson, *Ideology and Modern Culture* (1956) 56, quoted in Marks 2001, at 110.

102 Teubner and Korth 2012, at 37.

103 Koskenniemi 2005, at 600.

itself, but rather by external political forces that see international law as one more tool to achieve their needs. In this sense, a specialised regime such as this may play the part intended by the powerful. What is more, the Inter-American regime of human rights may have hegemonic ambitions, in the sense that it could seek to expand its world-view, placing its goal as more important (or universal) in detriment to the goals of other regimes.[104] Adopting such a unit of analysis could obscure important differences of power and, in fact, could perpetuate as neutral the structure of 'specialised regimes', which is a specific creation of the powerful.

This move, in turn, could end up empowering the narrowly defined experts that decide what the ultimate goal of the regime is. These are the actors that participate in the Inter-American community of practice, who become the ultimate insiders. Indeed, because the mindset of these regimes is wholly instrumental, then a certain a transnational elite that acts outside democratic or legal checks of accountability ends up being empowered by global specialised regimes.[105] Thus, the norm-making interaction approach could play into this expert-power base, legitimising what is only the result of the (functional) agenda of domination.

All of these are important challenges. The norm-making interaction approach, though, does not see specialised regimes as objects whose characteristics exist outside political choices. Quite on the contrary, this approach embraces the fact that the tunnel vision of specialised regimes is able to obscure differences of power. However, these differences of power may be foregrounded through a combination of three strategies. First, the inclusion of domestic political forces in the Inter-American community of practice may provide elements to compensate the 'tunnel vision' problem. It may allow for other variables, closer to domestic interests, to creep into the process of specialised legal reasoning, thus providing the decision-maker with more 'contextualising elements' when they adopt a decision. This strategy may not go too far, as domestic interests may in fact be represented by domestic elites seeking to favor specialised decision-making, instead of grass-roots movements seeking to democratise governance.[106]

104 A discussion of regimes as hegemons that seek to expand their sphere of influence can be found in Martti Koskenniemi, 'Hegemonic Regimes', in *Regime Interaction in International Law: Facing Fragmentation*, ed. Margaret Young (Cambridge: Cambridge University Press, 2012), 305–323.

105 For a discussion of expertise as a technology of governance in the specialised regime of global water governance, see Rene Urueña, 'Expertise and Global Water Governance: How to Start Thinking About Power over Water Resources', *Anuario Mexicano De Derecho Internacional* 9 (2010).

106 For this problem in the context of judicial reform in Colombia, César Rodríguez-Garavito, 'Towards a Sociology of the Global Rule of Law Field: Neoliberalism, Neoconstitutionalism, and the Contest over Judicial Reform in Latin America', in *Lawyers and the Rule of Law in an Era of Globalization*, ed. Yves Dezalay and Bryant Garth (New York: Routledge, 2011), 155–181.

A second strategy may prove more productive. Norm-making interaction occurs not only within a given community of practice (such as the Inter-American), but also of the contact between communities of practice belonging to different specialised regimes. Thus, new law emerges also when the Inter-American human rights community interacts with the environmental law community of practice, or the international investment law community of practice. In this 'external' interaction, tunnel vision may diminish and contestation may appear.

The most evident arena of contestation is, of course, definition. Such is the third strategy of foregrounding power in the context of specialised regimes. The rule-making interaction approach understands the Inter-American regime as ductile and porous, because its definition includes no act of formal public authority, but rather the decision of experts defining a specific issue as 'human rights' – a decision that can be contested. In fact, this definition is the necessary first step of resistance, as it prevents the deployment of the structural bias implicit in the regime that is not desired.[107] Moreover, this process of contested definition may imply that regimes are transformed as they interact: there is no reason why the Inter-American regime of human rights cannot become a regime of human rights/environment protection, or an Inter-American system of human rights and international humanitarian law.

## 4 Conclusion

This chapter proposes a different approach to thinking about postnational rule-making, in particular in the context of the Inter-American system of human rights. While the dominant view reads rule-making in Inter-American system as a constitutional process, with a strong Court on top, this chapter suggests that a more apt reading is that of a regulatory space. The IACtHR enters very populated contexts, where other institutions are already regulating (in one way or another) human rights issues. The Court needs to interact with these institutions, sometimes coordinating its actions with them, and sometimes controlling them. Rule-making is the result of this process of interaction, in which domestic law is transformed by international law, which is in turn transformed by the former, in a never-ending loop. In this context, the IACtHR as an 'actor' is not a discrete entity that exists independently from other institutions, but is part of a wider landscape (the regulatory space) that defines their 'actorness'.

Interaction allows us to focus on the dynamics of change in the global regulatory space, an approach that has certain advantages, as it helps us communicate process of interaction and incremental change that remains

107 On structural bias see Martti Koskenniemi, *From Apology to Utopia: The Structure of International Legal Argument*, 2nd edn (Cambridge: Cambridge University Press, 2005) at 600.

hidden in the standards view of change in international law. The challenge, though, is that this new vocabulary may be lacking in critical potential – it may end up working as an ideological device that justifies the reality it describes. This, I think, is no reason to reject it. It is not the case that the phenomena it describes will stop occurring because we have no conceptual way of grasping it. However, this challenge does point to the need to think of ways to enhance the incipient vocabulary of inter-actual rule-making in global governance.

Section III

# Interactions between actors in postnational rule-making

## Framing practices 'in the shadows' and beyond

# 7 The European Union: a shadowy global actor?

## The UN system as an example

*Jan Wouters, Anna-Luise Chané and Jed Odermatt*[1]

### 1 Introduction

The European Union (EU or Union) has for some time aspired to become a more influential and effective global actor. The Lisbon Treaty provided for a number of institutional and legal amendments to service these aspirations. However, the implementation of the Lisbon Treaty regarding the EU's external relations has been littered with incidents and turf battles between the EU institutions *inter se* and between them and the Member States. Acrimonious debates on external powers and representation have often given rise to rather unsatisfactory compromises, and there seems to be no clear sense of unitary purpose, especially as regards the manner in which the global multilateral system needs to be reformed and the exact place of the EU (as compared to its Member States) in this respect. EU Member States, whose preferences have only become more diffuse with the latest enlargement waves, often cling to their own diplomatic networks and membership positions of international organisations in spite of engaging into a joint strategic reflection on the way forward for the EU in the global order.

Partly as a result of this, the level of ambition concerning the EU's institutional position in international organisations is currently remarkably low within EU bodies such as the European Commission and the (newly created) European External Action Service. Worse, the external environment has, if anything, become less hospitable to the EU's ambitions in international relations. In many international organisations and fora, from the United Nations (UN) to the G20, there is a widespread sense that Europeans are already overrepresented, complicating an additional role/presence of the EU. The financial and Eurozone crises have been unhelpful, to say the least, for the EU's international standing, and the relative rise of the BRICS has made them far more vocal and resistant to EU-inspired institutional arrangements

1 This paper builds to a very large extent on research conducted by Professor Wouters while in Geneva at the Graduate Institute in the Spring of 2014, and in particular on our working paper Jan Wouters, Anna-Luise Chané, Jed Odermatt and Thomas Ramopoulos, 'Improving the EU's Status in the UN and the UN System: an Objective Without a Strategy?', Leuven Centre for Global Governance Studies Working Paper Series, No. 133, March 2014.

and policy recipes. Nevertheless, and in spite of these issues, the EU continues to exercise a rather important, though more subtle, global normative influence through the ongoing Europeanisation of its internal legislation and policies. The EU can therefore be seen as a 'shadowy' global actor, both in light of the limited formal role and position it has in many global multilateral settings, and in light of the substantive though often indirect influence it exercises through its internal lawmaking and policymaking.

The introduction to this volume sets out that EU law and public international law have been selected as two subjects on which to focus, since they 'arguably constitute the leading contemporary sources of study for postnational rule-making'.[2] The EU epitomises the complexities of postnational rule-making. Yet the Union is not only a forum in which postnational rule-making takes place; it is also an international actor in its own right, and seeks to influence the development of rule-making at the international level. The complexities of this relationship are made clear when one views the way in which the EU seeks to influence developments within the main sites of international law development, most notably at the UN and the UN system. The present chapter takes stock of the current situation by looking more specifically into the EU's 'shadowy actor' role within the UN and the UN system. The varied and indeterminate status of the Union in these bodies has both positive and negative elements. On the one hand, it allows the EU to continue to play a role in international legal developments, despite its lack of formal legal status within these bodies. On the other hand, it demonstrates the inability of the Union to assert itself fully as a distinct entity within these fora. The case study demonstrates the openness with which the EU seeks to upgrade itself in international organisations and the frequency of the 'second-best' roles it must accept, even in a preferential system. Moreover, as this case study outlines, the evolution of its place in the UN system is a constant battle between formalism and flexibility. It is not a case study about the pluralisation of actors, examined by other contributions to this edited volume, nor is it per se a case study of non-transparency, as examined by other contributions in this section.

Despite being a priority, the cooperation of the EU with the UN and UN system encounters several stumbling blocks that at times hamper the EU's efforts to have a unified and effective presence within the organisation. One of the most contentious issues in this respect is the division of powers between the EU and its Member States, most notably with regard to the right to speak or the right to negotiate international agreements. These issues of external representation are aggravated by the variation of statuses that the EU has in the different UN fora. While there are several bodies in which only the EU Member States are represented, the EU has obtained observer status in most fora, was given enhanced participation rights in some, and was even granted

2 See Introduction to this volume.

the status of a member organisation in very few exceptional cases.[3] The type of status depends not only on the competences of the EU, but also on the institutional framework of the respective UN bodies, which is in turn contingent upon the political circumstances.[4] Consequently, the EU's status in UN fora does not necessarily correspond to its competences and priorities, thereby hindering its effective representation.

In light of these shortcomings, European Commission President Barroso and Vice-President Ashton issued on 20 December 2012 a 'Strategy for the progressive improvement of the EU status in international organisations and other fora in line with the objectives of the Treaty of Lisbon',[5] ('Barroso-Ashton Strategy' or 'Strategy'), which contains a number of recommendations concerning EU representation in international organisations, including the UN framework. First, with regard to the EU's work in the UN General Assembly (UNGA), the Strategy recommends continued efforts to ensure the full implementation of UNGA Resolution 65/276 on the enhanced participation rights of the Union, as well as an evaluation of its possible extension to other UNGA subsidiary bodies. Second, with regard to other UN agencies and programmes, the Strategy makes a classification of the various situations, based on the potential for a status upgrade and on whether or not efforts are currently being undertaken. For each situation, recommendations and examples are provided, often indicating a number of priority organisations.

The case study sheds further light on the broader issue of the EU as a global actor, and how, despite being a goal of the Union, the representation of the EU in the system has encountered numerous obstacles. It examines some of the targets of the Barroso-Ashton Strategy and considers the manner in which the EU seeks to evolve itself in this framework and the internal and external facets thereof as the dual-faceted shadowy actor that the EU has become. It is dual faceted because the EU is evolving transparently, yet is also facing internal struggles and limited external concessions that it must continually engage with.

We argue that even after the entry into force of the Lisbon Treaty, which aimed to streamline the Union's external representation, the EU continues to struggle for more effective participation in the UN framework. The stumbling blocks are both internal – due to disagreements between the Union and its

3 Frank Hoffmeister, 'Outsider or Frontrunner? Recent Developments under International and European Law on the Status of the European Union in International Organizations and Treaty Bodies' (2007) *Common Market Law Review*, 41–68.

4 Catherine Flaesch-Mougin, 'Le statut de la Communauté Européenne au sein des organisations internationales', in 'Commentaire J. Mégret: Le Droit de la CE et de l'Union Européenne', vol. 12: Relations extérieures, Jean-Victor Louis and Marianne Dony (eds) (Editions de l'Université de Bruxelles 2005), 369–397, 369 *et. seq.*

5 Commission, 'Communication to the Commission from the President in Agreement with Vice-President Ashton: Strategy for the progressive improvement of the EU status in international organisations and other fora in line with the objectives of the Treaty of Lisbon, (Communication) COM (2012) 9420 final, 20 December 2012, on file with the authors.

Member States – and external – in particular due to gaps between the EU's status in most UN bodies and its competences and priorities. Although aligning the Union's internal and external dimensions thus remains a focal point of the EU's engagement at the UN, this chapter aims to demonstrate that the Barroso-Ashton Strategy lacks the required level of vision and precision to achieve this goal, and is thus inadequate for guiding the EU's efforts towards assuming its desired leadership role at the UN level. Nevertheless, the EU has still been able to assert a level of influence in the UN system despite this lack of formal status, and remains a 'shadowy' global actor.

The chapter first examines some of the legal and political issues that are at play as the EU attempts to enhance its cooperation with and representation in the UN and the UN system. Section 2 deals with general issues of EU external representation, which have recently played a role in EU-UN relations. Section 3 analyses difficulties with regard to the practical implementation of UNGA Resolution 65/276, as well as the possibility to extend its application to UNGA subsidiary bodies, using the example of the Human Rights Council (HRC or Council). Section 4 takes a closer look at UN bodies that were identified as targets for closer cooperation in the Barroso-Ashton Strategy and where the EU could potentially pursue upgraded status. It examines the EU's place in two main bodies: the Food and Agriculture Organization (FAO), the only example of a UN specialised agency in which the EU holds membership status; and the International Maritime Organization (IMO), a UN specialised agency in which the EU holds no status despite its prolific legislative and policy initiatives in maritime affairs.

## 2 EU representation at the UN after Lisbon

The EU's representation in multilateral fora has long been a contentious issue. The Lisbon Treaty had intended to deal with some of the obstacles that plagued EU external relations. However, problems have persisted, and the EU's relationship with the UN has not been immune to this.[6] Much of this can be traced to the fact that the EU can only be a full member in some of these organisations and instruments and cannot be a full member of the UN in general.[7] It therefore must rely on and cooperate with the EU Member States, who are full members of the UN and of most UN specialised agencies.

6 Sieglinde Gstöhl, 'EU Diplomacy After Lisbon: More Effective Multilateralism?', (2011) 17(2) *Brown Journal of World Affairs* 181–191; Nanar Hadeshian, 'European Union's External Relations: More Consistency?', (2010) 13 *Yearbook of Polish European Studies* 107–127; Niklas Helwig, 'EU Foreign Policy and the High Representative's Capability-Expectations Gap: A question of Political Will', (2013) 18(2) *European Foreign Affairs Review* 235–254.

7 See Article 4(1) UN Charter, which limits membership to states only. For literature examining the status and representation arrangements of the EU in different international organizations in accordance with the founding instrument of each organization, see Michael Emerson, Rosa Balfour, Tim Corthaut, Jan Wouters, Piotr Maciej Kaczynski and Thomas Renard, *Upgrading the EU's Role as a Global Actor: Institutions, Law and the Restructuring of European Diplomacy*, (CEPS 2011); Hoffmeister, note 3.

In order to ensure unity in the international representation of the Union,[8] the Member States and the Union have the duty to cooperate closely in their activities at the UN level.[9] This entails, among others, that Member States must collectively submit a Union position, whenever a matter in a UN body in which the EU does not have member status falls in an area of exclusive EU competence.[10] Member States are not entitled to table unilateral proposals, even in areas of shared competences, when the Union has remained passive pursuant to a common strategy not to submit a proposal.[11]

An issue that has prominently manifested itself in the UN has been the question in whose names statements are to be made. In particular, disagreement centred on the seemingly trivial issue of whether statements before the UN should be preceded by a short clause indicating if the statement was delivered 'on behalf of the EU', 'on behalf of the EU and its Member States', or 'on behalf of the Member States of the European Union'. In the second half of 2011, the United Kingdom blocked a significant number of EU statements in an ostensible attempt to safeguard its national competences in the field of shared competences,[12] thereby considerably impacting on the EU's

8 On the 'requirement' or 'principle' of unity in the international representation of the EU see *inter alia* European Court of Justice ('ECJ'): Case 1/78 *IAEA* [1978] ECR 2151, paras 34–36; Opinion 2/91 of 19 March 1993, *ILO* [1993] ECR I-1061, para 38; Opinion 1/94 of 15 November 1994 *WTO* [1994] ECR I-5267, para. 108; Case C-25/94, *Commission v Council* [1996] ECR I-1469 para. 48; ECJ; Case C-246/07, *Commission v. Sweden* [2010] ECR I-3317, paras 73, 104.

9 The case law of the ECJ has so far not established complete clarity on the legal foundations of the duty of cooperation in the Union's external relations. While the ECJ has frequently held that the 'obligation to cooperate flows from the requirement of unity in the international representation of the Community' (see e.g. Opinion 1/94, *supra*, n. 8, para. 108; *Commission v Council*, n 8 at para 48; *Commission v Sweden, supra*, n 8 at para 73), commentators interpret the recent judgments in the Cases C-459/03, *Commission v Ireland*, [2006] ECR I-4635 and C-246/07 to support the view that the Court derives the duty from the principle of sincere cooperation, enshrined in Article 4(3) *Treaty of European Union*. See Christophe Hillion, 'Mixity and Coherence in EU External Relations: The Significance of the 'Duty of Cooperation', in Christophe Hillion and Panos Koutrakos (eds), *Mixed Agreements Revisited: The EU and its Member States in the World* (Hart 2010) pp 91–92, and 87–115; Federico Casolari, 'The principle of loyal co-operation: A 'master key' for EU external representation?', in Steve Blockmans and Ramses A. Wessel (eds), *Principles and practices of EU external representation* in CLEER Working Papers 5/2012, 11–36; Marise Cremona, 'Case C-246/07, *Commission v. Sweden* (PFOS), Judgment of the Court of Justice (Grand Chamber) of 20 April 2010', (2011) *Common Market Law Review*, 1639–1666, 1650 *et. seq.*

10 Case C-45/07 *Commission v. Greece* [2009] ECR I-701, paras 14–38.

11 Case C-246/07, *Commission v. Sweden* [2010] ECR I-3317, paras 69–105; Geert de Baere, 'O, Where is Faith? O, Where is Loyalty?' Some Thoughts on the Duty of Loyal Co-operation and the Union's External Environmental Competences in the light of the PFOS Case' (2011) 36 *European Law Review* 2011, 405–419.

12 Toby Vogel, 'Split Emerges over Remit of the EU's Diplomatic Service', (*European Voice*, 25 May 2011) <http://www.europeanvoice.com/article/imported/split_emerges_over_remit_of_the_eu_s_diplomatic_service/71168.aspx> (accessed 30 January 2015); Julian Borger, 'EU Anger over British Stance on UN Statements', (*The Guardian*, 20 October 2011), <http://www.guardian.co.uk/world/2011/oct/20/uk-eu-un-statements-wording> (accessed 30 January 2015); Sebastian Barkowski and Katarzyna Wiatr, 'External Representation of the European Union and Shared Competences – an Unsolved Puzzle', (2012) 15 *Yearbook of Polish European Studies*, 155–175 and 166 *et. seq.*

external action.[13] The adoption of 'general arrangements' on EU statements in multilateral organisations by the Council on 24 October 2011[14] has ended the conflict for now, but these arrangements are far from offering a permanent solution. Their provision that 'Member States agree on a case-by-case basis whether and how to co-ordinate and be represented externally'[15] immediately triggered criticism by the Commission[16] and risks creating confusion for third countries regarding the allocation of competences within the EU.[17]

Other disagreements with regard to the delivery of statements have focused on the use of nameplates. When the Commission proposed in 2013 that in the FAO, 'all EU positions should be expressed from behind the EU nameplate',[18] the United Kingdom showed concern that this might prohibit EU Member States to speak from behind their national nameplate when supporting EU statements.[19] It highlights the unease with which some Member States react whenever the EU advances into territory previously reserved to State actors, and illustrates their latent fear of competence creep.

The negotiation of international agreements is another case where similar problems arose with regard to representation in the post-Lisbon era, particularly in areas of shared competences.[20] In negotiations on a legally binding

13 European External Action Service, Report by the High Representative to the European Parliament, the Council and the Commission, 22 December 2011, point 17.

14 *Council of the European Union*, EU Statements in Multilateral Organisations – General Arrangements, Doc No. 15901/11, 24 October 2011 ('General Arrangements'). For a commentary see Catherine Flaesch-Mougin, 'Représentation externe et compétences de l'Union européenne: quelques réflexions à propos des arrangements généraux du Conseil relatifs aux déclarations de l'UE dans les organisations multilatérales' in Chahira Boutayeb (ed.), *La Constitution, l'Europe et le droit – Mélanges en l'honneur de Jean-Claude Masclet Paris* (Publications de l'Université Paris-Sorbonne 2013), 571–592.

15 Ibid.

16 Statement by the Commission to be entered into the minutes of the Council session endorsing the General Arrangements, Council of the European Union, EU Statements in Multilateral Organisations – General Arrangements, note 13.

17 See Thomas Ramopoulos and Jed Odermatt, 'EU Diplomacy: Measuring Success in Light of the Post-Lisbon Institutional Framework', in Astrid Boening and others (eds), *Global Power Europe: Theoretical and Institutional Approaches to the EU's External Relations*, (Springer 2013) pp. 19–35, 27 *et. seq.*

18 Commission, 'Communication from the Commission to the Council, The role of the European Union in the Food and Agriculture Organisation (FAO) after the Treaty of Lisbon: Updated Declaration of Competences and new arrangements between the Council and the Commission for the exercise of membership rights of the EU and its Member States' ('FAO Communication') COM (2013) 333 final, annex 2, 13.

19 United Kingdom Department for International Development, 'Explanatory Memorandum on COM (2013) 333 final' (27 June 2013) Doc. No. 10368–13, para. 17.

20 See, for example, on the negotiations of a legally binding instrument on mercury, Tim Corthaut and Dries Van Eeckhoutte, 'Legal Aspects of EU Participation in Global Environmental Governance under the UN Umbrella', in Jan Wouters and others (eds), *The European Union and Multilateral Governance* (Basingstoke: Palgrave Macmillan, 2012), 145–170; Geert De Baere, 'International Negotiations Post-Lisbon: A Case Study of the Union's External Environmental Policy', in Panos Koutrakos (ed.), *The European Union's External Relations a Year After Lisbon*,

instrument on mercury, for example, the Commission held the view that it should be the negotiator on all Union competences, including shared ones, having to cooperate closely with the Member States. The Council, on the other hand, opted for a negotiating team comprising of the Commission and the Presidency as a means to attain unity of representation. The current compromise foresees that the Commission will be the Union negotiator in areas where the Union has competence and has acted upon it, but that it will do so 'in consultation with a special committee of representatives of Member States, and in accordance with [specific] negotiating directives'.[21]

The EU has managed to overcome many of these representation issues, mostly due to the desire of the Member States and the EU institutions to work together to find practical arrangements. Nevertheless, the representation problems that were exhibited in the post-Lisbon period were never fully settled, and could possibly arise again in the future.

## 3 The EU at the UNGA and the HRC: UNGA Resolution 65/276 and its aftermath

The issues regarding EU representation discussed above are further aggravated by the incoherent picture of EU status at the level of the UN and the UN system. Across the wide range of UN bodies, the Union holds a variety of different legal statuses, ranging from no representation to full membership. As indicated above, the level of status depends not only on the competences of the EU, but also on external factors, such as the institutional framework of the respective UN bodies and the political context.[22] This leads to the situation whereby the EU's status at UN bodies is not necessarily in line with its competences and priorities. Thus the EU frequently has very limited participation rights in those UN fora that are of high relevance for the effective exercise of its powers. Consequently, the Union has continuously pursued the objective of improving its representation at UN bodies.

One of the most prominent examples of such efforts is the 2011 upgrade of the EU's observer status at the UNGA. The Union had already been actively engaged at the UNGA for decades, ever since the European Economic

CLEER Working Papers 3/2011, 97–112, <http://www.asser.nl/upload/documents/772011_51358CLEER%20WP%202011-3%20-%20KOUTRAKOS.pdf>. Similar disagreements were observed with regard to the negotiation of the Arms Trade Treaty, see Foreign & Commonwealth Office, Review of the Balance of Competences between the United Kingdom and the European Union (Foreign & Commonwealth Office), 22 July 2013) <https://www.gov.uk/government/uploads/system/uploads/attachment_data/file/227437/2901086_Foreign_Policy_acc.pdf> (accessed 30 January 2015) at 38–39.

21 Council Decision on the participation of the Union in negotiations on a legally binding instrument on mercury further to Decision 25/5 of the Governing Council of the United Nations Environment Programme (UNEP), Doc. No. 16632/10, 6 December 2010.

22 Flaesch-Mougin, note 4.

Community (EEC) was invited to participate as an observer.[23] In light of the UNGA's high visibility and its rank as the premier forum to address the global community of States, it appeared to be the natural setting for the EU to seek an upgraded status.[24] Being one of the UN's primary organs, it was hoped that a status change in the UNGA would set a precedent for realigning the Union's participation rights in other UN bodies with its new internal institutional realities after the entry into force of the Lisbon Treaty. The Union aimed for an 'enhanced' observer status, which would allow the EU, as far as possible, to be represented in the UNGA in its own right instead of through the Member State holding the rotating Council Presidency. Diplomatic efforts suffered a serious setback in September 2010 when a first draft resolution was met with opposition by third states and failed to be adopted.[25] It was only after increased outreach and substantive amendments that the UNGA adopted Resolution 65/276 on 3 May 2011 and saved the EU from a diplomatic debacle.[26] Still, the EU achieved far less than it had initially intended, as the final Resolution secured participation rights that were far lower than what had been proposed at the outset.

### *3.1 Practical implementation*

Even though UNGA Resolution 65/276 was eventually adopted with a large majority voting in favour, its implementation in practice presented new challenges. Based on lingering concerns of endangering the principle of sovereign equality of the UN's Member States and the intergovernmental character of the organisation, a number of States, most vocally the CARICOM group, advocated a narrow interpretation of the Resolution. The disagreement centred in particular on the Union Delegation's right 'to be inscribed on the list of speakers among representatives of major groups, in order to make interventions'.[27] This had been interpreted by the UN Secretary-General

23 UNGA Res. 3208 (XXIX) 1974, Status of the European Economic Community in the General Assembly, 11 October 1974.

24 Cf. Geert De Baere and Esa Paasivirta, 'Identity and Difference: The EU and the UN as Part of Each Other', in Henri de Waele and Jan-Jaap Kuipers (eds) *The Emergence of the European Union's International Identity – Views from the Global Arena* (Boston, MA: Martinus Nijhoff 2013), 21–42, 26.

25 See Michael Emerson and Jan Wouters, *The EU's Diplomatic Debacle at the UN: What else and what next?*, Commentary, (CEPS 2010).

26 On the diplomatic saga involving the EU's upgraded status at the UNGA see Evan Brewer, 'The Participation of the European Union in the Work of the United Nations: Evolving to Reflect the New Realities of Regional Organizations', (2012) *International Organizations Law Review*, 181–225; De Baere and Paasivirta, note 24; Jan Wouters, Jed Odermatt and Thomas Ramopoulos, 'The Status of the European Union at the United Nations General Assembly', in Inge Govaere, Erwan Lannon, Peter Van Elsuwege, Stanislaus Adam (eds) *The European Union in the World: Liber Amicorum Professor Marc Maresceau* (Brill Publishers 2014), 211–223.

27 UNGA Res. 65/276, Participation of the European Union in the work of the United Nations, 3 May 2011, annex Article 1(a).

(UNSG) to mean that the EU shall be inscribed 'in the order in which the European Union signified its desire to speak'.[28] In an interpretive declaration of UNGA Resolution 65/276, CARICOM stated that it did not share the UNSG's interpretation, expressing the view that the Union should not take 'priority over other major groups that are represented by a State member of the United Nations'.[29] In order to maintain the clear hierarchy between States and observers, CARICOM concluded that 'in a speakers' list including multiple major groups, the European Union will not be able to speak prior to any major group represented by a full State Member of the United Nations'.[30]

The controversy had practical consequences when UNGA Resolution 65/276 was applied in the UNGA's 66th session. Speaking in the Third Committee, the representative of CARICOM reiterated its view, arguing that the UNSG's interpretation 'would appear to confer even more enhanced privileges to the European Union's observer'.[31] His view was shared by the representatives of Venezuela and Nicaragua. Poland, on the other hand, rejected any unilateral interpretation of the 'crystal clear' text of the Resolution, while the United States stated that the EU Member States should be able to decide who would speak on their behalf.[32] The dispute escalated in a later meeting, which had to be postponed when consensus on the list of speakers could not be obtained.[33] A similar conflict erupted in the Fifth Committee, when the EU intended to take the floor after Argentina for the G77 and China, which initially resulted in having the EU speak after all regional groups.[34] Other Committees, however, established pragmatic solutions apparently without opposition, such as the Second Committee, where inscription of the major groups on the list of speakers was made on a 'first-come, first-served basis'.[35] For the time being, the issue appears to have been settled and the

28 Note by the Secretary-General, Participation of the European Union in the work of the United Nations, A/65/856, para 5.

29 Letter dated 9 May 2011 from the Permanent Representative of the Bahamas to the United Nations addressed to the Secretary-General, A/65/834.

30 Ibid.

31 UNGA Third Committee, As World Struggles with Economic Crisis, 'Time Bomb' of Rising Social Inequality Could Tear Apart Moral Fabric of Societies, Third Committee Told (3 October 2011), GA/SHC/4004.

32 Ibid.

33 UNGA Third Committee, Landmark Election in Tunisia Superb Demonstration of UN Providing Advice, Support, while Fully Respecting National Leadership, Ownership Third Committee Told (25 October 2011), GA/SHC/4019.

34 Wouters, Odermatt and Ramopoulos, note 26, p. 214; but see Brewer, note 26, p. 208 *et. seq.* who identified that the EU spoke before many major groups represented by states.

35 Ad Hoc Working Group on General Assembly revitalization, Meeting devoted to the working methods of the Main Committees – briefing by the Chairs of the Main Committees, pursuant to operative paragraph 19 of GA resolution 66/296: Statement by H.E. Ambassador George Talbot (Guyana), Chair of the Second Committee.

Union Delegation regularly speaks before other major groups represented by States. Yet, without a common understanding about the scope of UNGA Resolution 65/276, the disagreement about its accurate interpretation results in unequal application across the UNGA's Main Committees and may cause further discussions in the future.

Another conflict focused on the right to submit an explanation of vote. It was argued by some Member States that this right could only be exercised by those entities that had a right to vote, given that the two rights were inextricably linked.[36] It would thus fall again to the EU Member States to submit explanatory statements on behalf of the EU. In some cases, the EU was granted the right to make a 'general statement' after the State Parties had delivered their explanations of vote; however, this practice has equally triggered criticism. When the UNGA President in a meeting on Resolution 65/281 gave the floor to the EU representative to make a general statement, the representative of Saint Vincent and the Grenadines, supported by Venezuela, raised a point of order, arguing that the Union should not be granted the exclusive privilege to make a general statement, when the same right was denied to Member States, and reiterating the view that the EU 'would not be able to speak after the vote since it had no vote'.[37]

Other difficulties in the practical implementation of Resolution 65/276 stemmed from the EU's allocation of competences and its external relations architecture. This includes the abovementioned disagreement between the United Kingdom and the Union on the question in whose name statements ought to be delivered, and the oftentimes inconsistent external representation, alternatively by the EU Delegation or by the Member State holding the rotating Council Presidency on its behalf.[38]

These hurdles prompted President Barroso and Vice-President Ashton to call for continued efforts to ensure the full implementation of the Resolution in their Strategy.[39] Nevertheless, despite certain setbacks, the overall application can be judged a success.[40] The Union Delegation has smoothly assumed its new responsibilities, EU representatives regularly address the plenary and the Committees, and Union communications are directly circulated as official documents. It is in this light that the President of the Commission and the HR/VP concluded in 2013: 'By now, the EU's enhanced participatory status in the work of UNGA, its committees and conferences, is broadly accepted at the UN; internal debates have largely subsided, although

36 UNGA, Five Years after Creation, General Assembly Maintains Human Rights Council as Subsidiary Body, Concluding Review of Work, Functioning (17 June 2011), GA/11101.

37 Ibid.

38 Brewer, note 26, 209 *et. seq.*

39 Barroso-Ashton-Strategy, note 5, 4.

40 Pedro Antonio Serrano de Haro, Participation of the EU in the work of the UN: General Assembly Resolution 65/276, CLEER Working Papers 2012/4, p. 32.

practical implementation requires permanent attention and vigilance by the EU Delegation in New York.'[41]

The EU's experience surrounding the 2011 upgrade at the UNGA not only demonstrates the challenges in seeking enhanced participation rights in the UN, it has been highly influential in shaping EU policy towards international organisations ever since. It is now clear that for the Union, securing upgraded status in international organisations is neither simple nor automatic, but requires a serious and careful diplomatic effort that takes into account the political sensitivities of third states, and even of the EU's own Member States. Moreover, this experience also makes clear that even once a higher status is reached, the EU may still have to fight for its place at the table to make sure the upgrade is given full effect. Consequently, the Union has adopted a more cautious and deliberate approach to similar efforts in other international organisations, especially those in the UN system. Although UNGA Resolution 65/276 is touted as a diplomatic success, since 2011 there has been no comparable effort to replicate the EU's upgraded status in other international organisations or UN bodies.

### *3.2 Extension to the Human Rights Council*

This does not mean, however, that the EU's ambitions to improve its status in the UN framework have been entirely crushed. As illustrated by the Strategy, Commission services and the EEAS are still evaluating and promoting options to remedy the perceived impediments for effective Union representation in UN bodies. Nevertheless, the Barroso-Ashton Strategy follows a significantly more cautious approach compared to similar EU communications dating from before the UNGA status upgrade. Written with a view to eventual EC membership in UN bodies, the Commission's 2003 Communication 'The European Union and the United Nations: The Choice of Multilateralism' boldly demanded that the EC 'should be given the possibility to participate fully in the work of UN bodies where matters of Community competence are concerned, and Member States should contribute effectively towards this,'[42] and stated – referring to EC membership in the FAO[43] and the Codex Alimentarius – that '[t]his option should also be pursued for other relevant organisations that belong to the UN

41 Note to the College of Commissioners from President Barroso and Vice-President Ashton on the implementation of the 'Strategy for the progressive improvement of the EU status in international organisations and other fora in line with the objectives of the Treaty of Lisbon, C(2012) 9420 final', INFO (2013) 115, p. 3 ('Information Note').

42 Communication from the Commission to the Council and the European Parliament – The European Union and the United Nations: The choice of multilateralism, COM(2003) 526 final, p. 23.

43 See for more detail below, ch. 4.A.

system'.[44] Almost 10 years later, the Barroso-Ashton Strategy is far less ambitious. It avoids a clear commitment to any fixed negotiation goal and merely refers to the 'improvement of the EU status and its alignment with the objectives of the EU Treaties'.[45] For the time being, full participation of the EU in the UN framework as a member organisation seems to have been abandoned as the final aim, giving way to a strategy of piecemeal steps towards modest upgrades wherever these appear to be legally and politically feasible.

One of the ways forward recommended by the Barroso-Ashton Strategy is the application of Resolution 65/276 in UNGA subsidiary organs.[46] In particular, the Strategy recommends to focus, among others, on the HRC and to avoid 'reopening the resolution, under which [subsidiary bodies] are not explicitly covered'.[47]

The HRC, which in 2006 replaced the UN Commission on Human Rights,[48] is a body of 47 elected UN Member States, tasked with the promotion of human rights and fundamental freedoms. It addresses cases of human rights violations, provides recommendations, and monitors the fulfilment of each State's human rights obligations through the universal periodic review ('UPR'). As one of the foremost global human rights fora, it is of significant importance for the Union's external action.[49]

The EU quickly developed into a strong supporter for the establishment of the HRC.[50] 'Welcom[ing] the presentation of a proposal reflecting the primacy of human rights by the creation of a Human Rights Council',[51] the EU actively lobbied for the realisation of its vision of the Council, which foresaw not only the creation of a standing body, possibly with the rank of a main organ of the UN, but whose membership should also be elected by a two-thirds majority of the UNGA and be smaller in numbers, admitting only those States that demonstrated genuine interest in the promotion of human rights.[52] Although the EU eventually had to compromise on many of its

44 Communication from the Commission to the Council and the European Parliament, *supra*, n. 41, p. 17.

45 Barroso-Ashton-Strategy, note 4, p. 1.

46 Ibid., 4.

47 Ibid.

48 UNGA Res. 60/251, *Human Rights Council*, 15 March 2006.

49 Cf. e.g. Council of the European Union, Council conclusions on EU priorities at the UN Human Rights Fora, Foreign Affairs Council meeting, 10 February 2014.

50 Jan Wouters, S. Basu, N. Bernaz, *The Role of the European Union in the Human Rights Council*, European Parliament, Directorate-General for External Policies, EXPO/B/DROI/2007/41, November 2008, p. 6 *et. seq.*; for a more recent analysis, see Jan Wouters and K. Meuwissen, 'The European Union at the UN Human Rights Council. Multilateral Human Rights Protection Coming of Age?', *European Journal of Human Rights* (forthcoming).

51 EU Presidency, Statement by the Representative of Luxembourg to the United Nations, Formal Plenary Session of the UN General Assembly, PRES05-032EN, 6 April 2005.

52 Wouters, Basu, Bernaz, note 49, p. 10.

positions, it commented favourably on the final outcome and welcomed the HRC as an improvement over the Commission on Human Rights.[53] The Union has remained an active supporter of the HRC ever since, participating extensively in the 2009–2011 review process,[54] supporting special procedures and the Office of the High Commissioner for Human Rights, and proposing or supporting resolutions. Despite several recent successes,[55] the Union's impact at the HRC has often been described as marginal due to its inability, at least until recently, to forge cross-regional coalitions. This was caused by a lack of credibility in light of the Union's persistent 'double-standards problem', but also by its inflexible negotiation practice, defensive stance and insufficient outreach.[56]

Effective EU participation is, among others, hindered by its legal status in the HRC. Full membership is only open to UN Member States. The Union has observer status, meaning that it cannot itself vote or sponsor resolutions, and while it has the right to make interventions, it may not do so in the speaking slots for States.[57] The EU thus remains dependent on the representation by a Member State, in particular by the rotating Council Presidency. Even after the entry into force of the Lisbon Treaty, the Union's participation in the HRC is clogged by cumbersome internal coordination processes, which often focus on burden-sharing rather than on substantive issues.[58] This heavy focus on the internal process often leaves insufficient time and resources to gather support for EU positions and to build successful coalitions. The necessary internal coordination also reduces the Union's flexibility during negotiations and with regard to new and unforeseen developments. Nevertheless, caution should be exercised to regard a status upgrade as a panacea that will solve all of the abovementioned issues. On the contrary, the Union must avoid contributing to the persistent bloc dynamics in the Council. In parallel

53 UNGA, EU Explanation of vote on the draft resolution on the Human Rights Council (L.48), Statement by Ambassador Gerhard Pfanzelter, Permanent Representative of Austria to the United Nations, on behalf of the European Union, 15 March 2006.

54 UNGA Res. 60/251, note 47, para. 1, 16.

55 See, for example, the initiative for the establishment of a new country mandate for Belarus, A/HRC/RES/20/13 of 16 July 2012.

56 Wouters and Meuwissen, *supra*, n. 49; Karen Smith, 'The European Union at the Human Rights Council: speaking with one voice but having little influence' (2010) *Journal of European Public Policy*, 224–241. A salient and frequently cited example of EU a 'failure' at the HRC includes the resolution terminating the expert mandate for the DR Congo where the EU joined the consensus although it had previously invested considerable diplomatic efforts for a renewal (HRC Resolution 7/20, Technical cooperation and advisory services in the Democratic Republic of the Congo, 27 March 2008), S. Basu, 'The European Union in the Human Rights Council', in *The European Union and Multilateral Governance: Assessing EU Participation in United Nations Human Rights and Environmental Fora*, Jan Wouters, H. Bruyninckx, S. Basu and S. Schunz (ed.), Basingstoke (Palgrave Macmillan 2012), 86–102, 91 *et. seq.*

57 S. Basu, note 55, p. 90; Wouters and Meuwissen, *supra*, n. 49.

58 Wouters and Meuwissen, note 49.

with efforts to improve its status in the Council, it should fully seize the possibilities offered by EU Member States participating in the Council, which can support the Union's message and bring invaluable expertise and third-country networks.[59]

While there appear to be no plans to eventually aim for full EU membership in the HRC, the Barroso-Ashton Strategy considers to promote the extension of Resolution 65/276 and thereby to grant the EU enhanced participation rights. This would permit the Union to participate in the work of the HRC 'in its own right', thus aligning its external representation with the requirements of Article 221 TFEU. However, the question remains whether it is legally and politically feasible to extend the application of Resolution 65/276 to the HRC. Adoption of the Resolution in the UNGA alone was not sufficient to modify the procedures of the HRC, given that the competence to decide on the granting of observer status and the modalities of participation rests with the Council.[60] Participation of and consultation with observers in the HRC is governed by Rule 7(a) of its Rules of Procedure, which provides:

> The Council shall apply the rules of procedure established for committees of the General Assembly, as applicable, unless subsequently otherwise decided by the Assembly or the Council, and the participation of and consultation with observers, including States that are not members of the Council, the specialized agencies, other intergovernmental organizations and national human rights institutions, as well as non-governmental organizations, shall be based on arrangements, including Economic and Social Council resolution 1996/31 of 25 July 1996, and practices observed by the Commission on Human Rights, while ensuring the most effective contribution of these entities.

Enhanced participation rights for the Union would be within reach, if, first, Resolution 65/276 was part of the rules of procedure established for the UNGA committees and if, second, the UNGA and the HRC did not decide against its application. As to the first point, in a narrow reading the term 'rules of procedure' in Rule 7(a) of the HRC's rules of procedure might refer only to the UNGA's rules of procedure *sensu stricto*, which in Section XIII contain provisions for the proceedings in the committees.[61] A broader understanding of the term, however, would not depend on the formal status of a provision, but on its substance, thereby widening the scope to include resolutions that

59 Ibid., 19; Gstöhl, note 5, 190.

60 The HRC has made use of its competence to adopt its own rules of procedure, cf. UNGA Res. 60/251, *supra*, n. 47, para. 11; HRC Resolution 5/1, Institution-building of the United Nations Human Rights Council, 18 June 2007; Jan Wouters, Jed Odermatt and Tomas Ramopoulos, The Lisbon Treaty and the Status of the European Union in the International Arena: The May 2011 Upgrade at the UN General Assembly, (2011) *IEMed. Yearbook* 2011, 166–170.

61 UNGA, Rules of Procedure of the General Assembly, A/520/Rev.17, 2008.

govern the procedure of the Assembly and its committees. This would also include the various resolutions granting participation rights to non-Member States and observers – matters on which the UNGA's rules of procedure *sensu stricto* are silent. Given that Resolution 65/276 contains 'modalities [. . .] for the participation of the representatives of the European Union, in its capacity as observer, in the sessions and work of the General Assembly and its committees',[62] it can be regarded as forming part of the rules of procedure referred to in Rule 7(a) of the HRC's rules of procedure and would therefore find application in the HRC.

Second, however, the question remains as to whether the UNGA or the HRC 'subsequently [decided] otherwise'. Neither body adopted an explicit decision against the application of Resolution 65/276 in the HRC. They may have done so implicitly, though. At first glance, the sweeping title of the Resolution ('Participation of the European Union in the work of the United Nations') suggests a broad scope of application across the entire spectrum of UN bodies.[63] But it was clearly not the intention of the drafters to modify the EU's status in the UN framework in general, first because this would entail a restriction in those fora where the EU obtained full participant or membership status and thus even broader participation rights; second because the UNGA lacks the competence to set the rules of procedure for the various UN bodies and fora.[64] Instead, Resolution 65/276 limits its application to the 'sessions and work of the General Assembly and its committees and working groups, in international meetings and conferences convened under the auspices of the Assembly and in United Nations conferences'.[65] While this list is not explicitly declared to be exhaustive, it reveals a conscious inclusion of several subsidiary organs, namely committees and working groups, while other subsidiary bodies, such as boards, commissions, councils and panels, were omitted. It could therefore be argued that Resolution 65/276 implies a decision by the UNGA against its application in the HRC, in the terms of Rule 7(a) of the HRC's rules of procedure.

Independent of the legal aspects, the political feasibility of a status upgrade remains doubtful. Significant resistance, both externally and internally, against an enhanced EU status at the HRC has caused the current cautious approach of the Union. States, including the EU Member States, continue to regard human rights as a state prerogative and hesitate to accept 'that actors at the level of the EU [. . .] take over the role of state actors'.[66] The extension of Resolution 65/276 to the HRC therefore remains a rather distant possibility, which seems also reflected in the fact that it has completely disappeared in

62 UNGA Res. 65/276, note 26, para. 2.
63 Wouters, Odermatt and Ramopoulos, note 59, 5.
64 Cf. Article 30 UN Charter (UNSC), Article 72 UN Charter (ECOSOC), Article 30(1) ICJ Statute (ICJ).
65 Note 61.
66 Wouters and Meuwissen, note 49, 19.

the 2013 information note on the implementation of the Barroso-Ashton Strategy.[67]

## 4 The status of the EU in the wider UN system

The EU has also pursued the objective of improving its representation at other UN agencies. In this regard, the EU is faced with an important question: which bodies should it prioritise? The Barroso-Ashton Strategy proposes a set of criteria based on interest and prospect: status enhancement should be sought in those organisations that have both a 'strategic or economic interest' for the EU and/or 'impact on policy areas where the EU has important competences', and in which 'an upgrade appears realistic in the short to medium term'.[68] Regrettably, neither of those factors is explained in more detail. It thus remains unclear which criteria the Strategy applies to determine the feasibility of a status upgrade. Also, the interest criterion is by far too broad to allow for a workable prioritisation of Union efforts. There remain very few issues dealt with by the UN that are not of strategic or economic relevance to the EU or which do not impact areas of important Union competences. This criterion, too, would have benefited from a more thorough definition in order to make the selection of priority organisations more transparent.

This section examines two bodies that were identified in the Barroso-Ashton Strategy as targets for resumed efforts for EU participation. These two case studies illustrate the 'shadowiness' of the EU as an actor in the wider UN system, a result of its indeterminate status in many of these bodies.

### *4.1 Food and Agriculture Organization (FAO)*

The Food and Agriculture Organization (FAO) is among those organisations for which the Strategy instructs Commission services and the EEAS 'to sustain their efforts with a view to a positive outcome', given that 'efforts to upgrade the EU status or improve the position of the EU within the existing arrangements are underway and progress is being made'.[69] The FAO is the second oldest UN specialised agency, founded against the background of the Second World War, which had given rise to the idea that 'international cooperation between nation states and the international regulation and supervision of economic sectors with strategic significance [. . .] could act as safeguards against future conflicts'.[70] Tasked with eradicating hunger, combatting

67 Information Note, note 40.

68 Barroso-Ashton-Strategy, note 4, 3.

69 Ibid., 2.

70 F. Schild, 'The Influence of the Food and Agriculture Organization (FAO) on the EU Legal Order', R.A. Wessel and S. Blockmans (eds), *Between Autonomy and Dependence: The EU Legal Order Under the Influence of International Organisations*, (Asser 2013), 217–241, 224.

poverty and promoting the sustainable use of natural resources, the FAO provides a network and forum of discussion for the dissemination of knowledge, expertise and up-to-date information.[71]

Although the EU has obtained the status of a Member Organisation[72] at the FAO, its effective representation continues to face serious challenges. These result first from the fact that, as a Member Organisation, the EU does not enjoy the same rights as Members: it may not hold office in the Conference, the Council and their subsidiary bodies,[73] it has no voting rights for elective places[74] or budget matters,[75] and no participation rights in the restricted committees[76] and the bodies dealing with the internal working of the conference.[77] In its FAO Communication, the Commission thus declared a need to address the limitations of the FAO Constitution in order to achieve coherence with the Lisbon Treaty and to achieve full and equal EU participation.[78] Given that any changes to the current modalities require a two-thirds majority in the biannual FAO Conference, the prospects of this initiative appear dim.

An additional complicating factor lies in the phenomenon of mixity. Since the EU acceded to the FAO as a Member Organisation alongside its Member States, speaking and voting rights have to be exercised on an alternative basis.[79] This causes a twofold problem of external transparency and internal coordination.

The biggest hurdle for effective EU participation at the FAO remains the cumbersome internal coordination process between Member States and EU institutions. In order to facilitate the procedure, the Commission and Council agreed in the internal 'Arrangement Between the Council and the Commission

71 J. Maersk Pedersen, 'FAO-EU Cooperation: An Ever Stronger Partnership', in Jan Wouters, Frank Hoffmeister and T. Ruys (eds), *The United Nations and the European Union: An Ever Stronger Partnership* (Asser 2006), 63–91, 63 *et. seq.* On the crisis of the FAO and the role of the EU in the reform process see R. Kissack, *Pursuing Effective Multilateralism: The European Union, International Organisations and the Politics of Decision Making*, (Basingstoke: Palgrave Macmillan 2010), 87–94.

72 Article II(3) FAO Constitution.

73 Article II(9) FAO Constitution; Rules XLIII (3), XLIV FAO General Rules.

74 Rule XLV (2) FAO General Rules.

75 Article XVIII (6) FAO Constitution.

76 Programme Committee, Finance Committee, Committee on Constitutional and Legal Matters, Art. II(9) FAO Constitution, Rule XLVI FAO General Rules.

77 In particular: Credentials Committee, General Committee, Rule XLIII (2) FAO General Rules.

78 FAO Communication, note 17, p. 6; cf. H. de Waele, '"Name me your friends, and I will tell you who you are" – The Union and the Member States in the global arena,' in *The European Union's Emerging International Identity: Views from the Global Arena*, Henri de Waele and Jan-Jaap Kuipers (eds), note 23, 239–256, at 242.

79 Article II(8), (10) FAO Constitution; on the exercise of voting rights see J. Heliskoski, 'Internal Struggle for International Presence: The Exercise of Voting Rights Within the FAO', in *The General Law of E.C. External Relations*, Alan Dashwood and Christophe Hillion (eds), (Sweet & Maxwell 2000), 79–99.

Regarding Preparation for FAO Meetings and Statements and Voting' that the EU exercises speaking and voting rights if the issue falls in the area of its exclusive competence and that the EU Member State holding the rotating Council Presidency is competent in case of Member State competence.[80] If an issue falls, both under EU and Member State competence, a common position should be sought, based on whether the 'thrust' of the issue falls in exclusive EU or Member States competence.[81] In case of disagreement, the matter will be referred to the COREPER.[82] This Arrangement has not only failed to avoid legal disputes in the past,[83] it also has not sufficiently streamlined the cumbersome process in which statements by the EU or the EU and its Member States are negotiated and agreed upon. Time-consuming discussions of procedural issues leave insufficient opportunity to focus on the substance, and weaken the EU's effective participation in the FAO. In an attempt to solve this problem, the Commission proposed a set of revised 'Arrangements between the Council and the Commission regarding the Exercise of Membership Rights of the European Union and its Member States in the Food and Agriculture Organisation (FAO)',[84] in Annex 2 of its 2013 FAO Communication. According to the draft arrangements, full statements shall in the future only be prepared in exceptional cases, while the new default modus for EU positions in the FAO shall be the one of 'lines to take'.[85] Although this would ensure greater flexibility for the external representative of the Union, fears of 'unscripted interventions with which Member States do not fully agree' have already been voiced[86] and indeed the additional effort, which Member States might invest to 'ensure lines to take [are] sufficiently tightly drafted to reduce these risks'[87] might negate any hopes of a more efficient coordination process. This is strongly suggested by a recent incident at the FAO, when the Commission representative deviated from the exact wording of a statement, which had been previously agreed during the Coordination Working Party, omitting or exchanging words that had been particularly contentious.[88] Nineteen EU Member States subsequently issued a joint statement in which they expressed their deep regret about the incident

80 Arrangement concerning preparation for the meetings of the FAO as well as interventions and voting ('Arrangement'), 18 December 1991, unpublished, reproduced in R. Frid, *The Relations between the EC and international organizations – Legal Theory and Practice* (Kluwer 1995), Annex VI, Article 2.1–2.2. The 1991 Arrangement was subsequently updated in 1992 and 1995.

81 Arrangement, Art. 2.3; Schild, *supra*, n. 69, p. 228.

82 Arrangement, Art. 1.12.

83 Case C-25/94, *Commission v. Council* [1996] ECR I-01469.

84 FAO Communication, note 17, Annex 2.

85 FAO Communication, note. 17, Annex 2, ch. 2.3.

86 United Kingdom, Explanatory Memorandum, para. 18.

87 Ibid.

88 Item 20.1 on the 148th session of the FAO Council, 4 December 2013.

and underlined that agreed statements should be fully respected.[89] A working method that accords a higher degree of flexibility to the Union representative might therefore fail to win the necessary support in the Council.

The example of the FAO shows that even though the Union obtained full membership status, its participation in the work of the organisation is still lagging behind.[90] This is not only due to the limitations that the FAO Constitution and the General Rules of Procedure impose on member organisations, but primarily results from EU internal procedures and quarrels. The Barroso-Ashton Strategy lists the FAO in the category of those international organisations where the prospects to improve the position of the Union are good, referring to the ongoing revision of the 1991 Arrangements between Council and Commission. In light of the above analysis, this evaluation of the Commission's FAO Communication might prove too optimistic. A two-thirds majority of the FAO Conference for the expansion of EU competences appears difficult to achieve, and EU Member States' fears of competence creep and loss of status might prevent the adoption of more flexible internal agreements.

### *4.2 International Maritime Organization (IMO)*

The IMO, a specialised agency of the UN, is an organisation where the EU may seek to upgrade its status in the near future.[91] It is one of the organisations that have been prioritised for a status upgrade in the Barroso-Ashton Strategy, based on the abovementioned criteria of interest and prospect.[92] The Union increasingly puts focus on the work of the organisation, especially with regard to working on international environmental issues (e.g. reduction in $CO_2$ emissions) and issues of ship safety.[93] While the EU currently has an emissions trading system that covers other fields of transport, including airlines operating in EU Member States,[94] it has not yet implemented a system that regulates

89 Council of the European Union, Joint statement concerning the representation of the EU and its Member States during the 148th session of the FAO Council, Doc. No. 17679/1/13, 13 December 2013.

90 Cf. Inge Govaere, J. Capiau and A. Vermeersch, 'In-Between Seats: The Participation of the European Union in International Organizations', (2004) *European Foreign Affairs Review* 155–187, 165.

91 Jan Wouters, de Jong, Axel Marx, and De Man, Study for the Assessment of the EU's Role in International Maritime Organisations, Final Report, April 2009.

92 Barroso-Ashton-Strategy, note 4, 3.

93 European Commission, Press Release, Transport: Vice President Kallas in talks with IMO Secretary General – focus on ship safety and reducing emissions, IP/13/409, 7 May 2013.

94 European Parliament and Council Directive 2008/101/EC of 19 November 2008 amending Directive 2003/87/EC so as to include aviation activities in the scheme for greenhouse gas emission allowance trading within the Community (O.J. 2009, L8/3).

emissions from maritime transportation. On 28 June 2013, the Commission set out its plan to integrate maritime emissions into the EU's policy for reducing its domestic greenhouse gas emissions.[95] Despite the slow pace of discussions within the IMO on this issue, the Union still views the IMO as the best international forum to regulate emissions from shipping, which currently constitute around 3 per cent of global greenhouse gas emissions.[96] The EU also plays an active role in other areas relevant to the IMO, such as maritime pollution and maritime safety. Apart from EU legislation in these fields, in 2003 the European Maritime Safety Agency (EMSA) was established to provide specialised technical assistance. Lastly, the EU and the IMO are both becoming active in the field of maritime security and piracy,[97] a topic that is increasingly important to the Union from a security standpoint. Besides, work undertaken by the IMO has led to amendments of the International Convention for the Safety of Life at Sea, 1974 (SOLAS Convention) and the International Ship and Port Facility Security Code (ISPS Code). Thus, interests as well as the significant EU legislation in fields covered by the work of the IMO support an enhanced status of the Union in the work of this organisation.

The European Commission (not the Community or the Union) has been an observer at the IMO since 1974. Although the Commission recommended to the Council to pursue full membership of the then EC in both the IMO and the ICAO back in 2002,[98] this was not supported by the EU Member States.[99] In the face of opposition from EU Member States that are IMO members, the Commission is now seeking instead to change the Commission's representation to that of the 'European Union' in accordance with the Lisbon Treaty. There are also significant external constraints that prevent the EU

95 Communication from the Commission to the European Parliament, The Council, The European Economic and Social Committee and the Committee of the Regions – Integrating maritime transport emissions in the EU's greenhouse gas reduction policies, COM(2013) 479.

96 Ibid., 4.

97 See IMO, Piracy and Armed Robbery Against Ships, 'Guidance to shipowners and ship operators, shipmasters and crews on preventing and suppressing acts of piracy and armed robbery against ships', MSC.1/Circ.1334, 23 June 2009; European Commission, Recommendation of 11 March 2010 on measures for self-protection and the prevention of piracy and armed robbery against ships, 2010/159/EU.

98 European Commission, Recommendation from the Commission to the Council in order to authorise the Commission to open and conduct negotiations with the International Civil Aviation Organization (ICAO) on the conditions and arrangements for accession by the European Community, SEC/2002/0381 final.

99 Cf. de Baere who observed that 'external sovereignty seems to be regarded as rather more sacred than internal sovereignty: the Member States are quite happy to accept Community-imposed restrictions on their regulatory competences with regard to internal policy areas, while refusing to accept parallel restrictions for the external aspects of the same areas', Geart de Baere, *Constitutional Principles of EU External Relations* (OUP 2008), 249–250, see also Govaere, Capiau and Vermeersch, note 89, 164.

from becoming a full IMO Member.[100] The IMO Convention is only open to States,[101] and EU membership would require the inclusion of a REIO clause, as was the case with the FAO. There is little incentive, however, to go through the process of treaty modification that would be necessary to amend the Convention, which would require the ratification of two-thirds of the IMO membership.[102]

The IMO therefore represents yet another organisation where, even though the Union has significant competences, legislation and interests in the fields dealt with by this IO, its lack of membership means that it must continue to rely on its Member States. This can cause problems within the EU's legal order. When the EU is not a formal member of an IO where significant Union competences are concerned, this can create a gap in legal obligations between the EU and its Member States, since only the Member States are formally bound under international law. For instance, in the *ATAA* case, the EU's non-membership of ICAO, another UN specialised agency, meant that the EU was not formally bound by a significant body of international law regulating air transport.[103] EU membership in international organisations such as ICAO and IMO would go a long way to filling this gap. Moreover, the Union's membership in global regulatory bodies such as IMO is important for it to safeguard its own significant regulatory framework. However, the prospects for status upgrade look rather dim, as illustrated by the 2013 information note on the implementation of the Barroso-Ashton-Strategy, which states that 'little or no progress could be achieved due to a changed political context' and recommends that '[s]ervices will sustain their efforts in order to unlock the situation'.[104]

## 5 Concluding remarks

Although cooperation with the UN is a significant political priority for the EU within a preferential system, efforts to enhance the Union's representation in the various UN bodies, and to become an influential 'actor' in this respect, have encountered stumbling blocks. The Union continues to deal with problems regarding representation in those fora where the EU Member States remain highly active, due to disagreements concerning the distribution of tasks, in particular with regard to speaking rights and negotiating mandates.

100 For further discussion on these constraints, see L. Nengye and F. Maes, 'Legal Constraints to the European Union's Accession to the International Maritime Organization' (2012) *Journal of Maritime Law & Commerce* 279–291.

101 Article 4 IMO Convention.

102 Article 66 IMO Convention.

103 Case C-366/10 *Air Transport Association of America and Others v. Secretary of State for Energy and Climate Change*, [2011] ECR I-1133.

104 Information Note, p. 3.

Moreover, the EU's efforts to upgrade its status at the UN, as illustrated by the diplomatic saga around the adoption of UNGA Resolution 65/276, did not go as smoothly as planned, and the gaps between the EU's status in most UN bodies and its competences and priorities significantly hinder the effective representation of the Union. Its position as a shadowy actor in the global legal order remains unchanged in light of the manifold strategies it pursues, the variety of means employed and its continued assertion of autonomy, irrespective of its transparency.

The EU epitomises the complexities of postnational rule-making. The Union is not only a forum in which postnational rule-making takes place, it is also increasingly an international actor in its own right, and has sought to influence international legal developments. Yet the EU's path to 'actorness' in the UN and the UN system has been met with numerous legal and political obstacles, both internal and external. The EU's status within these bodies is also an example of the tension between formalism and flexibility that was discussed in the introduction to this volume. Unable to secure full rights as a member in many UN bodies, the EU has had to employ flexible methods that would allow it to continue to assert influence within the World Organization.

# 8 Lawmakers in the shadows

## Legal academics in the construction of European private law

*Ruth Sefton-Green*[1]

> The role of legal science then is not as a handmaiden to the powers that be; nor as an autonomous source of law; but as a transmission belt between the social and political sphere in an organic process.[2]

The fact that legal academics, *qua* experts, help construct European private law, or more precisely, are involved in its rule production, can be regarded from two perspectives: first, the legitimacy of legal academics' activity, from a democratic point of view; second, the scientific legitimacy of such an enterprise. Although much has been written about the latter, the focus of this paper will be on the former, which means that as a legal academic, as opposed to a political scientist, I need to open up the boundaries of my enquiry. I am, therefore, going to explore the process in which European private law is fabricated. I am interested in the actors[3] of the process and the processes themselves, rather than the object, i.e. the construction of European private law, in terms of production of legal knowledge, or even European legal science.[4] In other words, legal academics are the subject of this enquiry,

1 I would like to thank Jacobien Rutgers for her perspicacious comments on an earlier draft of this paper.

2 H. Schepel, 'The European Brotherhood of Lawyers: the Reinvention of Legal Science in the Making of European Private Law', (2007) 32 (1) *L & Social Inquiry* 183–199, 193. The no doubt ironic use of the term 'European brotherhood of lawyers' by Schepel is attributed originally to Ole Lando, 198.

3 Max Weber famously coined the phrase of 'legal *honoratioren*'. The focus on actors can be contrasted with an institutional approach, see e.g. K. Purnhagen, 'The Architecture of Post-National Contract Law from a Phenomenological Perspective. A question of Institutions' (2013) *The Rabel J of Comparative and Intl Private L* 592–619.

4 For example, see R. Zimmermann, 'Civil Code and Civil Law – The Europeanization of Private Law within the European Community and the Re-emergence of a European Legal Science' (1994–1995) 1 *Colum J Eur L* 63; C. Schmid, 'The Emergence of a Transnational Legal Science in European Private Law' (1999) 19 *OJLS* 673–689; Schepel (n 1); M.W. Hesselink, 'A European Legal Science? On European private law and scientific method?' (2009) 15 *Eur LJ* 20–45; T. Lundmark, 'Legal Science and European Harmonisation' (2014) 130 *LQR* 68–82. It is noteworthy that the idea of a European legal science does not appear to preoccupy legal academics from common law countries.

not the object. However, for obvious reasons, an external viewpoint of legal academics' production and activity is adopted.[5]

As a preliminary, we need to clarify the meaning of the expression 'lawmakers in the shadows'. According a lexicographical definition, a shadow signifies: (i) something dark; (ii) figuratively close, sad or gloomy; and more pertinently (iii) an inseparable attendant or companion who follows the main actor.[6] Extrapolated from this third meaning, another dark side emerges. An inseparable attendant, or handmaiden, to adopt Harm Schepel's metaphor, can work in tandem, as well as in opposition, with the protagonist, or master. The significance of this nuance, illustrated in expressions such as the shadow cabinet (of the opposition) or the shadow economy (the unofficial or black-market), will be the cynosure of the enquiry.

It is uncontroversial that legal academics operate as lawmakers in the shadows in the sense that they follow, or work behind the scenes of, official legislative institutions and actors. These official actors include, of course, both the legislator and the judiciary,[7] though I will concentrate on legislative, rather than judicial, instances. It is quite customary, on a national level, for legal academics to be appointed on ad hoc committees,[8] to draw up recommendations about law reform, or draft proposed legislation. Examining the production process in the field of European private law, and in particular the role that legal academics play within it, will thus enable us to ascertain whether European lawmaking is distinctive, and can be differentiated from national lawmaking,[9] or whether it is more of the same. The fact that legal academics may have multiple and potentially split interests to promote, *inter alia*, national and European claims, requires our special attention. The link, whether interpersonal or a question of political orientation, between policymaking and rule production, is another promising line to follow.

The role of legal academics on the European legal scene is manifold, ranging from: (i) giving opinions to European institutions in the prior stages of European legislation; (ii) participating as stakeholders in consultation processes; (iii) being involved in purely academic projects, such as the Draft Common Frame of Reference; (iv) assuming an official function on a committee for drafting instruments, such as the draft Common European Sales Law; and (v) advising national governments on European projects, including how to transpose European Directives into national law. In addition to the roles played on stage, the voices of the critics, the players 'off scene', should not

5 H.L.A. Hart, *The Concept of Law* (2nd edn, Clarendon Press 1994); See N. Jansen, 'The Authority of an Academic CFR' in F. Cafaggi and H.W. Micklitz (eds), *European Private Law After the CFR* (Edward Elgar 2010) 147–172.

6 See *Oxford English Dictionary* entry under 'shadow' and 'shadows'.

7 See, for example, A. Vauchez, *Dans la fabrique du droit européen, Acteurs, scenes et publics de la Cour de justice des communautés européennes* (Bruylant 2009).

8 For example, The Law Commission of England and Wales.

9 J. Gordley, 'The State's Private Law and Legal Academia' (2008) 56 *Am J Comp L* 639–654.

be neglected. Evaluating the lawmaking process is a quintessential attribute of the legal community and legal academics in particular, of which the Social Justice Study Group's Manifesto on European Private Law is a paradigmatic illustration.[10]

This multifaceted and potentially ambivalent nature of legal academics' roles in the process of constructing European private law merits further enquiry. After an initial identification of legal academics' diverse roles, this chapter will focus on critically assessing them.

## 1 An improvisation in five scenes. Who plays which part?

In order to examine the nature of legal academics' role in the construction of European private law in depth, a short description is required. Of course, abundant literature about the Europeanisation of private law, as a construction process, already exists.[11] Certain special characteristics of European lawmaking process need to be highlighted in order to examine the role legal academics play in it. This survey is not exhaustive and takes the form of an empirical observation: it attempts to follow a temporal reality by examining one instance of the construction of European law, so as to connect the enquiry to a concrete series of events. The focal point is the role numerous legal academics have played in the construction of a particular European legislative project, which has been named variously the European Civil Code ('ECC'), the Draft Common Frame of Reference ('DCFR'), the Common Frame of Reference ('CFR') and now the Common European Sales Law ('CESL'). In particular, attention will be paid to the design, which appears to be an improvised rather than preconceived, or properly thought out, product and process.

### *1.1 Scene 1: The birth of the European Civil Code idea*

To do this, I need to construct my own narrative,[12] or even become a dramaturge. One of the difficulties about this plot, like many others, is to unravel where it starts. An obvious starting place would be the European

10 Study Group on Social Justice in European Private Law (2004) 10 *Eur L J* 653–674.

11 Consequently, reference to such prolific literature is inevitably selective: see, for example, the contributions in S. Grundmann and J. Stuyck, *An Academic Green Paper on European Contract Law* (Kluwer Law International 2000); C. Joerges, 'The Challenges of Europeanization in the Realm of Private Law: A Plea for a New Legal Discipline' (2004) 14 *Duke J. Comparative and International Law* 149–196; S. Grundmann, 'European Contract Law(s) of What Colour?' (2005) 1 *Eur Rev Contract L* 184–210; R. Michaels and N. Jansen, 'Private Law Beyond the State? Europeanization, Globalisation, Privatization' (2006) 54 *Am J Comp L* 843; L. Miller, *The Emergence of EU Contract Law, Exploring Europeanization* (OUP 2011); C. Twigg-Flesner, *The Europeanisation of Contract Law. Current Controversies in Law* (2nd edn, Routledge 2013).

12 J.B. Baron, 'The Many Promises of Storytelling in Law' (Book review) (1991–1992) 23 *Rutgers L J* 79.

Commission's consultation paper of 2001,[13] which suggested four options, two of which could be taken seriously. The first soft option was to promote the development of common contract law principles, leading to greater national convergence. The second hard option was to adopt comprehensive legislation at EU level.[14] However, as Harm Schepel has already related: the Commission's idea was initiated a long time before that, over dinner in the Tivoli gardens, where Winfried Hauschild of the European Commission suggested to Ole Lando that 'we' needed a European Civil Code.[15] Following this suggestion, the Lando Commission was established in 1982,[16] and drew up the Principles of European Contract Law ('PECL'), published in 2000 and 2003. Notice that the Lando Commission research group received funding from the European Commission.[17] In between setting up the first research project and its publications, two noteworthy resolutions of the European Parliament must be recorded: its 1989 call for a 'common European Code of private law',[18] as well as its 1994 reminder to codify European private law, mentioning the Lando Commission's work explicitly.[19] History repeats itself. In 1998, Christian von Bar set up the Study Group on a European Civil Code (the 'SGECC'),[20] which superseded, rather than competed with, the Lando Commission.[21] We could now call this scene one of the academic projects relating to European contract law.

### *1.2 Scene 2: Withdrawal and a new gestation period*

Consultation duly followed the Commission's 2001 paper, along with a vehement academic controversy. Academics divided into fierce partisans for and against what was considered to be the Commission's proposals for a veiled

13 Communication from the Commission on European contract law, COM (2001) 398; D. Staudenmayer, 'The Commission Communication on European Contract Law and the Future Prospects,' (2002) 51 *ICLQ* 673–88.

14 The European Parliament follow-up was to suggest these two options be carried out one after the other. See European Resolution on the approximation of the civil and commercial law of the Member States, (2002) OJ C 140 E/538. G. Dannemann and S. Vogenauer (eds), *The Common European Sales Law in Context* (OUP 2014) 5 call these different responses the 'remedial' and 'grand' solutions, respectively.

15 Schepel (n 1) 188.

16 O. Lando, 'European Contract Law' (1983) 31 *Am J Comp L* 653–659.

17 H. Beale and O. Lando (eds), *Principles of European Contract Law – Parts I and II* (Kluwer 2000) preface.

18 European Parliament Resolution on action to bring into line the private law of Member States (1989) OJ C 158/400.

19 European Parliament Resolution on the harmonization of certain sectors of the private law of the Member States (1994) OJ C205/ 518.

20 Details of the organisation and members of the SGECC can be found on <www.sgecc.net> accessed 28 October 2014.

21 Schepel (n 1) 189, DCFR (n 30) Introduction, para 49.

European Civil Code.[22] The Commission's now famous Action Plan of 2003[23] was published as a sequel and scene 2 took place in the aftermath. In its Action Plan, the Commission used a back-tracking strategy; rather than proposing to promote comprehensive hard legislation, it favoured investigating an optional instrument instead, coming up with a new proposal for a Common Frame of Reference ('CFR'),[24] subsequently nicknamed a 'Trojan horse'[25] and a 'sheep in wolf's clothing'.[26] Following the proposal for a CFR, and subsequently an additional discussion of the revision of the *Acquis communautaire*,[27] round two was thus the setting-up of Joint Network on European Private Law, a network of excellence, heavily funded by the Commission's Sixth Framework Programme from May 2005 onwards ('CoPECL').[28] Notice that on two separate occasions, the Commission has steered and invested in legal academic research projects relating to European private law. Is this an exclusively European model, or an exaggerated copy of national actors' behaviour? In any case, it is obvious that the respective roles of politics and production of legal knowledge overlap. This did not escape the notice of the

22 Again, the literature is too copious to be cited in full. See, for example, against: P. Legrand, 'Against a European Civil Code' (1997) 60 *MLR* 44–63; Y. Lequette, 'Vers un code civil européen?' (2003) 107 *Pouvoirs* 97–126; in favour: C. von Bar, 'From Principles to Codification: Codification Prospects for European Private Law, (2002) 8 *Colombia J Eur L* 379–88; for a critical discussion, U. Mattei, *The European Codification Process. Cut and Paste* (Kluwer 2003).

23 Commission Communication, A More Coherent European Contract Law – An Action Plan, COM (2003) 68 final OJ C 140 E/538.

24 Ibid. para 59 16.

25 H. Collins, 'The Common Frame of Reference for EC Contract Law: A Common Lawyer's Perspective', in M. Meli and M.R. Maugeri (eds), *L'Armonizzazione del diretto privato Europe* (Giuffre Edn 2004) 107, 124: 'the common frame of reference, may like a Trojan horse, smuggle into Europe a Code of Contract law (. . .) Let's just call it a Code;' European Union Committee, House of Lords, 12th Report of Session 2004–5, European Contract Law – The Way Forward? Report with Evidence (5 April 2005) HL Paper 95, HMSO, paras 27–28. For a critical overview, see H. Collins, *The European Civil Code. The Way Forward* (CUP 2008) ch III The Hidden Code.

26 B. Lurger, 'The Common Frame of Reference/Optional Code and the Various Understandings of Social Justice in Europe,' in T. Wilhelmsson, E. Paunio and A. Pohjolainen (eds), *Private Law and the Many Cultures of Europe* (Kluwer International 2007) 177–199.

27 Commission Communication, European Contract Law and the Revision of the *Acquis*: the Way Forward, COM (2004) 651 final. It became apparent subsequently that the European Parliament was not duped by the Commission's strategy: see European Parliament, Resolution on European Contract Law and the revision of the Acquis, 23.03.2006, A6–0055/2006: 'even though the Commission denies that this is the objective, it is clear that many of the researchers and stakeholders working on the project believe that the ultimate long-term outcome will be a European code of obligations or even a fully blown European civil code.' Schepel (n 1) 190, suggests that the European Parliament is 'prone to conspiracy theories'.

28 See for information about the participants and activities of CoPECL available at: <www.copecl.org> accessed 28 October 2014; Schepel (n 1) 189–190 indicates funding was 'to the tune of 5 million euros'. See Dannemann and Vogenauer (n 13) 7–9 for a more detailed description of the 'fusion of political and academic activities'.

Social Justice Group, which has criticised the legitimacy of the Commission's methods on a number of grounds.[29]

### *1.3 Scene 3: Project babies*

Scene 3 marks the birth of a number of academic projects. The period between 2005 and 2009 was highly fertile; but the cynics might add that the stakes were high. Legal academics produced various books to fulfil the requirements of CoPECL, namely in chronological order: (i) the Principles of Existing European Contract Law: the *Acquis* Principles in 2007;[30] (ii) the Draft Common Frame of Reference, interim (in 2008), then outline edition in 2009;[31] (iii) *Terminologie contractuelle commune*;[32] and (iv) *Principes contractuels communs*, by the *Association Henri Capitant des amis de la culture française* and the *Société de legislation comparée* in 2008.[33] The *Acquis* Principles and the DCFR were then subject to assessment and academic evaluation, as part of the network of excellence,[34] as well as both internal[35] and external criticism.[36] Once again, there is nothing more natural than that: a great many academic productions are subject to academic scrutiny. The distinctive characteristic of academics' behaviour in this respect is to take off a European group hat and don an external and critical perspective. For example, certain legal academics, such as Martijn Hesselink, have been part of the European research project network, at the same time as they have also undertaken to respond to certain foundational questions, linked to the end-goals of the research.[37]

29 Study Group on Social Justice (n 9). See also the contributions of the special issue of (2006) 2 *Eur Rev Contract L* publishing a conference of the Social Justice Group of June 2005.

30 Research Group on the Existing EC Private Law (Acquis Group) (ed), *Principles of the Existing EC Contract Law (Acquis Principles): Contract I* (Sellier 2007).

31 C. von Bar, E. Clive, H. Schulte-Nölke (eds), *Principles, Definitions and Model Rules of European Private Law: Draft Common Frame of Reference (DCFR) Interim Outline Edition* (Sellier 2008); C. von Bar and E. Clive (eds), *Principles, Definitions and Model Rules of European Private Law: Draft Common Frame of Reference (DCFR) Full Edition* (Sellier 2009).

32 B. Fauvarque Cosson and D. Mazeaud (eds), *Terminologie contractuelle commune vol* 6 (Société de législation compare 2008).

33 B. Fauvarque Cosson and D. Mazeaud (eds), *Principes contractuels communs vol* 7 (Société de législation compare 2008).

34 L. Antoniolli and F. Fiorentini (eds), *Academic Commentary on the DCFR. A Factual Assessment* (Sellier 2010).

35 For an example of internal criticism, see e.g. R. Schulze and T. Wilhelmsson, 'From the DCFR towards European Contract Law Rules' (2008) 4 *Eur Rev Contract L* 154–168 (both authors were members of the Acquis Group).

36 E.g. M. Oderkerk, 'The CFR and Methods of Comparative Legal Research' (2007) 3(3) *Eur Rev Contract L* 350; N. Jansen and R. Zimmermann, 'Restating the Acquis Communautaire? A Critical Examination of the Existing EC Law' (2008) 71 *MLR* 505–534.

37 M.W. Hesselink was a member of the steering committee of the SGECC, the Social Justice Group and contributed, *inter alia*, to the following scholarly productions: Martijn Hesselink,

Or Bénédicte Fauvarque-Cosson, whose actions as a member of the steering committee of the SGECC, then CoPECL, as well as the *Association Henri Capitant* and *Société legislation comparé*, remain enigmatic. Normally members of national law commissions do not criticise their own work within their own legal community. They leave this to other members of the same legal community. Moreover, the evaluation and assessment process has engendered some internal competition between official and unofficial actors. For instance, the European Parliament, when taking stock of the evaluation process, warned the DCFR group that their project was unlikely to see the light of day in its contemporaneous format, thus putting the record straight as to exactly who was running the show.[38] The rivalry for political hegemony between the European Parliament and the European Commission is a leitmotif of this construction project. Furthermore, legal academics have indeed become engaged in a specifically European role, in that the battles for scholarly leadership[39] have enhanced international and national competitiveness.[40] German scholars on the outside criticised German scholars on the inside.[41] French scholars competed within CoPECL in that the works produced by the *Association Henri Capitant* amount to rival projects, which was not the original

Jacobien W. Rutgers, Odavia Bueno Díaz, Manola Scotton and Muriel Veldmann (eds), *Commercial Agency, Franchise and Distribution Contracts, Principles of European Law* (Sellier 2006); M.W. Hesselink, J.W. Rutgers and T.Q. de Booys, *The Legal Basis for European Contract Law; Short study for the European Parliament on the different options for a future instrument on a Common Frame of Reference (CFR) in EU contract law, in particular the legal form and the legal basis for any future optional instrument*, PE 393.280 (February 2008); M.W. Hesselink, *The CFR and Social Justice* (Sellier 2008). With respect to the latter, S. Grundmann, 'The role of competition in the European codification process', in Cafaggi and Micklitz (n 4) 36–55; 40 fn 6, intimates that 'this contribution (and criticism made there) should be assessed against the background that Martijn Hesselink is a member of the Study Group [sic for Social Justice].'

38 Resolution of the European Parliament of 3.9.2008, P6-TA-PROV (2008) 0397: 'D. whereas the DCFR is merely an academic document and the possible selection of what parts of the DCFR are to be integrated into the forthcoming Commission document is a highly political exercise.'

39 U. Mattei, 'The Issue of European Civil Codification and Legal Scholarship: Biases, Strategies and Developments' (1998) 21 *Hastings Intl and Comp Rev* 883–902.

40 For an enquiry linking regulatory competition and nationalism in this context, see R. Sefton-Green, 'Concurrence normative, performance juridique et nationalisme juridique à la lumière de l'instrument optionnel en droit commun européen de la vente', in R. Sefton-Green and L. Usunier (eds), *La concurrence normative: Mythes et réalités* (Société de législation de droit comparé 2013) 189–208.

41 H. Eidenmüller, N. Jansen, E-M. Kieninger, G. Wagner, R. Zimmermann, 'The Common Frame of Reference for European Private Law – Policy Choices and Codification Problems' (2008) *OJLS* 28; N. Jansen and R. Zimmermann, '"A European Civil Code in all but name": Discussing the nature and purpose of the DCFR' (2010) 26(1) *CLJ* 98–112; Grundmann (n 35); K. Riesenhuber, 'A Competitive Approach to EU Contract Law' (2011) 7 *Eur Rev Contract L* 115–134; S. Grundmann, 'The Costs and Benefits of an Optional European Sales Law' (2013) 50 *CMLR* 225–242, esp. 234ff.

intention of the research project.[42] Legal academics within[43] and outside the EU[44] have criticised and commented on these academic projects.

Throughout the prolonged deliveries of the various scholarly books, legal academics, *qua* stakeholders, were simultaneously involved in consultation processes relating to other aspects of European contract law, such as the Consumer Rights Directive, for example, which was finally adopted in 2011.[45] Legal academics could thus respond as stakeholders in these processes, as many indeed did, defending national and professional interests, while working on European-funded projects for European contract law. There was nothing unusual about legal academics' part in the elaboration of the Consumer Rights Directive. However, it was complicated by the fact of its chronological overlap with other academic projects on European private law, illustrating once again the Commission's indecisiveness about the scope and ambit of European private law.

### *1.4 Scene 4: Handing the baby over to a wet nurse: the expert group*

Scene 4 establishes a new scenario, explicitly altering the nature of legal academics' role, even though some of the characteristic features outlined above reappear. It marks the setting up of a formal committee of experts, nominated by the Commission, along the familiar lines of a Commission expert group (the 'Expert Group').[46] In April 2010, one project baby, the academic DCFR, was thus handed over to the Expert Group appointed to draft another Common Frame of Reference. Unsurprisingly, this in turn gave rise to a further consultation process.[47] The time frame for action was extremely short: a mere

42 R. Sefton-Green, 'The DCFR, the Avant-projet Catala and French Legal Scholars: A Story of Cat and Mouse?' (2008) *Edinburgh L Rev* 351–373. For a national call to join the European race, see B. Fauvarque-Cosson, 'Droit européen des contrats : les offre sont faites, les dés non encore jetés' (2008) n° 9 *Dalloz* 2–3.

43 Again the literature is abundant, for a famous example, see P. Legrand, 'Antivonbar' (2006) 1(1) *J Comp L* 13–40. Adde Y. Lequette, 'De la France et de l'Europe: la nation ou l'empire' in B. Ancel (ed.), *Etudes à la mémoire du professeur B. Oppetit* (Litec 2009); various contributions in Cafaggi and Micklitz (eds) (n 4).

44 For an external view, see, D. Caruso, 'The Baby and The Bath Water: The American Critique of European Contract Law' (2013) 61 *Am J Comp L* 479–500; Conference on European Contract Law at the University of Chicago: A Law-and-Economics Perspective, published in a special issue (2013) 1 *CMLR*.

45 Consumer Rights Directive 2011/83/EU, OJ L 304/64, 22.11.2011.

46 Commission Decision 2010/233/EU of 26.04.2010 setting up the Expert Group of the Common Frame of Reference in the Area of European Contract Law, OJ L 105, 27.04.2010, 109.

47 See Green Paper Policy of 1 July 2010, Options for progress towards a European Contract Law for Consumers and Businesses, COM (2010) 348. The responses to the consultation process are available at <http://ec.europa.eu/justice/news/consulting_public/news-consulting_0052.en.htm>, archived on 1 August 2011, now available: <europa.eu/rapid/press-release_MEMO-11-55_en.htm> accessed 21 November 2014.

18 months, unless one considers that the process has been going on for 10 years since 2001. In fact, the Expert Group set to work before the consultation process was finished, which would indicate that the outcome was to some extent predetermined.[48] The plot thickens. Retrospectively, this slice of European legislative activity can be described as circuitous yet intense, zigzagging in several directions, until it veered off to its final destination. Whether its final destination is unexpected or not, depends on one's powers to see through the European Commission's tergiversations.

### *1.5 Scene 5: The official offspring: the CESL*

In May 2011, the Expert Group published a feasibility study, with a draft regulation for CESL in the form of an optional instrument in the annexe.[49] A consultation with stakeholders was carried out concurrently. In August 2011, the European Commission published a work in progress report[50] followed by the launch of the official CESL project in October 2011, differing in some respects from the Expert Group's proposal, which was thus not adopted wholeheartedly.[51] In short, the draft regulation for a CESL contains an optional instrument to be used in cross border European sales contracts, of which two distinct categories are identified, known in the current jargon as B2C and B2B. In June 2011, the European Parliament expressed its approval of the optional instrument[52] and the legal committee of Parliament then carried out further enquiries and instructed more expert opinions from academics.[53] In February 2014, the European Parliament curtailed the scope of the instrument when it approved the 'blue button' approach, namely that the instrument will apply to cross-border electronic sales only.[54] Before this

48 See for a more detailed description of how events were orientated from an early stage, Riesenhuber (n 40).

49 European Commission, A European contract law for consumers and businesses: Publication of the results of a feasibility study carried out by the Expert Group on European Contract law for stakeholders' and legal practitioners' feedback (03.05.2011) <http://ec.europa.eu/justice/contract/files/feasibility_study_final.pdf> accessed 29 October 2014.

50 European Commission, 'European Contract Law: Work in Progress' (version of 19 August 2011) <http://ec.europa.eu/justice/contract/files/feasibility_study_final.pdf> accessed 29 October 2014.

51 European Commission Proposal for a Regulation of the European Parliament and of the Council on a Common European Sales law, 11.10.2011, COM (2011) 635 final.

52 Resolution of European Parliament 08.06.2011, TA_2011_0262, in favour of the optional instrument.

53 See European Parliament Committee on Legal Affairs, 'Working Document on the proposal for a regulation of the European Parliament and of the Council on a Common European Sales Law, 08.10.2012, JURI_DT (2012) 497786. The European Parliament has also requested that certain investigative studies be carried out, e.g. M. Behar-Touchais, member of TEE, 'Le fonctionnement du DCEV dans le cadre du Réglement Rome I, 2012, PE-462.477 <http://www.transeuropexperts.eu/index.php?part=4&sujet=177> accessed 29 October 2014.

54 Resolution of 26.02.2014, P7_TA (2014) 0159.

most recent development, several national governments had expressed their reluctance about the proposed regulation, *inter alia* on the basis of failure to respect subsidiarity,[55] and the proposal is still awaiting further discussion by the Council of Ministers. Once again, the CESL has also been subject to another round of academic gunfire, and of course more commentary.[56] The establishment of the European Legal Institute in June 2011 has increased the number of actors on the European scene. An independent non-profit-making organisation, the ELI describes its remit as 'the quest for better law-making in Europe and the enhancement of European legal integration'.[57] Of special interest is its evaluation report on the draft CESL.[58] Once again, legal academics have assumed the role of evaluating the 'doers' in the lawmaking process: a perfectly natural phenomenon.

The descriptive overview above has emphasised that the construction of European private law has been a strikingly improvised process, not only in terms of distributing roles to the actors, but most significantly in terms of the content and form of the play. If the play is about European private law, then the official and unofficial actors appear to have changed the meaning and structure of the play's subject matter as they went along. We may come out of this performance genuinely wondering what this play was all about. It is thus time for a critical review of the actors' performance and roles.

## 2 Critical review: the protagonist's role reversal

Much has been and still remains to be said about the overall design of the play, in terms of democratic transparency, democratic legitimacy and methods of policymaking. Yet this particular critical appraisal has its attention fixed on the actors and their democratic, as opposed to scientific, legitimacy. Two main threads emerge, after unearthing who was playing which role. First, the knotty triad of policymaking, technicality and expertise needs to be untied. Second, the nature of the relationship between official and unofficial actors

55 See e.g. for the UK, Ministry of Justice and Department for Business, Innovation and Skills, 'A Common European Sales Law for the European Union – A Proposal for a Regulation from the European Commission: the Government Response', 13.11.2012 <https://consult.justice.gov.uk/digital-communications/common-european-sales-law> accessed 29 October 2014.

56 R. Zimmermann, 'Codification. The Civilian Experience Reconsidered on the eve of the CESL' (2012) 8(4) *Eur Rev Contract L* 367. For some commentaries, see e.g. O. Deshayes (ed.), *Le droit commun européen de la vente. Examen de la proposition de réglement du 11 octobre 2011* (Société legislation comparé 2012); R. Schulze (ed.), *The Common European Sales Law. A Commentary* (Hart Publishing 2012); Dannemann and Vogenauer (eds) (n 13).

57 <https://www.europeanlawinstitute.eu/about-eli/> accessed on 29 October 2014. See also R. Zimmermann, 'Challenges for the European Law Institute' (2012) 16 *Edinburgh L Rev* 5–23.

58 Statement of the European Legal Institute on the Proposal for a Regulation on a Common European Sales Law Com (2011) 635 final, 2012 <http://www.europeanlawinstitute.eu/projects/publications/> accessed 29 October 2014.

will be explored: collaboration or competition? In other words, we need to find out who exactly is serving whom.

### *2.1 The symbiotic nature of policy-making and expertise*

Many political scientists have examined the role of experts in the EU, exploring questions such as how they appointed, how they become habitual or repeat experts, showing that social, cultural and professional contingencies may have a significant impact, rather than expertise per se. In general, such studies have shown how expertise and policymaking are closely intertwined.[59] The use of legal academics *qua* experts can be linked to an extended or, some would criticise, excessive use of expertise in consultation processes in the EU more generally and is thus the tip of a much bigger iceberg.[60] Many interrelated questions arise out of the use of experts and consultation processes as a form of governance and lawmaking, of which the political dimensions of European contract law and the legitimacy of legal academics due to lack of transparency, as well as their impartiality, are of special interest to us.

#### *2.1.1 The political dimensions of European contract law expertise*

##### 2.1.1.1 TECHNICAL EXPERTISE DOES NOT EXCLUDE POLICYMAKING

It is no longer possible to oppose the political and the technical. Cecile Robert, an expert on experts in the EU, has demonstrated thoroughly how expertise and political consensus are not in opposition.[61] According to her, experts' behaviour in the EU breaks down all the traditional antithetical barriers between: policymaking versus science and production of knowledge; interested parties versus impartial, objective experts; negotiation versus deliberation and even domination versus persuasion.[62] Hence, politicians no longer have the

59 See A. Gornitza and U. Sverdrup, 'Who Consults? Expert Groups in the European Union', Arena, Centre for European Studies, Working paper n° 12, August 2007 <http://www.sv.uio.no/arena/english/research/publications/arena-publications/workingpapers/working-papers2007/> accessed 29 October 2014; V. Vassalos, 'Secrecy and Corporate Governance, A study on the composition and transparency of European Commission Expert Groups,' ALTER-EU, 2008 <http://www.alter-eu.org/documents/2008/03/secrecy-and-corporate-dominance> accessed 29 October 2014; C. Robert and A. Vauchez, 'L'Académie européenne. Savoirs, experts et savants dans le gouvernement de l'Europe', (2010) 23 *Politix* 9–34; H. Michel and C. Robert (eds), *La fabrique des 'Européens' Processus de socialisation et construction européenne* (Presse Universitaire Strasbourg 2010).

60 See Gornitza and Sverdrup (n 58); C. Robert in Michel and Robert (eds) (n 58), 'Etre socialisé à ou par "l'Europe". Dispositions sociales et sens du jeu institutionnel des experts de la Commission européenne', 313–386; spec. 328–329.

61 C. Robert, 'Les groups d'experts dans le gouvernement de l'Union Européenne. Bilans et perspectives de recherché' (2010) 32 *Politique européenne* 7–38.

62 Ibid. 32.

exclusive monopoly over policymaking, partiality, negotiating and the ability to dominate. Consequently, it has become difficult to differentiate the specific zones of competence of the respective actors of lawmaking in the EU. Cécile Robert and Antoine Vauchez contend that expertise is eminently political, not objective and scientific; technicality can no longer disguise the political dimension of EU lawmaking.[63] The DCFR group's claim that their 'project was an academic text, not politically authorised',[64] has already been decried.[65]

The ability of the European Commission to steer academic research, as well as impact assessments,[66] whether by European instruments, such as Eurobarometers,[67] the kind of geared questions asked in consultation green papers,[68] or indeed the input of European funding for research projects, which the Commission wants produced,[69] are but a few examples. In any case, it is obvious that legal academics are not being asked to pursue purely academic technical research, which is depoliticised. Legal academics cannot plausibly claim just to be plumbers, or technicians, fiddling with nuts and bolts, which require purely technical expertise. The introduction to the DCFR admits this, though it both confronts and avoids the issue in its long list of underlying principles.[70] Indeed, legal academics' expertise is required precisely because they are able to assess the practical implications of political choices. The famous 'best solution' objective of the Commission's Action Plan[71] fits perfectly into this category. In part, this objective requires legal academics to make policy choices about the legal rules they propose. Surely it is better to call a spade a spade and admit that legal academics are involved in policy choice when they draw up legal rules, even in a so-called 'academic project'.[72] Hans Schulte-Nolke, a member of CoPECL and the Expert Group, has explained how the politicians had the final say and how the academics were left to work in the dark, i.e. that academic research is steered by the political-administrative actors.[73] Be that as it may, political scientists suggest it is far more complex

63 Robert and Vauchez (n 58) 11.

64 *DCFR* (n 30) Introduction, para 4.

65 For criticisms of the non-political pretentions of the project, see the numerous contributions in A. Somma (ed.), *The Politics of the DCFR* (Kluwer 2009).

66 See e.g. Caruso and contributions in (2013) *CMLR* (n 43).

67 For references to further enquiries, see Robert and Vauchez (n 58) 15.

68 For a discussion of the kind of leading questions the Commission asks in consultation with stakeholders, see J.W. Rutgers and R. Sefton-Green, 'Revising the Consumer Acquis: (Half) Opening the Doors of the Trojan Horse' (2008) 3 *Eur Rev Private L* 427–442.

69 For a naïve, or perhaps disingenuous, perception of the Commission's funding and aid for academic projects, see H. Schulte-Nölke, 'The Scope and Function of the Optional Instrument on European Contract Law' in R. Schulze and J. Stuyck (eds), *Towards a European Contract Law* (Sellier 2011) 35–45.

70 *DCFR* (n 30) paras 9–25.

71 See n 21.

72 R. Sefton-Green, 'The DCFR: A Technical or Political Toolbox' in Somma (ed.) (n 64) 39–50.

73 Schulte-Nölke (n 68).

than this since 'real decisions are often made in the early stages of the decision-making process'.[74] Hans Micklitz has pointed out how conforming to a model of 'apolitical neutral experts' leads to a paradox: both the drafters of the DCFR and CESL were caught in their own trap, as they were 'cut off from the more visible political issues', while at the same time were expected to find solutions to them.[75] In the same vein, a former expert of the EU, Jean-Michel Eymeric Douzan, has suggested experts are used as a soft power by the Commission, as a testing ground for sounding out policies,[76] while Nils Jansen has aired the idea of the DCFR as soft law, as a model with potential for influencing further legislation.[77]

Furthermore, the links between political-administrative actors and legal academics may be interpersonal, but exist nonetheless. The paradigm is Walter Hallstein, law professor and first president of the European Commission.[78] More specifically, in the field of European private law, it has already been pointed out that Dirk Staudenmayer of the European Commission was appointed an honorary degree at one or more universities where legal scholars deeply involved in CoPECL belong.[79] It is no secret that Benedicte Fauvarque-Cosson and Christian von Bar, both members of CoPECL, were appointed legal advisors to the Vice-President Commissioner, Viviane Reding, or that a Member of the European of Parliament, such as Diana Wallis, is a fellow of the ELI. It is not simply a question of ascertaining the politics of the law professors:[80] the description of legal academics involved in shadow lawmaking suggests that the relationship between the various actors is more sophisticated, infinitely more sinuous and permeable, rather than simply branding people with names and political labels.

#### 2.1.1.2 THE DEEPLY POLITICAL AGENDA OF RESEARCH: WHICH EUROPEAN CONTRACT LAW?

The functional market integration approach, proposed by the European Commission, has led to a split between legal academics in the field of European

74 Vassalos (n 58) 14.

75 H.W. Micklitz, 'A Certain Future for the Optional Instrument' in R. Schulze and J. Stuyck (eds), *Towards a European Contract Law* (Sellier 2011) 181–193, 183: 'complies with the still dominant understanding of academics as apolitical neutral experts'.

76 J-M. Eymeric-Douzan, in Michel and Robert (eds) (n 58) 311–312, esp. 307–308, where he suggests Eurocrats use experts as a sounding board to test out action plans on them as 'hommes ressources'.

77 Jansen (n 4).

78 See Robert and Vauchez (n 58) 14.

79 Grundmann (n 36) 53; Grundmann (n 40) 235, fn 18 where the author highlights the extraordinarily sedentary position of Staudenmayer, despite rules about rotating Commissioners.

80 M.W. Hesselink, 'A European Legal Method? On European Private Law and Scientific Legal Method' (2009) 15 *Eur L J* 20–45.

contract law: described as the European legal science camp let by Christian von Bar versus the *ius commune* camp led by Reinhard Zimmermann.[81] Is the division political or technical or both? The fact that the field, European contract law, is a malleable and ever-shifting domain complicates the enquiry. Legal academics do not all agree on what European contract law is or should be. This indeterminacy or uncertainty impacts on their democratic legitimacy, as well as their scientific objectivity. Questions such as where does European contract law begin and end, particularly in terms of the scope of legislation, highlight the real quandary the official and unofficial lawmakers in the EU are up against: what belongs to national and EU law? The competence question means that legal academics are forced to take sides.[82] These arguments thus show that the very object of legal academics' study is politically controversial, never mind the process leading to its elaboration. In short, the lawmaking process shared by official and unofficial actors in the EU corroborates the idea that policymakers and legal academics are dependent on one another: their relationship could be qualified as mutually parasitic, or symbiotic.

### *2.1.2 The legitimacy of legal academics: lack of transparency*

The legitimacy of legal academics *qua* experts can be criticised on the grounds of lack of transparency in several respects.[83] First, the method and content of the DCFR while it was in process was extremely opaque. Even though a CFR network was set up to monitor and give feedback on the CoPECL project, several academics who participated in the project admitted that it was inadequate and did not function properly.[84] The lack of transparency as to method was compounded by the publication of an unexpected rival project by the *Association Henri Capitant*, which had as its mandate, under CoPECL, to evaluate the DCFR. Moreover, the final production of the DCFR largely exceeded the scope of its research remit, producing 10 books on European private law, including extra contractual liability and property law, some of which no one was expecting, for instance Book X on Trusts,[85] or Book V on the Benevolent Intervention of Another's Affairs,[86] which hardly correspond to market integration imperatives. It is thus difficult to counter allegations of lack of transparency, since the DCFR ended up being an academic production, which did not correspond to its stated objective. Indeed, many have pointed out that the DCFR looks like a German Civil Code in English,

81 Schepel (n 1) 193.
82 Hesselink, Rutgers and de Booys (n 36).
83 Study Group for Social Justice (n 9).
84 See e.g. Hesselink (n 79).
85 See A. Braun, 'Trusts in the Draft Common Frame of Reference: the "Best Solution" for Europe?' (2011) 70 *CLJ* 327.
86 C. von Bar (ed.) *Benevolent Intervention of Another's Affairs* (Sellier 2006).

although that was not what the CFR was meant to be, according to the Commission's Action Plan.[87] Moreover, the fact that the CoPECL network was given a monopoly over the design and construction of European contract law has been disparaged.[88]

A second criticism about transparency relates to the appointment of legal academics as experts, this time in relation to the Expert Group, which drafted a provisional CESL. This criticism is an epiphenomenon, since the Commission's extended use of expertise is a more generalised problem, not limited to legal academics. However, it is worth pointing out here that it is not very clear to anyone exactly what criteria the European Commission use to appoint experts, since the process is somewhat obscure. These difficulties were compounded in our example. Just as criticisms were levelled at how membership of the CoPECL network was neither representative nor proportionate of all Member States, so the Expert Group is susceptible to the same objections.[89] Indeed, it is highly controversial whether membership of the Expert Group constituted good governance for a number of reasons.[90] Originally, the committee was composed of 18 members, seven of whom were members of the SGECC, two of the Acquis Group. [91] One could ask why some leading members of the CoPECL were nominated to the Expert Group, while others were conspicuously absent.[92] Fourteen of these members were legal academics, two of whom were invited as representatives of the legal professions. Or 12 members were legal academics and five were other legal experts, two of whom were also legal experts. After Simon Whittaker's resignation, the nine members of the CoPECL network had a majority within the Expert Group. Of the final 17 members, four were women and 14 men.[93] The membership of the Expert Group can thus be questioned on the following grounds: (i) lack of proportionate representation of Member States; (ii) lack of parity; (iii) the potential conflict of interests, or impartiality, of the legal academics appointed; and (iv) the quantitatively high representation of legal academics as opposed to other legal experts. Of course, those who took part in both CoPECL and sat on the Expert Group have responded to these allegations.

87 H. Collins, 'Review of the DCFR' (2008) 71 *MLR* 840–844.

88 Grundmann (n 36); Riesenhuber (n 40).

89 The various criticisms levelled at the composition of the Commission's expert groups exceeds the scope of this enquiry. For a recent survey in general, see <http://www.ombudsman.europa.eu/cases/correspondence.faces/en/54300/html.bookmark> accessed 21 November 2014.

90 See Riesenhuber's astute critical review ibid., which suggests that the principle of *nemo iudex in sua causa* applies to academic discussion.

91 See Annex to the press release, 'European Commission convenes legal expert group to seek solutions on contract law' 21 May 2010, IP/10/595/. The members of the SGECC are as follows: H. Beale, E. Clive, M.W. Hesselink, T. Hästad, I. Kull, H. Schulte-Nölke, A. Veneziano and those of the Acquis Group: L. Grynbaum and P. Mota Pinto.

92 It has already been pointed out that Bénédicte Fauvarque Cosson and Christian von Bar were appointed advisors to Vice-President Commissioner Viviane Reding.

93 <http://ec.europa.eu/transparency/index_en.htm> accessed 29 October 2014.

The stock answer that academic expertise signifies autonomy could be used,[94] but is it still true today? The appointment of certain members of the Expert Group seems to have blurred the lines between, on the one hand, an allegedly purely academic project and, on the other hand, a project formally oriented by the Commission. The Expert Group for the draft CESL thus runs the risk of failing to respect the requirements of democratic, as well as scientific, legitimacy.

### *2.1.3 The impartiality of legal academics*

We have seen that the European Commission makes use of academic expertise on the basis that impartiality is one of their core characteristics. I want to discuss whether, or to what extent, legal scholars are in fact neutral. Three aspects of the impartiality of legal academics *qua* experts will be examined. First, if expertise becomes increasingly politicised, the autonomy, or neutrality, of experts becomes compromised. Second, inferences can be drawn from the fact that academic research and expertise have become commodified. Third, what characterises legal academics as experts in the EU, and seems to distinguish them from the role legal academics play on a national playing field, is their juggling diverging interests: a phenomenon that shall be referred to as the multiple hats syndrome.

#### 2.1.3.1 THE POLITICISATION OF ACADEMIC RESEARCH AND EXPERTISE

The political steering of research on European private law projects has been discussed above. There is a risk that once the subject matter of expertise becomes explicitly politically oriented, it is more difficult for experts to maintain their political independence, though this may be hard to prove. Aside this difficulty, the highly political aspects of research in the field of European private law may have a more devastating effect on the neutrality, or complete autonomy, of experts. Again, this is a speculative rather than verifiable proposition. However, if it becomes increasingly difficult to differentiate the political and technical dimensions of research in European private law, the core of legal academics' expertise – their impartiality – is potentially compromised. For instance, Hans Schulte-Nölke's famous 'blue button' idea,[95]

94 Robert, in Michel and Robert (eds) (n 58) 337: 'La présomption d'autonomie don't bénéficient les universitaires constitue l'une des raisons qui concourent à la forte representation de ces derniers dans les groups d'experts. Au délà dex enjeux d'affichage et de l'efficacité sympbolique des titres universitaires, ce qui est ici recherché c'est à nouveau, la liberté de parole et le jugement dont dispenseraient les auteurs du monde "académique" à l'endroit de leurs gouvernements et administrations respectifs et, plus généralement, des politiques conduites au niveau national.'

95 H. Schulte-Nölke, 'EC Law on the Formation of Contract. From the Common Frame of Reference to the Blue Button' 3 (2007) *Eur Rev Contract L* 332–349.

relating to cross-border electronic sales contracts, is beginning to look prophetic today, now that the European Parliament has recently approved it.[96] We will never know whether Schulte-Nölke had access to information about the Commission's plans for the direction it really wanted the project on European contract law to go in 2005, or whether the Commission simply followed the direction that was initially suggested by a legal academic.

#### 2.1.3.2 ACADEMIC RESEARCH HAS BECOME COMMODIFIED

Even if the members of the Expert Group were not remunerated, expertise has its price. For instance, legal academics are paid for producing expert opinions and reports in the EU, even if remuneration is sometimes given to institutions and not to the reporters personally.[97] Expertise does not always come free; the CoPECL project was funded by the European project of excellence. There may be no relation of cause and effect. Sometimes legal academics give their expertise gratuitously in the EU, whereas sometimes they work on projects that receive an injection of European funding for research. Hans Micklitz has indicated how easy it is to identify 'the desire and readiness of the European Commission to "outsource lawmaking" to legal academics'.[98] Outsourcing is not usually carried out gratuitously.

The above observations raise many difficult questions. More specifically, legal academics' impartiality becomes more porous and suspicious, if the same academics put on different hats for varying purposes. Is it problematic if an academic responds to steered research and produces an opinion, for which she is paid, and then sits on a committee to draft legislation, for which she is not paid, on the same topic? Does remuneration have a qualitative impact on results? Is remuneration of certain legal academics' expert reports and opinions made for instrumental purposes in order to orientate results in a certain direction? Does the scientific objectivity of legal experts suffer a setback in this respect? Notice that legal academics may be innocent and unwitting pawns in this game.[99] None of these remarks may be surprising and may be

96 European Parliament Resolution of 26 February 2014 (n 53).

97 E.g. Hesselink, Rutgers and de Booys (n 36); Behar-Touchais (n 52).

98 H.W. Micklitz, 'A Certain Future for the Optional Instrument' in R. Schulze and J. Stuycke (eds), *Towards a European Contract Law* (Sellier 2011) 181–193, 189: 'the DCFR which has found no political recognition and still stands as a monolith in legal scholarship, documenting the desire and readiness of the European Commission to outsource law-making to legal academics, would in turn become a "toolbox" to serve the needs of the AGs and the ECJ for elaborating (inventing?) principles to fill gaps in the self-standing system of the European Contract Law. I have reservations on all points.'

99 See, for example, Y. Lequette, 'Le code européen de retour' (2011) 3 *Revue de droit des contrats* 1028, who refers to legal academics on the European scene who play the role of 'idiotes utiles', borrowing Lenin's phrase, which, he suggests, is not pejorative at all, but reflects an honest and idealistic personality who turns out to have been manipulated by the more unscrupulous.

the simple consequence of basic political manoeuvres. However, the fact that legal academics are actors playing several roles in the same play may be of particular relevance to the European political scene.

#### 2.1.3.3 THE MULTIPLE HAT SYNDROME

We have seen the title of expert may no longer necessarily guarantee neutrality and impartiality, if it is recognised that expertise has become highly politicised in the EU. Consequently, it looks as if certain characteristic features of academic expertise diminish in the field of European private law. Over and above academic rivalry, or battles for scientific hegemony on an international and European level, is the fact that certain legal academics have accumulated a number of roles, which may be incompatible or compromising. Their role in European contract law is complicated by a fundamental tension between the European and the national.[100] On one level, most legal academics working on the European scene are pro-European, otherwise they would have stayed at home. However, it is not quite as simple as that. Just as it does not follow that legal academics who remain exclusively on the national scene are not pro-European, nor lacking in European law expertise, nor does it follow that legal academics operating on the European scene are exclusively pro-European.

In fact, some legal academics operate on two levels, being experts on the European scene and back home; others just on one. Let's take English law professors as an example. Simon Whittaker was appointed to the Expert Group, but then resigned. He had advised the UK Ministry of Justice after the DCFR's publication and prior to this appointment, he subsequently advised again after the CESL was publicised.[101] In 2006, Stefan Vogenauer was auditioned by the House of Lords, as was Hugh Beale, though only the latter was a member of CoPECL and later the Expert Group. Moreover, it is no doubt erroneous to refer to legal academics as if they have a sole identity, linked to being scholars.[102] Legal academics may also be legal professionals and may have corporatist, as well as national, interests to defend, while being pro-European at the same time. It may be too much to ask of legal academics to be totally neutral, unbiased and impartial. They simply cannot be all of these in the sense that experts are educated and trained in a certain way, using their conceptual working frameworks in order to carry out the required

100 See the contributions in the special issue of (2012) 8 *Eur Rev Contract L* relating to the seminar on private law and nationalism, organised by CESL on 3 January 2012.

101 S. Whittaker, *The Draft Common Frame of Reference. An Assessment* (Commissioned by the UK Ministry of Justice) (2008) <http://webarchive.nationalarchives.gov.uk/20110201125714/> <http://www.justice.gov.uk/publications/docs/Draft_Common_Frame_of_Reference__an_assessment.pdf> accessed 21 November 2014.

102 A. Sen, *Identity and Violence* (Norton & Co 2006).

research and deliver their expert opinions. This does not prevent them from being open-minded, of course, but it raises the question just quite who is serving whom, and for what purpose. Is the European Commission trying to form and train a new set of experts with expertise in European legal science and culture, or are they simply reaping the benefits of existing expertise, for their own ends?

### *2.2 Who is serving whom?*

I am conscious that this paper may raise more questions than it answers, but the choice to adopt an external critical perspective, eschew certainty and dig under the surface is deliberate. The focal point of this enquiry has been directed at the actors involved in the ongoing process of constructing European private law. We have already seen that the various actors have adopted multiple stances: How exactly do the official and unofficial actors commingle? Do they collaborate or compete with one another? More specifically, legal academics may be both actors and the audience of this play. We thus need to think about whether or not the question as to who is the director is straightforward.

Harm Schepel has suggested that it is inaccurate to describe the role of legal science as the handmaiden of the powers to be.[103] The approach taken in this paper highlighting legal academics as actors also shuns a traditional approach conceiving of legal science as an autonomous source. Not only is this conception overly abstract; it is inexact in that legal academics are clearly not autonomous: they work hand-in-hand with other actors involved in the lawmaking process in the EU. Is the metaphor of legal academics 'as a transmission belt' a good one? Are legal academics merely transmitters; do they not also provide impetus for transmission?

It may be premature to answer this particular question. Taking stock of the present climate cultivating the growth of European private law, the presence of the CESL, now reduced to regulating electronic cross-border sales, can be envisaged as a very small expansion, in terms of European encroachment on Member States' private law rules, especially as it is contained in an optional instrument. This overly formalist approach should be handled cautiously. First, we do not know yet if the CESL will receive approval from the Council of Ministers one day and be enacted. Second, even if this does occur, does this necessarily mean that all the groundwork of the various other academic projects in this field will never see the light of day, in any form whatsoever? This line of speculation is predicated on imagining the official and unofficial actors of this process in competition with one another; however, an alternative paradigm may be possible.

103 Schepel (n 1).

*2.2.1 A relationship of master and servant?*

Once it is recognised that the relationship between official and shadow, or unofficial, actors in the construction of European private law is porous and malleable, a number of avenues need to be explored. Are the official lawmaking actors, the European Parliament and Commission, in competition with the shadow actors, namely legal academics? If so, who are the winners and losers? Is it appropriate to imagine the EU lawmaking instances as the master giving orders to the servant, or inseparable companion? If one academic project, namely the DCFR, seems to have been put in a drawer and forgotten, does this mean that the official actors have won? A pertinent legal argument, which might be helpful in this respect, is to evaluate legislative projects in terms of their influence and authority. If the CESL is enacted, its authority will be uncontroversial. However, even if this were the case, this might not relegate the academic DCFR to dust. Karl Riesenhuber has examined in detail the permutations and implications for competitive models of European contract law both before and after legislative enactment.[104] Although this line of enquiry is mere speculation, it is also possible that the DCFR be used as a model of soft law for inspiration, or indeed counter-inspiration.[105] Indeed, the DCFR has already been referred to by the CJEU. Conversely, as mentioned earlier, a reference by the European Parliament to academic projects merely acknowledges their existence, but has no effect on their authority or influence. Indeed, we could ask ourselves quite why the European Parliament chooses to refer to certain academic projects and to what end. Are legal academics just pawns in a game between the various institutional actors? I consider that the relationships between actors are infinitely more adulterated; nor should the potential of legal academics as a lobbying power be underestimated.[106] More importantly, we should not forget that the ultimate destiny of academic projects does not rest solely in the hands of the powers-to-be. Indeed, we, as legal academics in the audience and off scene, may have a say in the matter. It is in part our reception of academic projects, which may determine their outcome, or their influence. A great deal of metaphorical ink has already been spilt over the DCFR, and there may be some reason to believe that academics do not like their ink going to waste. In other words, it is conceivable that a hard law does not preclude a soft law model emerging. *A fortiori*, if the CESL is not enacted in the future, the influence or unofficial authority of the DCFR

104 Riesenhuber (n 40).

105 Jansen (n 4).

106 The French network, Trans Europe Experts, may be a good example; the ELI another potential lobbying power. For instance, the TEE collects together French responses to consultation and publishes them collectively, thus reinforcing a (mostly) French entity of legal academics, see e.g. M. Behar-Touchais and M. Chagny (eds), *Livre vert sur le droit européen des contrats: réponses du réseau Trans Europe Experts* (Sociéte legislation comparée 2011).

could increase or diminish, depending on what we as legal academics, and other actors, particularly the CJEU, decide to do with it: use it as model, counter-model, or ignore it altogether. These possibilities indicate that the unilateral master-servant relationship may not be the most accurate explanation of a much more complex picture. As suggested above, the construction process is not necessarily unidirectional. It is not easy to identify who is in the driving seat: the European Commission or legal academics. Even envisaging the relationship between official and shadow actors as a competition, where some must win and others lose, may miss the point.

### *2.2.2 An improvised organic collaboration*

This survey has demonstrated that the construction of European private law is an ill-conceived, or unsystematic, process. The Commission has constantly changed gears and direction over the last 10 years or more. It is impossible to assess the relative strengths and weaknesses of the various actors on the European legal scene, which looks like an improvisation, more than a finely devised play. Whether deliberately or not, the European Commission has given legal academics the possibility to train themselves in the field of European private law: the shadow lawmakers have created their own terrain, thereby acquiring a knowledge in a European legal culture, just as much as the Commission has benefitted from their expertise. It can thus be inferred that the construction of European private law is a cooperative, bidirectional and organic process, in the sense that it is alive and growing.[107] The official and shadow actors may have political agendas that blow the winds in opposite and converging directions; each has a certain degree of power to influence the other in a variety of ways. Envisaging the relationship between the various actors involved in the construction of the EU as collaborative or cooperative is not meant to be naïve. I hope to have shown that the actors are mutually dependent on each other, just as actors need an audience. Whether the official actors are the protagonists or whether we will witness their role reversal yet remains to be seen. The dénouement of the play will occur over time as we assume our own roles and responsibilities, as the audience and voices of the critics. We, too, are involved in this particular organic process.

In conclusion, this enquiry has investigated the respective roles of the official and shadow actors involved in the construction of European private law. While in some respects we have seen that legal academics assume certain roles similar to those played on a national scene, the scenario is infinitely more complex, the roles and hats more multiple and entangled, on the European one. No doubt this is because constructing European private law is an ongoing

107 See the *Oxford English Dictionary* for the meaning of organic as 'alive', as opposed to 'structured, coherent, harmonious'.

organic and highly improvised process, which neither resembles the top-down systematisation of codification known to many Member States, nor the gradual, evolutionary metamorphosis of the English common law.[108] The role of legal academics is unique for several reasons, among which is the possibility to exercise power and influence on national and European levels simultaneously, as well as their ability to collaborate with the official actors. The various actors seem to take it in turns to give one another directions. Legal academics are indeed lawmakers in the shadows but the flickering limelight shifts our attention continuously.

108 I do not have time to develop this idea here but European private law's evolution is more directed and not just subject to an aleatory production of legal rules through litigation, as was at first the case in the early development of the English common law.

# 9 EU lobbyists

## Rule-makers 'in the shadows'?*[1]

*Emilia Korkea-aho*

### 1 Introduction

In May 2014, a British newspaper, *The Guardian*, published a lengthy piece on Brussels lobbyists, arguing that 'shadowy agitators are estimated to influence 75 per cent of European legislation'.[2] According to the newspaper, tens of thousands of lobbyists, such as banks, companies, law firms and trade associations, are engaged in influencing the content and form of EU action. Stories such as this have become commonplace in the European press, leading to the perception of lobbying[3] as an unavoidable aspect of our daily political life in a growing range of policy sectors. One specific type of lobbying – lobbying on legislation – gathers most attention. But, as I claim in this contribution, lobbyists have an as yet unrecognised and potentially immensely powerful role to play in rulemaking: instead of trying to influence the proposed rules from outside the decision-making process, lobbyists have become rule-makers in their own right.

EU rule-making, a constitutional process through which the Commission and in some cases EU agencies create rules to implement legislation passed

* The author thanks Andrea Bianchi, Elaine Fahey, Benedict Kingsbury, Hans-W Micklitz, Panu Minkkinen, Silke Trommer, and Kaarlo Tuori for comments on the earlier draft of this chapter.

1 Max Weber, *The Vocation Lectures: 'Science as a Vocation' and 'Politics as a Vocation'* (Rodney Livingstone tr., David Owen and Tracy B. Strong (eds), first published 1919, Hackett Publishing Company 2004) 70.

2 Ian Traynor, '30,000 lobbyists and counting: is Brussels under corporate sway?' *The Guardian* (London, 8 May 2014) <http://www.theguardian.com/world/2014/may/08/lobbyists-european-parliament-brussels-corporate> accessed 16 January 2015.

3 The definition of lobbying is by reference to that adopted in art 7 of the Interinstitutional Agreement: 'all activities . . . carried out with the objective of directly or indirectly influencing the formulation or implementation of policy and the decision-making processes of the EU institutions, irrespective of where they are undertaken and of the channel or medium of communication used'. See Agreement between the European Parliament and the Commission on the transparency register for organisations and self-employed individuals engaged in EU policy-making and policy implementation [2014] OJ L277/11 (revised Interinstitutional Agreement).

by the European Parliament (EP) and the Council,[4] does not at first seem the place to attract lobbyists. However, at least four reasons may suggest why EU rule-making is worth the lobbyist's attention. First, legislative lobbying tends to be subject to intense public scrutiny and press coverage. Lobbying that is directed at lower-profile areas of policymaking, such as rule-making, does not disturb the public quite so much, hence providing lobbyists with greater ability to influence beyond the public gaze. Second, and relatedly, regulation of lobbying is premised on the need to respect and protect the integrity of the legislature, and rules governing lobbying often target the legislative process, e.g. many US states expressly prohibit campaign contributions from lobbyists 'while the legislature is in session'.[5] Lobbyists are (in the US: constitutionally)[6] entitled to offer information to the legislator but they are prevented from entering, thus having to remain in the 'lobby' of,[7] legislative chambers. No comparable rules have been established for executive rule-making.

Third, lobbying on legislation is not easy: 'securing a single, clearly defined imprint of a "rubber stamp" on legislation is difficult given the inter-institutional bargaining that results in blurred and smudged legislative imprints at the best of times'.[8] Now, rule-making that occurs after legislation has been passed, that is, after the inter-institutional give-and-take stage has been reached, seems to create new opportunities for lobbyists. The lessening of inter-institutional tensions is not the only reason why rule-making attracts lobbying. New EU legislation is, to a growing extent, drafted in an open-

4 This definition excludes formal legislative procedures provided for in the EU treaties. However, the definition includes preparation of legislation, since, as argued below in Section 2, the same actors often both prepare legislation and adopt rules in order to implement it.

5 Richard Briffault, 'The Anxiety of Influence: The Evolving Regulation of Lobbying' (2014) Columbia Law School, Public Law & Legal Theory Working Group Paper <http://ssrn.com/abstract=2384645> accessed 16 January 2015, 31.

6 In early US case law, lobbying was perceived to fall 'on the corruption side of the corruption/legitimate advocacy divide'. Only later did lobbying become endorsed as a First Amendment constitutional right. See Briffault (n 5) 19. Cf. Zephyr Teachout, 'The Forgotten Law of Lobbying' (2014) Fordham Law Legal Studies Research Paper No. 2383317 <http://papers.ssrn.com/sol3/papers.cfm?abstract_id=2383317> accessed 16 January 2015. According to Teachout, no historical consensus can be found on lobbying as a constitutionally protected right, and lobbying became increasingly accepted as a result of changes in the contract law paradigm: judges began enforcing lobbying contracts instead of nullifying them on the basis of good morals.

7 Lobbying takes its name from the medieval Latin words 'laubia', 'lobia', meaning 'covered walk in a monastery'. In contemporary political usage, the word has come to refer to the lobbies or hallways situated outside legislative chambers where those seeking to influence legislators gathered to wait for elected representatives. See Online Dictionary Etymology, <http://www.etymonline.com/index.php?allowed_in_frame=0&search=lobby&searchmode=none> accessed 16 January 2015.

8 David Earnshaw and D. Judge, 'No Simple Dichotomies: Lobbyists and the European Parliament' (2002) 8 *The Journal of Legislative Studies* 61, 61.

textured manner, hence emphasising the rule-making level for the specification of legislative requirements. Consider the following example. The EU Chemicals Regulation REACH was celebrated (for a good reason or not) for the reversal of the burden of proof that it introduced nearly 10 years ago.[9] This shift of informational responsibility from authorities to industry was seen as a victory for the EU model of consumer protection and environmental regulation and, consequently, an emphatic defeat for multinational chemicals corporations.[10] However, with reversal being the main rule, the actual 'bite' and costs of REACH regulation for businesses ultimately depend on how data requirements are interpreted and applied in practice. Battles over what the law means or requires move to the concretisation and implementation of legislation. As a result, very few lobbyists find themselves out of a job when the final text is published in the Official Journal of the EU: 'the life-span of lobbying doesn't end', as one of the participants in the seminar aptly observed.

Fourth, lobbyists' interest in rule-making can be explained by reference to changes in rule-making itself. In this contribution, I refer to these changed rule-making conditions under the rubric of 'postnational rule-making'. In today's pluralised and fragmented societies, the regulator attempts to contain all sorts of challenges, threats and risks by improving the knowledge base of its rules. Science-based regulation is crucial in several areas of governmental activity, such as food safety, data protection, energy efficiency or environmental protection. To satisfy these informational needs in different fields of regulatory attention, the staff numbers of administrations have significantly increased. Additional outside expertise is also necessary, a phenomenon particularly pronounced in the EU due to the fact that its wide-ranging regulatory tasks have not been matched with equal administrative capacities. This is also where lobbying comes into play: the level of lobbying is argued to have increased in the EU to meet the need for expertise.[11] In recent years, however, this highly technical vision of rule-making has come under attack on account of concerns for transparency and accountability. In particular, a cascade of rules and regulations from the EU has led to worries being expressed about democratic accountability, and attempts have been made to increase the role

9 Regulation (EC) No 1907/2006 of the European Parliament and of the Council of 18 December 2006 concerning the Registration, Evaluation, Authorisation and Restriction of Chemicals (REACH), establishing a European Chemicals Agency [2006] OJ L33.

10 Elizabeth Fisher, 'The "Perfect Storm" of Reach: Charting Regulatory Controversy in the Age of Information, Sustainable Development, and Globalization' (2008) 11 *Journal of Risk Research* 541.

11 For lobbyists as a source of (technical) information for policymakers, see e.g. Adam William Chalmers, 'Trading information for access: informational lobbying strategies and interest group access to the European Union' (2013) 20 *JEPP* 39; Henry Hauser, 'European Union Lobbying Post-Lisbon: An Economic Analysis' (2011) 29 *Berkeley Journal of International Law* 680; Justin Greenwood, *Interest Representation in the European Union*, (3rd revised edn, Palgrave Macmillan 2011).

of civil society in rule-making – to the extent that open and transparent administration with active participation by civil society actors has now become a staple of research and practice in EU policies.[12] In today's society, everyone is a stakeholder: 'elected and nonelected government officers, nongovernmental organizations, political parties, interest groups, policy entrepreneurs, "epistemic communities", and "networks" are all relevant actors in the decision-making processes that produce government action'.[13]

What I intend to show in this chapter is that these two trends of modern EU administration are increasingly important for lobbying, too.[14] They explain not only the interest of lobbyists in rule-making, but also how they have been able to enter rule-making. My argument is that lobbyists have moved into rule-making, acquired rule-making powers, and they have done so by tapping into the two influential ideals of expertise and democratic accountability. When suggesting that lobbyists are involved in making the rules, I do not refer to the practice, often deplored by the press, in which lawmakers copy and paste amendments prepared by lobbyists. Rather, I claim that by positioning themselves as either *experts* or *stakeholders* in rule-making, lobbyists play a role in making the rules alongside more traditional rule-makers. By analysing lobbyists as rule-makers, however, this contribution appears to come close to the above-mentioned discussion of lobbyists as 'unelected legislators', the question whether lobbyists write laws which are subsequently only 'rubber stamped' by public authorities. While I would reject that understanding simply because I believe, as pointed out above, that EU lobbying is more complicated than this claim suggests, another difference important to mention is conceptual. The definition of legislator is a closed concept in the sense that it is easy to say who exercises legislative powers and who does not, whereas the notion of 'rule-maker' is open-ended and encompasses a wide variety of actors, as will be seen in Section 2. In other words, while the boundary between 'elected' and 'unelected' is relatively straightforward to establish, the same boundary between a 'formally authorised'

12 E.g. Francesca Bignami, 'Three Generations of Participation Rights Before the European Commission' (2004) 68 *Law and Contemporary Problems* 61; Carol Harlow, 'Civil society organisations and participatory administration: a challenge to EU administrative law?' in Stijn Smismans (ed.) *Civil Society and Legitimate European Governance* (Edward Elgar 2006) 115; Deirdre Curtin and others, 'Constitutionalising EU Executive Rule-Making Procedures: A Research Agenda' (2013) *ELJ* 1.

13 Martin Shapiro, 'Administrative Law Unbounded: Reflections on Government and Governance' (2001) 8 *Indiana Journal of Global Legal Studies* 369, 369.

14 Little research has been done on lobbying by administrative law scholars. Lobbying is usually mentioned in connection with debates on civil society, where lobbyists are depicted as representatives of business interest groups, prone to outnumber and outweigh non-business interests. Another context where lobbying is mentioned in passing is the issue of transparency in public decision-making. See e.g. Joana Mendes, *Participation in EU Rule-Making* (OUP 2011) 114.

rule-maker and an 'informally (or non-) authorised' rule-maker is not. This difficulty in drawing the distinction stems from two factors: first, general rule-making powers tend to be only vaguely defined in order to ensure the discretion of the rule-making authority, and, second, the fact that the 'formally authorised' rule-maker can adopt both legally binding as well as non-binding norms further blurs the boundaries between formal, informal and non-formal authority. This blurring in formal rule-making capacity eases the task of lobbyists in establishing themselves as rule-makers.

In explicating the new roles of lobbyists, I use an ideal type categorisation of politician, introduced in the essay 'Politics as a Vocation' by Max Weber.[15] As the typology was originally developed to characterise and analyse a professional politician, an explanation is in order. Lobbying can be, and has usually been, studied as a form of interest representation, with lobbyists as actors *outside* the political process. What I propose to do in this chapter is to approach lobbying as an integral part of the democratic decision-making process with lobbyists as *inside* actors, bringing the views of those whom they represent to bear on law and policy, alongside politicians and other rule-makers. In this new role, lobbyists come so close to politicians that their assessment from the perspective of a neighbouring profession, that of the professional politician, is justified.[16]

This particular aim to acknowledge lobbyists as actors inside the policy process connects the analysis to the question of actors 'in the shadows', and, ultimately, to the issue of the legitimacy of lobbyists. According to popular usage, shadow means something that is dark, not visible to us.[17] Translated into the lobbying context, this would mean that lobbyists operate in a space that is hidden from view. Now, this argument is increasingly difficult to make given that transparency practices involving lobbyists, such as electronically swiping in and out of the EP, being on various registers, are quite strong. With respect to this case study, my argument is that a shadow is not created by lack of regulation or by lobbyists hiding behind semi-legitimate practices, but by our inability to acknowledge the new roles of the lobbyist.[18] Admittedly, this is difficult because rule-making practices in the EU are complex and incomprehensible to all but experts. However, as argued, an account of postnational rule-making is helpful in framing these new lobbyist roles and in so doing goes some way towards eradicating the shadow.

15 Weber (n 1).

16 One could also argue that a lobbyist is a political parasite, for lobbying as a profession would not exist without politicians.

17 See also Ruth Sefton-Green in this collection. Note that the expression 'shadow' or 'shadowy actor' can imply illegitimacy or malpractice, but such practices are not analysed in this chapter.

18 An excellent illustration of this tendency is the point made in the introduction. EU rule-making has long been interested in stakeholder participation, without seeing participation by lobbyists as a distinct phenomenon. See Elaine Fahey, 1.

This chapter is organised as follows. Section 2 sets out the conditions for postnational rule-making in the EU, arguing that the rule-making environment is fragmented as a result of the emergence of EU agencies and administrative networks as actors with rule-making powers. Then, in Section 3, I proceed to provide a brief overview of lobbying on EU rule-making. Drawing upon Weberian ideal types of legitimate political authority, I show in Section 4 how lobbyists position themselves as actors in postnational rule-making and identify two principal ways in which they seek to legitimise their role. In Section 5, I deploy these insights in evaluating the effectiveness of EU lobbying regulation to ensure that lobbyists as rule-makers operate within the parameters of legitimate conduct. Finally, I conclude.

## 2 Postnational rule-making in the EU

In a much-generalised notion of rule-making, the legislature enacts laws on the basis of which expressly authorised officials provide more detailed rules. Specifically in the EU context, the EP and the Council adopt norms (legislation), and the Commission prepares more detailed rules needed in the application of norms (rule-making). This definition of rule-making excludes from its scope formal legislative procedures provided for in primary EU law. Rule-making can also be understood in a wider sense to include legislation but, for present purposes, I have limited the term 'rule-making' to encompass such activities taken by the Commission, EU agencies or these in collaboration with administrative networks, thus excluding lawmaking practices. However, even the narrow definition adopted in this chapter covers preparation of legislation in EU expert and advisory committees, for the same actors often wear multiple hats, that is, they are involved in both drafting and implementing legislative rules. Rule-making gives rise to rules that can be either binding or non-binding.[19]

As the most important rule-maker in the EU, the Commission has both the delegated and implementing powers (Articles 290 and 291 of the Treaty on the Functioning of the European Union, TFEU). While a delegated act is adopted by the Commission acting alone, adoption of an implementing measure is a joint exercise between the Commission and a committee of Member State representatives (comitology committee). Unsurprisingly, the Commission prefers delegated acts whereas the EP and the Council often decide on adoption of the implementing act. Given this tension and the fact that the Treaties do not offer clear guidance to demarcate between these two types of act, inter-institutional contests are easily provoked. What underlies these skirmishes is not only general disagreement about who does what and according to which procedure, but about who has the upper hand in EU

19 For rule-making, see Matthias Ruffert in this collection.

rule-making.[20] Interestingly, the continued confusion is believed to harm the EU's external credibility for, as argued below, lobbyists from outside the EU have signalled a wish to see a strong centralised EU rule-maker, operating as a one-stop shop for contact.

In the light of recent developments in the EU, these hopes will be dashed. The increasing fragmentation of rule-making loci, that is, the establishment of EU agencies and the emergence of networks with at least soft rule-making powers, has considerably weakened the claim that rule-making is a privilege enjoyed by the Commission only.[21] For example, an increasing number of EU agencies operate with specific rule-making tasks given to them in sectoral legislation. While agencies with formal rule-making powers still form the minority among nearly 40 EU agencies, recent agencies have all been established with rule-making authority, a strong indication of a continuing trend.[22] On the other hand, the EU rule-making landscape has changed due to administrative networks. Often operating in connection with implementation of EU law, networks have been set up to produce non-binding yet highly influential interpretative guidance with a view to clarifying the norms governing a particular sector or sphere of activity. The relevance of these networks for rule-making can be explained by reference to the fact that, despite their often unofficial status, they lay down definitions and establish authoritative interpretations of underlying legislative norms. In other words, networks may also discharge functions that we tend to associate with the formal rule-making authority.[23] How inclusive are they of outside interests? Virtually all EU agencies are duty-bound by express provisions in their founding regulations to seek public input. Moreover, those who wish to become involved in the activities of agencies can do so in manifold ways, from leaving comments on the website to participating in advisory groups. In the same vein, administrative networks, composed of the Commission and Member State authorities and experts, are committed to establishing open and participatory processes to include civil society actors and other stakeholders, these often being major pan-European NGOs with niche (technical) expertise.[24]

In conclusion, two things should be noted about EU rule-making. First, it is an important field for influencing policy developments. The observation

20 See, e.g., Case C-427/12 *Commission v EP and Council* ECLI:EU:C:2014:170.

21 A. (Ton) van den Brink and Linda Senden, Checks and Balances of Soft EU Rule-Making (Policy Department C: Citizens' Rights and Constitutional Affairs, April 19, 2012) <http://ssrn.com/abstract=2042480> accessed 19 January 2015, 8.

22 Most recently, see founding regulations of European Financial Supervisory Authorities.

23 For networks' activities in environmental law, see Emilia Korkea-aho, 'Legal Interpretation of Framework Directives. A Soft Law Approach' (2015) 4 ELRev 70.

24 For the legitimacy of networks in EU environmental law, see e.g. Bettina Lange's contribution in Olaf Dilling and others (eds), *Transnational Administrative Rule-Making. Performance, Legal Effects and Legitimacy* (Hart Publishing 2011).

made specifically in the US agency context generally fits EU rulemaking, too: 'Tasked with filling in the details and gaps in congressionally passed legislation, agencies routinely propose and promulgate rules, and the subjects and effects of these rules are often far from trivial,'[25] hence rule-making being: 'the most important way in which the bureaucracy creates policy'.[26] Second, the EU rule-making environment is fragmented: as shown above, EU agencies and administrative networks now occupy rule-making space alongside the Commission, multiplying potential contexts for lobbying activities.

## 3 Lobbying on EU rule-making

Some universal rules about lobbying exist. One of these is that lobbying follows power. When the EU gained new powers with the Single Market Act in the late 1980s, lobbyists quickly discovered new opportunities presented to them. Lobbying similarly intensified after the entry into force of the Lisbon Treaty, again attesting to the link between lobbying and power. Focusing on the changes wrought by the Lisbon Treaty, two reasons in particular can be suggested to explain the growth of lobbying activity. First, lobbying provides the EU with the expertise it needs to exercise its new 'Lisbon' powers. Second, and more controversially, lobbying connects to the political and legal obligation of the EU to enhance the civic engagement of its citizens and promote stakeholder participation. In other words, the legitimacy of increased EU powers, evident in a range of sectors, from business, education and culture to health, environment and welfare, is claimed by a more inclusive vision of policymaking.[27] How do lobbyists take advantage of these new developments when lobbying on rule-making?

Since lobbying takes place outside established processes of consultation, information is not abundant for the operation, resources and actors involved in lobbying. Information specific to lobbying on rule-making is even scarcer than data available about lobbying more generally.[28] Two recent reports

25 Susan Webb Yackee, 'The Politics of *Ex Parte* Lobbying: Pre-Proposal Agenda Building and Blocking During Agency Rulemaking' (2011) *Journal of Public Administration Research and Theory* 1, 3.

26 William West, 'Administrative Rule-making: An Old and Emerging Literature' (2005) 65 *Public Administration Review* 655, 655.

27 See also Hauser (n 11) 681.

28 Being much broader in scope than EU literature, US lobbying scholarship has focused on lobbying in rulemaking. A recent focus has been on what US scholars call 'informal' lobbying, lobbying that leaves no traces. For instance, Wagner argues that most agency rules result from hidden negotiations among agencies and interested parties. See Wendy Wagner, 'Administrative Law, Filter Failure, and Information Capture' (2010) 59 *Duke Law Journal* 1321, 1366. For lobbying in agenda setting, see Webb Yackee (n 25). The different political context and differences in the regulation of lobbying somewhat limit the usefulness of US literature for analysis of EU lobbying.

published by Europe-wide transparency NGOs try to fill the gap and to remove the ambiguity surrounding lobbying on EU rule-making. The first report, entitled 'The Fire Power of the Financial Lobby', by the *Corporate Europe Observatory* claims that 700 different financial industry groups spend over €120 million a year in lobbying and employ more than 1,700 lobbyists.[29] These figures almost certainly understate the actual numbers but give a rough estimate of the situation for one particular lobby sector. What is profoundly interesting is that according to the report, lobbyists have recently moved into rule-making, for the financial lobby knows where the 'show is quickly moving'.[30] In rule-making, lobbyists often work as part of so-called 'expert groups', set up and coordinated by the Commission.[31] These expert groups prepare rules to implement EU legislation. They are also involved in drafting future legislation, to the extent that expert groups' final reports often provide the basis for new legislation. Members can be appointed in a personal capacity or as representatives of interests or organisations. Besides the Commission, EU agencies have also increasingly set up advisory groups to assist in the adoption of implementing rules. Both types of group, expert and advisory, are dominated by industry representatives.[32]

The second report published by a European transparency NGO, *ALTER-EU*, provides numerical information on the (over)representation of business interests in expert groups. Its report offers a follow-up to the high-level disagreement that arose between the EP and the Commission on the role of industry representatives in expert groups. The EP questioned the Commission on the issue several times but where its pressure did not translate into changes, the EP froze the budget for expert groups twice, first in 2011 and briefly again in 2012, before the institutions reached an informal compromise in 2012. Taking up the task of analysing all new expert groups set up in the 12 months between 2012 and 2013, ALTER-EU set out to review the current situation, in particular whether the Commission had complied with the conditions that the EP imposed on it. In ALTER-EU's analysis, the situation had not been satisfactorily addressed by the Commission; indeed, 'business as usual' has continued to date, although some variation exists depending upon

29 Corporate Europe Observatory, ÖGB Europabüro (Brussels office of the Austrian Trade Union Federation), and AK EUROPA (Brussels office of the Austrian Chamber of Labour), *The Fire Power of the Financial Lobby. A Survey of the Size of the Financial Lobby at the EU level* (April 2014) <http://corporateeurope.org/financial-lobby/2014/04/fire-power-financial-lobby> accessed 19 January 2015.

30 Ibid. 17.

31 The Commission maintains a register on expert groups, see the Public Register of Expert Groups and Other Similar Entities, see <http://ec.europa.eu/transparency/regexpert/> accessed 19 January 2015. See also Communication from the Commission on the collection and use of expertise by the Commission: principles and guidelines 'Improving the knowledge base for better policies', COM(2002) 713 final.

32 Fire Power (n 29) 16.

the policy area in question.[33] Among the worst-performing directorates-general are DG Taxation and Customs Union and DG Enterprise and Industry, as well as the Commission's Secretariat-General, whereas new supervisory authorities (the European Banking Authority (EBA), the European Insurance and Occupational Pensions Authority (EIOPA) and the European Securities and Markets Authority (ESMA)) are hailed for setting a better standard of performance in stakeholder consultation and transparency.[34]

Reflecting the controversial nature of the issue, in 2014 the European Ombudsman opened an investigation into how Commission groups are composed, who their members are and whether they operate transparently and openly.[35] One of the biggest concerns raised by the transparency NGOs, and a point of interest for the EO inquiry, relates to lobbyists sitting in expert groups in their personal capacity. In one instance, out of 28 individuals appointed in their personal capacity, only two were truly independent experts while the rest, a total of 26 nominees, had potential conflicts of interest. As noted by the reporting NGO, whether those conflicts of interest do in fact have an effect on rule-making is not relevant; but the mere fact that they exist is.[36] Another worrying practice is mislabelling of lobbyists in registers, that is, the use of terms such as 'consultancy', 'international organisation' or 'association' to conceal corporate interests.[37] In one estimate, two-thirds of mislabelling cases involve business representatives, with the exception of DG Taxation and Customs Union, where the figure is 100 per cent.[38]

This brief overview focuses attention on two issues in particular. First, lobbying on rule-making is an important yet insufficiently studied area. While perhaps slightly one-sided, the above-mentioned NGO reports should be taken as the first significant steps towards establishing the fact that lobbying on rule-making *does* take place. The second issue concerns the extent to which lobbying on rule-making takes place 'in the shadows'. Certain

33 Alliance for Lobbying Transparency and Ethics Regulation (ALTER-EU), *A Year of Broken Promises. Big business still put in charge of EU Expert Groups, despite commitment to reform* (November 2013) <http://www.alter-eu.org/sites/default/files/documents/Broken_Promises_web.pdf> accessed 19 January 2015.

34 Fire Power (n 29) 17; see also van den Brink and Senden (n 21) 34.

35 The EO published her preliminary views in January 2015 and invited the Commission to respond by 30 April 2015. Her main conclusion was that the Commission should 'consider putting in place a new framework for Commission expert groups'. See Letter to the European Commission requesting an opinion in the European Ombudsman's own-initiative inquiry OI/6/2014/NF concerning the composition of Commission expert groups, <http://www.ombudsman.europa.eu/cases/correspondence.faces/en/58861/html.bookmark> accessed 2 February 2015.

36 Broken Promises (n 33) 16. In her preliminary analysis, the EO strongly urged the Commission to ensure that 'no individual with any actual, potential or apparent conflict of interest will be appointed to an expert group in his/her personal capacity'.

37 Ibid. 27.

38 Ibid. 19.

questionable practices such as registration of lobbyists under ambiguous institutional credentials can lead to the perception of lobbyists acting in the shadows but, as I argued above, the shadow is primarily created by our inability to acknowledge the new roles of the lobbyist. The best example of this is the EU's Transparency Register, a voluntary lobby register set up by the Commission and the EP in 2011. The institutions revised the Interinstitutional Agreement on the register in 2014, and the 'second generation' Register was launched in January 2015.[39] Its mission is to provide 'citizens with a direct and single access to information about who is engaged in activities aiming at influencing the EU decision making process'.[40] Its Article 12, however, includes a limitation providing that all 'direct' and 'individual' requests from EU institutions for factual information, data or expertise are not covered by the Register. However, this is a significant improvement from the previous regime, for the 2011 Interinstitutional Agreement extended this exemption also to cover activities of expert groups and consultative committees.[41] Among other things, this meant that those lobbyists who participated in Commission expert groups were not obliged to register; the exception that has now been removed from the text of the revised Interinstitutional Agreement.

Drawing these observations together, it appears that lobbyists are analysed from the standpoint of the Commission, while their own distinct 'actor role' is underdeveloped: indeed, the identities, strategies and pathways of lobbyists (and how they change over time) are given much less attention, for two obvious reasons. First, lobbying is not a unidirectional activity, and the EU plays an important role in increasing the demand for lobbying, as well as in regulating access by lobbyists to rule-makers.[42] As I will later argue, it is especially the Commission that is implicated in the growth of the lobbying business in the EU. Second, and relatedly, the fact that NGOs fix their attention on the Commission makes sense given that the quickest way to address corporate domination in the formation of expert groups is through reformed Commission practices. However, it is my view that the reform will be misdirected and only half-successful if we do not have an understanding of lobbyists as actors. This is the question to which I shall now turn.

39 <http://europa.eu/rapid/press-release_IP-15-3740_en.htm> accessed 28 January 2015.

40 When last accessed, the number of registrations was 7,492. See more at: <http://ec.europa.eu/transparencyregister/info/homePage.do> accessed 19 January 2015.

41 Ex Article 10c of the 2011 Interinstitutional Agreement. Note though that although the Transparency Register now covers expert groups, registration in the Register is not required for appointment to expert groups. This is one of the EO's suggestions for improvement.

42 Pieter Bouwen, 'Corporate Lobbying in the European Union: The logic of access' (2002) 9 *JEPP* 365, 368. See also Christine Mahoney, 'The Power of Institutions: State and Interest Group Activity in the European Union' (2004) 5 *European Union Politics* 441, 445.

## 4 Lobbyists as actors in postnational rule-making

### *4.1 Definition of a lobbyist*

As already indicated, not a great deal is known about lobbyists as actors. This is easily evidenced by looking at some of the available definitions of lobbying. Scholarly writings define lobbying but only seldom address the same question about the lobbyist. Most definitions, in identifying lobbying as an attempt to influence public action, remain silent about who it is that is engaged in influencing.[43] This silence masks deeply rooted confusion over the terms of lobbying, for instance whether 'lobbying' and 'interest representation' mean the same or if they are different concepts, whether the term lobbying should be reserved for activities intended to represent private interests only or whether they encompass public (civil society) interests too. The Green Paper on the European Transparency Initiative, which eventually led to the establishment of the European Transparency Register in 2011, is an instructive example of difficulties with terminology. The Green Paper, which includes a rare definition of a lobbyist, paints with a broad brush: '"lobbyists" are defined as persons carrying out such activities [influencing public action], working in a variety of organisations such as public affairs consultancies, law firms, NGOs, think-tanks, corporate lobby units ("in-house representatives") or trade associations'.[44] Though civil society is not mentioned in the definition, the Commission, when elaborating the definition, includes lobbying carried out by 'civil society organisations'.[45] For the Commission, then, the lobbyist is an umbrella concept, covering all those seeking to represent their interests.

For the Council of Europe's advisory body on constitutional matters, also known as the Venice Commission, civil society/NGO actors and lobbyists are very different (if not opposite) actors. The former actors form a particular group of 'lobbyists' underpinning the pluralist model of democracy, hence qualifying for stronger human rights guarantees than lobbyists representing commercial interests.[46] Finally, lobbyists' self-perception has not been systematically studied, and it can only be speculated how differently NGOs and corporate lobby units perceive their interest representation activities. Civil society actors have signed up in significant numbers to the European Transparency Register for lobbyists but this may have more to do with the benefits of registration

43 See e.g. Cornelia Woll, 'Lobbying in the European Union: From Sui Generis to a Comparative Perspective' (2006) 13 JEPP 456, 465 fn 1.

44 Green Paper on European Transparency Initiative COM(2006) 194 final, 5.

45 Ibid.

46 European Commission for Democracy Through Law (Venice Commission) Report on the Role of Extra-Institutional Actors in the Democratic System (Lobbying). Adopted by the Venice Commission at its 94th Plenary Session (Venice, 8–9 March 2013) CDL-AD(2013)011, paras 37 and 39.

(i.e. facilitated entry to the EP and better information flow) rather than having a strong lobby identity. In this chapter, the lobbyist, following the Commission, is understood as a comprehensive concept covering all kinds of actors in interest representation.

The observations above show divergences in definitions of the lobbyist. Clearly, a more comprehensive review of the relevant literature would be needed to specify and substantiate these observations; but, this not being possible here, something should be said about the conclusion reached by LaPira and Thomas, the authors of a recent empirical work on revolving door lobbyists in the US.[47] Namely, their conclusion is representative of the feeling one is left with after browsing through the literature: 'both good theory and good data on individual lobbyists-agents and their impact on the policy process' are lacking.[48] In other words, what seems still to be missing is a more fully fledged narrative or understanding about lobbyists as individual actors in the policy process. Therefore, I turn to Weber immediately below.

### *4.2 Typology of lobbyists: Weber's 'Politics as a Vocation'*

Applying Weber's categorisation of ideal types of the professional politician, I now attempt to provide a preliminary conceptualisation of the lobbyist as actor in the rule-making process.[49] The conceptualisation is not considered only as a descriptive tool, but also as an analytical vehicle through which to offer content to an evaluation of the legitimacy of lobbyists and their practices.[50]

Following the order in which he himself introduced the three types in an essay, 'Politics as a Vocation', based on a lecture given in 1919, the first figure is what might be called the *expert-lobbyist*. A lobbyist of this kind is not renowned for being an eloquent and engaging public speaker, and as a lobbyist his expertise lies elsewhere altogether, that is, in an excellent command of, and knowledge about, rules and procedures. It is hardly surprising that in

47 Timothy LaPira and Herschel Thomas III, 'Revolving Door Lobbyists and Interest Representation' (2014) 3 *Interest Groups & Advocacy* 4, 24.

48 Ibid. 24.

49 For the typology in the context of Weber's other works, see Panu Minkkinen, '"Here I stand, I can do no other": Politics, Violence, and Ends in Themselves' (2013) 25 *Law & Literature* 226, 236.

50 The type of legitimacy used in this chapter is social. Weber has no strong normative criteria for legitimacy and he emphasises the (social) context in which legitimacy is constructed. This kind of social understanding of legitimacy corresponds to what people think is legitimate behaviour. In the context of lobbying this understanding draws our attention to two sources: what actors themselves (lobbyists) regard as morally or legally legitimate and how those who are the subject of their activities respond to their claim to legitimacy. For the relevance of social legitimacy to analysis of actors in postnational rulemaking, see also Fahey in this collection.

Weber's account, this first type of a competent managerialist is the child of a mature capitalist system, where corporations need the technical skills of trained lawyers to decipher the mysteries of modern administration and to solve problems brought about by technological advances in production. This connects nicely to a more contemporary observation that with the creation of the internal market, the EU has also created a niche market for the type of expertise offered by the expert-lobbyist.

The second type excels exactly where the expert-lobbyist fails to impress. This character, which we, paraphrasing Weber, call the *demagogue-lobbyist*, possesses skills in persuasion and artful speaking and assumes leadership by communicating emotions effectively. Having a way with words, he can turn a bad case into a good one, just like a skilful advocate, which Weber gives as an example of this type.[51] Another major difference between the expert-lobbyist and the demagogue-lobbyist is that the latter delivers his services in public and does not shy away from being openly associated with the clients whose interests he promotes. To envisage the third figure, Weber uses the English term 'der Boss', modelling the type on an American industrialist with near-infinite resources. This type seems to capture the modern archetype of a lobbyist. Unlike the demagogue-lobbyist, the *entrepreneur-lobbyist* does not appear in public arenas, prompting Weber to talk of acting 'in the shadows'.[52] As a lobbyist, his most distinctive trait is a tendency to work behind the scenes and a lack of interest in public approval, hence not being embarrassed to be seen working his way upwards using money and connections.

These are ideal types, not to be found in a pure form in the real world, and, as will be seen below, lobbyists conveniently mix and match different strategies and techniques. However, even these ideal types seem to claim legitimacy on two grounds: expertise or stakeholder representation (or neither). While the expert-lobbyist tries to distance himself from the interests he represents, and rather links, as far as possible, the legitimacy of lobbying action to technical skill or expert knowledge, the demagogue-lobbyist, putting his personality to work, argues that rule-making is legitimate insofar as the interests that he represents are given consideration.[53] Finally, the entrepreneur-lobbyist is guided by avoidance of public arenas for he shows no interest at all in defending what he does, nor does he seek legitimisation. Immediately below, I offer concrete examples of these types in the light of actual EU lobbying, starting with the lobbyist as expert.

51 Weber (n 1) 53.

52 Ibid. 70.

53 Ibid. 63: 'a demagogic leader with a powerful personality'.

### *4.3 The lobbyist as expert*

As EU rule-making increasingly happens 'on the basis of facts',[54] the deployment of expertise has become an important tool both to gain access to rule-makers and to legitimise lobbying activities.[55] As a result, lobbyists see and present themselves as experts, of which the following is an instructive example. The Commission was recently reported to have axed its plans to legislate on shale gas production in the EU, proposing instead a set of recommendations. The announcement was immediately followed by press coverage on both sides of the Atlantic that raised suspicions about lobby influence on the Commission.[56] Shale gas is a growing business, especially in the US, and the adoption of EU shale gas legislation would have had huge and potentially damaging implications for the energy industry around the world. In an article in the *New York Times*, an American law firm, Covington & Burling, was reported to be organising an expert 'industry group' to offer its assistance to the Commission in drafting non-mandatory rules. According to the newspaper, oil companies such as Chevron and Statoil are allegedly included in the firm's clientele.[57] Lobbyists' desire to be seen as experts is also apparent in a recent comment by the US industry spokesperson, advocating greater transparency in EU rule-making. He (cleverly), speaking for the whole transatlantic business community, noted that 'both European and American businesses want to provide a *meaningful analysis* for proposed EU legislation and regulation, but to do this we need to see and comment on the actual text that is being considered'.[58]

54 The then ECHA Member State Committee Chairman (Anna-Liisa Sundquist) pointed out that she does not have a 'fear of lobbying' and that 'it is up to the members to decide whether lobbies are received, but I do not see any problems. All Committee members have signed a commitment of independence and declared their conflicts of interest. They can listen to lobbyists if they choose, but they should decide on the basis of scientific and technical facts only . . . I have a lot of experience in being lobbied in my previous work, more information does not harm, but decisions have to be made on the basis of facts' <http://newsletter.echa.europa.eu/home/-/newsletter/entry/1_08_committees;jsessionid=2678A660A5A40D59E6A3E4EE6E522E48.live2> accessed 21 January 2015.

55 When comparing US and EU lobbying styles, Woll notes that 'instead of confronting public officials, European lobbyists typically gain access through expert consultations'. See Cornelia Woll, 'The Brash and the Soft-spoken: Lobbying Styles in a Transatlantic Comparison' (2012) 1 *Interest Groups & Advocacy* 193, 200.

56 Benjamin Fox: 'EU ditches plan to regulate on shale gas' (*EU Observer*, 22 January 2014) <http://euobserver.com/news/122835> accessed 21 January 2015.

57 Eric Lipton and Danny Hakim: 'Lobbying Bonanza as Firms Try to Influence European Union' (*The New York Times*, 18 October 2013) <http://www.nytimes.com/2013/10/19/world/europe/lobbying-bonanza-as-firms-try-to-influence-european-union.html?_r=0> accessed 21 January 2015.

58 Shawn Donnan: 'US pushes for greater transparency in EU business regulation' (*The Financial Times*, 23 February 2014) <http://www.ft.com/cms/s/0/6e9b7190-9a65-11e3-8e06-00144feab7de.html#axzz2xWyldSfI> accessed 21 January 2015 (emphasis mine).

What is readily inferred from these two instances is that lobbyists do not explicitly name or identify themselves as experts. They do so indirectly: by calling outputs they prepare 'expert reports' or 'policy analyses'; they present themselves as experts, thus also influencing and guiding the way in which these outputs are received by decision-makers and the general public. Sometimes it is the institutional environment in which the lobbyist works that sends the message of the expert-lobbyist. The most obvious example of this is a Commission *expert* group, to which members are appointed either as representatives of interests or organisations or in their personal capacity (expert category). Given that expert-lobbyists are often appointed in the latter category despite conflicts of interest, interests that are private are thus reframed in the language of experts that claims to be neutral and free from influence. An additional problem is that expertise is recast as a personal rather than a professional feature, allowing the expert-lobbyist to divert attention away from the interests or the organisation in the background.

The second issue that should be observed is the simple demand and supply story: the interest of lobbyists to appear as experts can be explained as a response to a growing demand from the Commission for these services. When the Commission considers setting up a new expert group it is required to publish an open call. The NGO report referred to above, going through the entire corpus of Commission expert groups set up within the last 12 months, showed that calls for application are drafted in highly technical language. Whether or not this a deliberate effort to limit the pool of qualified applicants, as suggested by the NGO,[59] matters perhaps less than the fact that the EU's gatekeeper role is so strong that lobbying comes to be seen as an exercise in mutual interdependence where public institutions are not simply the objects of lobbying, but lobbyists themselves can be seen as objects of the EU's desire to increase its rule-making legitimacy and the knowledge base of its rules.

The third observation relates to the uses and nature of expertise.[60] I argue that EU expert-lobbyists deploy both scientific 'substantive' expertise as well as general 'regulatory' expertise; this latter kind of expertise is especially relevant to those lobbying in rule-making. I further assume this kind of expertise is legal expertise. In Weber's typology, lawyers (more accurately, advocates) were mentioned in connection with the second type of lobbyist,

59 Broken Promises (n 33) 15.

60 Space precludes an in-depth discussion of the meaning and the uses of expertise. Generally about experts in EU and international decision-making, see Monika Ambrus and others, *The Role of 'Experts' in International and European Decision-Making Processes: Advisors, Decision Makers or Irrelevant Actors?* (CUP 2014). For the question what constitutes expertise and what experience, see Jacob Jacoby and others, 'Experience and Expertise in Complex Decision Making' (1986) 13 Advances in Consumer Research 469; Kathleen McGraw and Neil Pinney, 'The Effects of General and Domain-Specific Expertise on Political Memory and Judgment' (1990) 8 Social Cognition 9.

'demagogue', but my argument is that the increasing complexity of the EU decision-making process boosts demand for lawyers as expert-lobbyists. There is an expanding marketplace for lobbyists who have a specialised knowledge of, and who can genuinely understand, the inner workings of the EU and the rules governing its various institutions. Not only do lawyers offer legal consultation, but they also provide PR, as well as economic and management services.[61] Consequently, lobbying is increasingly seen as a long-term project, the aims of which can best be realised with help hired from (cross-border) law firms.[62] The steady growth in the numbers of law firms and legal businesses offering consultancy services attests to this claim.[63]

Here, expertise and complicated decision-making processes are assumed to go together, but in fact their relationship is more multifaceted than that. On the one hand, complexity, both in terms of process as well as substance, does indeed drive into the arms of lobbyists organisations and businesses that wish to influence decision-makers. Further, complexity encourages decision-makers to seek lobbyists' help, in particular if lobbyists can convince them that they have information and knowledge which decision-makers themselves lack, or lack resources to access.[64] On the other hand, the increasing complexity of decision-making makes it more difficult for lobbyists to get their points across and to leave their distinct mark on policy or legislation. In the same vein, complexity may serve to decrease the risk that decision-makers are captured by lobbyists as decision-makers are flooded with a mass of facts and figures from competing lobby groups. Does all of this then mean that the rise of expert-lobbying is likely to reduce ideological tensions in decision-making? In particular, does the expert-lobbyist make the demagogue-lobbyist redundant? Quite interestingly, the answer seems to be 'no'. It has been argued that experts can *de facto* strengthen ideologically motivated decision-making. Empirical work undertaken by Miller and Curry in agency decision-making shows that:

> in complex areas of law . . . ideological decision making is normatively difficult or unattractive for nonexperts because they lack the underlying motivation to view legally or factually complex cases within an ideological framework. However, experts are likely to have greater interest

61 See Christian Lahusen, 'Law and Lawyers in the Brussels World of Commercial Consultants' in Antoine Vauchez and Bruno de Witte (eds) *Lawyering Europe. European Law as a Transnational Social Field* (Hart Publishing 2013) 178.

62 Yves Dezalay, 'Opportunities and Limits of a Weak Field: Lawyers and the Genesis of a Field of European Economic Power' in *Lawyering Europe* (Hart Publishing 2013) 276. Dezalay also points to the alleged 'neutrality' of legal language rendering it suitable for lobbying purposes.

63 For the growth of US law firms in Europe, see Daniel Kelemen, *Eurolegalism. The Transformation of Law and Regulation in the European Union* (Harvard University Press 2011) 80–81.

64 Earnshaw and Judge (n 8) 62–63.

> in imposing an ideological framework on these kinds of cases since they are likely to see them as crucial policy-making opportunities and will not have difficulty understanding the subject matter . . .[65]

As for lobbyists, similarly, a solid legal or factual background in the matters under discussion is beneficial as it frees up a lobbyist's resources to hone demagoguery skills and to deliver knowledge engagingly.

Generally, however, demagoguery, understood as the use of emotions and passionate arguments, is presented as an opposite to expertise and facts. Bjorn Hansen, head of the chemicals unit in the Commission's environmental Directorate-General, was recently quoted as saying that the chemicals industry 'must stick to the facts and *not to resort to emotional arguments* when attempting to persuade decision-makers on how EU chemicals should be regulated', continuing that due to opposition by the industry, 'a sensible technical discussion' is impossible.[66] Whether this is a genuine concern or whether the Commission played the emotions card in order to exclude certain issues from the discussion is, however, impossible to say without more information about the underlying disagreement. The process leading up to the adoption of the REACH Chemicals Regulation offers additional examples of demagogic lobbying. In May 2003, the Commission published a draft proposal for REACH and requested interested actors to comment online, receiving over 6,400 comments by the deadline. The majority were from workers 'mobilised by their respective companies and trade-unions in order to complain about potential job-losses'.[67] For the demagogue-lobbyist, mass mobilisation is one among many potential strategies; the only apparent limit is imagination. Demagogic skills are also at play in the example we consider next.

### *4.4 The lobbyist as stakeholder*

Another way to access rule-making and to legitimise lobbyists' presence there is to adopt the point of view of a stakeholder. The success of this claim rests on the ability of a (demagogue-)lobbyist to convincingly argue that the interests which he represents should be incorporated as part of regulatory discretion. These kinds of claims are often associated with non-EU lobbying,

65 Banks Miller and Brett Curry 'Experts Judging Experts: The Role of Expertise in Reviewing Agency Decision Making' (2013) 38 *Law & Social Inquiry* 55, 68.

66 Philippa Nuttal Jones: 'EU Commission urges factual communication from industry' (*Chemical Watch*, 19 November 2013) <http://chemicalwatch.com/17293/eu-commission-urges-factual-communication-from-industry> accessed 21 January 2015 (emphasis mine). For the role of emotions in legal regulation, see Bettina Lange, 'The Emotional Dimension in Legal Regulation' (2002) 29 *Journal of Law and Society* 197.

67 Christian Hey and others, 'Better Regulation by New Governance Hybrids? Governance Models and the Reform of European Chemicals Policy' (2007) 15 *Journal of Cleaner Production* 1859, 1869.

a phenomenon that has allegedly become more common lately. No figures are available but a German Green MEP interviewed by the *Guardian* noted that over a half of the companies contacting him are from outside the EU, usually from the US.[68]

Stakeholder logic is in ample evidence from the following two examples. In early 2014, the *Financial Times* reported that US companies 'complain that they are often shut out of the regulatory process in Europe because the EU system can depend on closed consultations with local industry groups that make it difficult for outsiders to register their concerns'.[69] Their solution to the problem was to introduce the US notice-and-comment procedure in the EU. US companies did not explicitly claim to have any specialist knowledge but suggested – invoking a sense of exclusion – that they have a special place or role in EU rule-making for which reason their interests should be given consideration by the EU. Of course, and as I have argued above, several techniques can be in play simultaneously, and often those jostling for stakeholder status also base their claims on the knowledge they could bring to the table. The US statement is an expert example of this combination, carefully crafted to create an image of (political) exclusion and of expertise being let to go to waste. The US opening was widely quoted in the European press, and many high-profile commentaries suggest that although it was welcomed with scepticism the proposal made an impression on European business and political elites. In another recent instance, countries from outside the EU contacted the Commission about potential barriers to trade triggered by the provisions for treated articles in the new Biocidal Products Regulation, in particular the interpretation adopted in the guidance document during rule-making. These concerned countries were Japan and the US, which were both referred to as 'stakeholders'. Following the request by these foreign stakeholders to 'correct' the interpretation in the document, the authorities competent in the field of EU biocides gathered to address the concerns that were raised. The Commission has now asked both Member States and non-EU 'stakeholders' to share their views and suggest solutions.[70]

The use of 'stakeholder' language brings in the notion of participation, recognition of lobbyists as participants, from within and without the EU. Yet there is almost an intuitive discomfort with the vocabulary of participation, in particular in the latter situation, and a whole host of sceptical questions rushes to one's mind. Is participation imbued with overly strong (nation state) democratic connotations? Does the notion of 'transboundary' participation have a conceptual potential or concrete value here? What about

68 Traynor (n 2).

69 Donnan (n 58).

70 All citations from Vanessa Zainzinger, 'Biocides Stakeholders Want Further Clarification on Treated Articles' (*Chemical Watch*, 17 March 2014) <http://chemicalwatch.com/18734/biocides-stakeholders-want-further-clarification-on-treated-articles> accessed 21 January 2015.

multinational companies that are virtually stateless? These questions cannot be answered here but should be addressed by future research on lobbying. Suffice it to say that the current decision-making mode of the EU is constructed through inclusion and societal engagement, hence offering a fertile breeding ground for demands for stakeholder status from (non-EU country) lobbyists too.

### *4.5 Where is the entrepreneur-lobbyist?*

A dark figure with bags of money appears to capture the image of the lobbyist cherished by the general public. However, for analytical purposes, 'der Boss' is a difficult character. Falling outside the typology, the entrepreneur-lobbyist is not easy to pinpoint on actual examples.

Recent experience, though, especially in the US, offers interesting evidence that modern lobbyists strive to define themselves freely, outside the straight-jacket of legal categorisations and sociological typologies. A modern-day entrepreneur-lobbyist does not come up with ingenious techniques to prevent himself from falling on the corruption side of the corruption/legitimate behaviour divide; instead, the entrepreneur-lobbyist removes himself from the realm of lobbying altogether. In the US, this tendency has led to massive deregistration among lobbyists and the emergence of a new lobby species. This is the 'strategic adviser' who 'shape[s] lobbying strategy behind the scenes but do[es] not engage in the direct contact with policymakers that triggers the statutory definition of lobbying'.[71] In Europe, where registration is not mandatory for lobbyists, actors simply decline to register. Among those who resist registration, one particular group comprises law firms and other legal consultancy businesses. Despite vocal criticism from transparency NGOs, law firms have not signed up to the European Transparency Register.

In Weber's typology, the most distinctive feature of the entrepreneur-lobbyist is the fact that this type does not seem to be bothered about negative public opinion. For instance, Newt Gingrich, a prominent Republican politician and one-time presidential candidate, was 'widely mocked' when he explained that he did not register as a lobbyist for the Federal Home Loan Mortgage Corporation, which paid him about $1.7 million, because he acted as a 'historian', not as a lobbyist.[72] Gingrich, as well as other high-profile 'political consultants', not to mention law firms in Europe, remain politely indifferent to public ridicule and, in respect of the law firms, to repeated appeals by civil society, and continue to attract clients.

71 Briffault (n 5) 4.

72 Lee Fang, 'Where Have All the Lobbyists Gone?' (*The Nation*, 10–17 March 2014) <http://www.thenation.com/article/178460/shadow-lobbying-complex> accessed 21 January 2015.

## 5 EU lobby regulation and the limits of the procedural approach

Above, I have sought to adduce evidence for my argument that lobbyists have become actors in rule-making by positioning themselves either as experts or stakeholders; as actors inside the government. But surely this is a threat to democratic self-government, certainly not something that we would like to see more of. Should we not rather work harder at keeping lobbyists at arm's length from those who make the rules? Lobbying studies regularly report on the dangers of too cosy a relationship between lobbyists and decision-makers, in which lobbyists have come to be seen 'not as lobbyists but as colleagues'.[73] It is precisely this cosy collegialism between decision-makers and lobbyists that lobbying regulation tries to eradicate.

In this penultimate section, I examine the way in which the EU has been seeking to provide a check on lobbying.[74] In my view, the EU has chosen a procedural approach to regulation of lobbying: its many initiatives, such as setting up the Transparency Register and a recent decision of the Commission to publish, as of 1 December 2014, all contacts and meetings with lobbyists,[75] are premised on the idea that transparency is a cure, if not for all, then at least for many, ills of lobbying. But how does the procedural approach succeed in controlling lobbyists who resort to expertise or claim stakeholder status? Starting with those lobbyists who claim stakeholder status, it needs to be borne in mind that registration is of limited value, especially if the lobbyist is from outside the EU, because third country governments are exempt from registration. Would the general EU framework for consultations be of help in increasing transparency about lobbying activities by foreign stakeholders? Presumably, the concerns raised by Japan and the US, noted above, were taken into account in an ad hoc, informal manner, thus reducing overall transparency in rule-making.[76] Similarly, registration is not an answer to the legitimacy

73 Alex Warleigh, 'The hustle: citizenship practice, NGOs and "policy coalitions" in the European Union – the cases of Auto Oil, drinking water and unit pricing' (2000) 7 *JEPP* 229, 235 (emphasis removed).

74 US lobbying is a heavily regulated business, and the trend seems to hold. For instance, in the US since 2010, registered lobbyists have been excluded from sitting on advisory committees. See Presidential Memorandum, *Lobbyists on Agency Boards and Commissions* (White House, 18 June 2010) <http://www.whitehouse.gov/the-press-office/presidential-memorandum-lobbyists-agency-boards-and-commissions> accessed 21 January 2015. For regulation more generally, see Briffault (n 5) 6.

75 Commission Decision of 25 November 2014 on the publication of information on meetings held between Members of the Commission and organisations or self-employed individuals.

76 I say 'presumably' as the Commission organised a public consultation on the evaluation of efficacy of wood preservative products in 2013. As the consultation concerned a technical note for guidance document, it was not published on the Commission website 'Your Voice in Europe', listing all public consultations, and it is thus unclear whether the Japanese and US authorities submitted comments within or without the public consultation.

problem raised by the expert-lobbyist. On the one hand, the Transparency Register covers only those who lobby the Commission or the EP, not the Council (working groups) or EU agencies, although the latter actors are important targets for lobbyists seeking to influence rule-making.[77] On the other hand, the Transparency Register, although now covering the expert group structure used in particular by the Commission, still excludes individual requests from EU institutions for data and expertise. It remains to be seen if this shifts emphasis from expert groups to bilateral and informal data exchange.

To me, it then seems clear that the procedural approach has its limits, and that the choice of transparency as a prime regulatory strategy has been made with one type of lobbyist in mind, that is, the entrepreneur-lobbyist. Registration is believed to tackle the particular threat posed by the dark figure of 'der Boss' and to increase information on such lobby activities for the benefit of open government.[78] Although EU lobbying regulation is clearly crafted to shed light on, and temper, the influence of the entrepreneur-lobbyist, the analysis in this chapter strongly suggests that the future challenge may lie in controlling the legitimacy of claims by the expert-lobbyist. Unlike entrepreneur-lobbyists who are, at least for the time being, near-celebrities and thus easy to identify, expert-lobbyists are difficult to spot. Operating under a range of institutional identities, they are prone to mask representation of (private) interests as production and communication of (public) expertise.

Are alternatives to the current system available? To a certain extent, the procedural approach, and the Transparency Register as its prime manifestation, is justifiable and advisable. It is justifiable as the Commission does not have the expertise to countercheck what lobbyists assert as expert knowledge, leaving the EU with little choice but to build on transparency as an overall strategy. It is also advisable as it treats lobbying as legitimate irrespective of who is engaged in influencing. In other words, the procedural approach is indiscriminate, avoiding the categorisation of lobbyists in two groups: good and bad. For instance, not so long ago the EU adopted a new tobacco directive, despite heavy lobbying by the tobacco industry. According to one report, health associations were on the 'good' side, acting allegedly 'as a sort of *anti-lobby*'.[79] The legitimacy of the cause or the association employing the lobbyist should not be relevant to the analysis of lobbying and should not be allowed to influence the parameters of lobbying regulation. What is relevant and what decides the question whether lobbyists are on the 'right' side is whether or

77 Article 35 of the revised Interinstitutional Agreement.

78 However, experience with public registers especially in the US has shown that mandatory registration does not work for the entrepreneur-lobbyist either. Rather, stringent regulation has created an incentive for lobbyists to go underground under titles such as 'strategic adviser', resulting in waves of deregistration.

79 Traynor (n 2) (emphasis mine).

not lobbyists adhere to conditions we perceive as necessary for decision-making and rule-making in a democratic society.

But how to ensure that lobbyists do in fact comply with these conditions? This is where I return to the argument about lobbyists as actors. In order to bring lobbyists out of the shadows and ensure that their conduct is consistent with legal and ethical standards, lobbyists should be recognised as *de facto* actors in the policy process. In my view, public decision-making is still the best place to put to the test the legitimacy of claims made by lobbyists, as to both factual accuracy and respect for procedural rules.[80] One of many ideas debated in connection with the EU Transparency Register is a 'legislative footprint'.[81] Although the idea never got off the ground, it nevertheless prompted discussion of its merits. Accompanying each EU legislative act, it would have served as a public record of all the information relating to the legislative process, such as the number of meetings held with lobbyists, suggestions for draft amendments or other such input received from interest groups, and so on. The responsibility to report this information would have fallen on individual MEPs. Although perhaps insufficient alone, the proposal is a step in the right direction in perceiving lobbyists as actors inside the legislative process.

## 6 Conclusion

This contribution is an attempt to analyse the new roles of lobbyists in the context of EU rule-making practices. The way in which EU administration is currently organised, highlighting expertise and stakeholder access to policymaking, has also profoundly affected the rationale of lobbying and diversified the strategies that lobbyists pursue. As a result of these organisational shifts, and contextualising the argument in relation to postnational rule-making in the EU, I have posited above that lobbyists have become actors in rule-making by positioning themselves either as experts or stakeholders.

The analysis proceeded in three steps. By drawing on Weber, I first offered a typology of lobbyists and then, in the light of concrete examples from EU rule-making, argued that the most pressing legitimacy concerns are raised by the practices of the expert-lobbyist. I finally deployed these insights in evaluating the effectiveness of the procedural approach which the EU has promoted in lobbying regulation. It seems that the EU's current vision, in

80 For the argument that the EU is the right level to supervise experts and their activities in transnational norm-making contexts, see Caroline Devaux, 'The Role of Experts in the Elaboration of the Cape Town Convention: Between Authority and Legitimacy' (2013) 19 *ELJ* 843, 861.

81 EP resolution of 8 May 2008 on the development of the framework for the activities of interest representatives (lobbyists) in the European Institutions (2007/2115(INI)).

seeking to increase transparency, primarily through registration of lobbyists, is not as effective as desired, failing to provide a check on lobbyists who exchange expertise for access to rule-making. In conclusion, while broadening the scope of the Transparency Register to include participation in expert groups, committees and similar structures was a welcome first step, a second and more crucial step is to lift the shadow that has been created by our inability to perceive lobbyists as actors as they factually are in rule-making practices. Only this way can we begin to ensure that lobbyists remain within the bounds of legal and ethical requirements for public decision-making and rule-making.

# Concluding reflections

This publication has sought to embrace the *tabula rasa* of postnational rule-making. The subjects of EU and public international law are demonstrated here to be significant leading case studies of postnational rule-making but they also remain disciplinary 'problem children'. Flexibility and also pragmatism remain the dominant guiding force in the evolution of contemporary EU and public international law. The inquiry here in all accounts has focused upon 'blind spots' in these subject areas because certain actors may receive little attention if considered only within a strict doctrinal prism for analysis, for example, lobbyists or academia. The study of contemporary postnational rule-making necessitates the study of many practices, and this particular edited volume has specifically 'zoomed in' upon the behavioural dimension to postnational rule-making and the relevance of sociological understandings of practice.

The contributions here demonstrate how the social legitimacy of practices of rule-making is an increasingly salient concern in legal scholarship. Nevertheless, as the accounts of Korkeo-aho or Sefton Green demonstrate, the social reality of postnational rule-making is murky and often problematic to isolate. Urueña makes a compelling case that the study of actors requires a sophisticated understanding of the dynamics of action and interaction, usefully captured, for example, within his case study within a specific spatial context. The empirical breadth of many individual contributions, for example, Jancic, amply supports the thesis that the 'blind spots' of postnational rule-making are rich and lively research fields in and of themselves. The contributions have also sought to demonstrate the limits of the *Trias Politicas* beyond the Nation State and instead focus upon its vibrant manifestations in this context – as, for example, in De Waele's detailed account of the evolution of the European Council.

Otherwise, this publication has sought to bring transparency to the study of rule-making beyond the Nation State. It has used the frame of the shadows to methodologically narrow the focus but also as a motif for the study itself conducted. The focus of the accounts here has been particularly narrow and largely focused, isolating upon certain types of practices and even certain types of actors, as unregulated/non-regulation/non-existent formats, depicted well in the foreword by Cassesse. Many of the accounts demonstrate the merit in probing actors operating in the shadows. The limited prism of doctrinarism and formalism is demonstrated here to be self-evident from the accounts outlined.

The contributions to this publication draw attention to the significance of empirical studies of contemporary postnational rule-making. Postnational rule-making is derived from seemingly isolated studies of evolving practice that somehow unify as a state of affairs. The contributions demonstrate amply how they challenge prevailing narratives, for example constitutionalism, and in many instances traverse subject domains and boundaries unquestionably. Indeed, it is hard to see how a contemporary account of postnational rule-making could be otherwise. In this regard, the contributions demonstrate the virtues of adopting mixed methods – mapping, empirics and theoretical inquiries – some inductive and others more deductive.

Some contributions here have sought to couch their contributions explicitly in terms of recommendations to improve rule-making techniques. The output of postnational rule-making scholarship is often high on legitimacy concerns and low on practical techniques for rectification, and such concerns are argued here to be essential. In this vein, the contributions form part of the open-textured dialogue that is the context for the *tabula rasa* of postnational rule-making.

# Index

www.ingramcontent.com/pod-product-compliance
Ingram Content Group UK Ltd.
Pitfield, Milton Keynes, MK11 3LW, UK
UKHW022134190926
475702UK00013B/1801
* 9 7 8 1 1 3 8 7 1 7 2 3 7 *